HIT THE TARGET

HIT THE TARGET

EIGHT MEN WHO LED

THE EIGHTH AIR FORCE TO VICTORY

OVER THE LUFTWAFFE

BILL YENNE

NAL
CALIBER

NAL Caliber
Published by the Penguin Group
Penguin Group (USA) LLC, 375 Hudson Street,
New York, New York 10014

USA | Canada | UK | Ireland | Australia | New Zealand | India | South Africa | China
penguin.com
A Penguin Random House Company

First published by NAL Caliber, an imprint of New American Library,
a division of Penguin Group (USA) LLC

First Printing, July 2015

LIBRARY OF CONGRESS CATALOGING-IN-PUBLICATION DATA:

Yenne, Bill, 1949–
Hit the target: eight men who led the Eighth Air Force
to victory over the Luftwaffe / Bill Yenne.
pages   cm.
Wartime service of Tooey Spaatz, Ira Eaker, Jimmy Doolittle, Curtis LeMay, Hub Zemke,
Maynard "Snuffy" Smith, Bob Morgan, and Rosie Rosenthal.
Includes bibliographical references.
ISBN 978-0-425-27417-0
1. United States. Army Air Forces. Air Force, 8th—Biography.   2. United States. Army Air
Forces. Air Force, 8th—Officers—Biography.   3. United States. Army Air Forces. Air Force,
8th—Aerial gunners—Biography.   4. Air pilots, Military—United States—Biography.
5. Leadership—United States—History—20th century.   6. World War, 1939–1945—Aerial
operations, American.   7. World War, 1939–1945—Campaigns—Western Front.   I. Title.
II. Title: Eight men who led the Eighth Air Force to victory over the Luftwaffe.
D790.228th .Y46   2015
940.54'49730922—dc23   2015001506

Printed in the United States of America
1   3   5   7   9   10   8   6   4   2

Set in Palatino
Designed by Elke Sigal

★

EIGHT OF THE EIGHTH

Carl Andrew "Tooey" Spaatz
(1891–1974)

Ira Clarence Eaker
(1896–1987)

James Harold "Jimmy" Doolittle
(1896–1993)

Curtis Emerson LeMay
(1906–1990)

Maynard Harrison "Snuffy" Smith
(1911–1984)

Hubert A. "Hub" Zemke
(1914–1994)

Robert "Rosie" Rosenthal
(1917–2007)

Robert Knight Morgan
(1918–2004)

CONTENTS

CONTENTS

CONTENTS

NOTE ON ORGANIZATION

The Eighth Air Force was one of 16 numbered air forces that comprised the US Army Air Forces (USAAF) during World War II. Numbered air forces were composed of "commands," defined by function and typically designated with a Roman numeral that was the same number as that of the air force. The Eighth was composed of the VIII Bomber Command and the VIII Fighter Command—long-range heavy bombers and the fighters to escort them—as well as the VIII Air Force Base Command to manage its base infrastructure. The VIII Air Support Command was added to operate medium bombers in a tactical role, but was later peeled off to form the nucleus of the Ninth Air Force.

Within the USAAF table of organization, the "group" was the basic building block, and was contained within the commands. Groups initially contained three squadrons, although larger organizations, such as the Eighth Air Force, later added a fourth squadron to many groups. As the numbers of groups increased in 1943–1944, "wings" were activated to contain multiple groups, and "divisions" were later activated to contain multiple wings. Both wings and divisions were technically contained within commands, although, beginning in 1944, those within the Eighth Air Force answered directly to the Eighth Air Force headquarters.

INTRODUCTION

The Eighth Air Force is not the subject of this book but the stage upon which the climactic act of eight stories takes place. It was the wartime home of these eight individuals, whose lives intersected beneath its roof.

These are eight parallel lives chosen from among those of around 350,000 men who were part of this unique organization during a crossroads of world history. These eight came from widely varied backgrounds, in a dozen states, from North Carolina to Alaska (then a territory).

Tooey Spaatz, Ira Eaker, and Jimmy Doolittle each served as commander of the Eighth Air Force during World War II, but their careers were much more than their time with the Eighth. Their aviation careers were closely intertwined with one another and with the early evolution of American aviation and American airpower.

Curtis LeMay and Hub Zemke were also accomplished prewar military pilots, and they became important leaders in the middle tier of command at the Eighth. With LeMay commanding bomber units and Zemke commanding fighters, both led large numbers of men, but both also flew combat missions themselves.

Maynard "Snuffy" Smith, an anomaly among the eight, was the only enlisted man. He was the first living airman in the European Theater to receive the Medal of Honor, but his medal was a shining island in a lifetime of mischief and failure. Recalling Smith's life is like looking at a train wreck. Though it is unsettling to watch, we cannot avert our eyes. Yet he is an icon of the Eighth who is not forgotten, and who symbolizes how service with the Eighth brought out the very best in even the most unlikely people.

Bob Morgan piloted the *Memphis Belle*, probably the best remembered of the tens of thousands of B-17 Flying Fortresses that were operated by the Eighth—and he later served under LeMay in the Pacific. Just as Doolittle led the *first* American raid on Tokyo in 1942, Morgan led the *next* mission to Tokyo in 1944.

Rosie Rosenthal flew Flying Fortresses with the 100th Bomb Group, known as the "Bloody Hundredth" for the terribly heavy losses that it suffered in combat. On his third mission with the Bloody Hundredth, Rosenthal was the only member of the group on that mission who came back. He interrupted his career as an attorney to fly with the Eighth, and then returned to Germany after the war as part of the prosecution team at Nuremberg.

Though the Eighth Air Force was only one of 16 numbered air forces within the US Army Air Forces (USAAF) during World War II, it was the largest, and today it is probably the most famous. At the National Museum of the Mighty Eighth Air Force in Pooler, Georgia, we are reminded that the Eighth suffered half the casualties of the entire USAAF during World War II.

These eight lives are representative of those of more than a third of a million men who rose to a challenge and helped wield the relentless hammer that pounded the Third Reich into submission, earning an indelible place in the annals of world history for the Eighth Air Force.

CHAPTER 1

⭐

SPAATZ, EAKER, AND DOOLITTLE

Three of the eight were born on the cusp of two centuries, in which the paradigms that had defined the nineteenth were recognized to have expired but the defining characteristics of the twentieth were not yet known. These men, who were born when manned, powered flight was still a pipe dream, would be among the shapers of twentieth-century military aviation.

Carl Andrew Spatz came into the world on June 28, 1891, in the southeastern Pennsylvania community of Boyertown, a village of 1,436 people by the reckoning of the previous year's national census. A second-generation American of German extraction, he was the eldest son and second child of Anne Muntz Spatz and her husband of two years, Charles Spatz, a politically active newspaperman whose own parents, Karl and Juliana Amalie Busch Spatz, had emigrated from Prussia in 1865. Karl was an accomplished commercial printer fluent in several languages; Juliana was related to the Krupp family, the powerful German industrialists.

Later in the coming century, a second "a" was added to the surname to give it a "Dutch" appearance. According to David Mets, Carl Andrew's

BILL YENNE

biographer, the second "a" was also intended to encourage the correct pronunciation of the surname ("spots") rather than "spats," which was synonymous with the pretentious and outmoded footwear accessory.

Karl bought the *Boyertown Democrat* newspaper, running it until his death in 1884, after which it was taken over by Charles, then only 19 years old. By 1891, when young Carl Andrew was born, the paper was still going strong and Charles was gaining influence in the Boyertown community.

On the editorial page, Charles expressed a sentiment for an expansionist foreign policy, such as the intervention in Cuba on behalf of its independence from Spain. Today, small-town papers usually restrict themselves to local news, but in those days—before cable news networks or even radio—people got all their world news and journalistic opinion from newspapers.

In 1896, Charles Spatz was elected to the state assembly, and young Carl Andrew joined him in Harrisburg as a page before joining the staff of the paper, now called the *Berks County Democrat*, where he was described as the youngest Linotype operator in the state.

Ira Clarence Eaker and James Harold Doolittle were both born in 1896, a year in which hints of the transition to a new age in the coming century were seen and discussed. It was the year that Henry Ford first putted down a Michigan lane in his gasoline-powered "Quadricycle," though no one but Ford himself—and perhaps not even him—grasped the importance of this turn of events. In Dayton, Ohio, Wilbur and Orville Wright were imagining technology that was even further from the imagination of the average person than that which Ford was exploring.

Eaker was born on April 13, 1896, in Field Creek in Llano County, Texas, about 100 miles north of San Antonio, near the Old Chisholm Trail. Doolittle was born eight months later, on December 14, at the western edge of the continent in Alameda, California, a Navy town within sight of San Francisco.

Field Creek, where the post office was closed in 1976, still doesn't ap-

2

pear on most maps. Ira was the eldest of the five sons of a farmhand and part-time cowboy named Young Yancy "Y.Y." Eaker and his wife, Dona Lee Graham Eaker, who was only 17 when Ira was born. As Eaker later told Colonel Joe Green of the US Military History Institute, the family was "poor by any modern standard, but we didn't know it. We were comfortable and had plenty of food and we considered that our status enabled us to move forward and encouraged us to do so."

The family, originally called Ecker, had emigrated from the Pfalz (Palatine) region in what is now southwestern Germany in the early eighteenth century. They originally settled in upstate New York, but later generations drifted west. Ira's grandfather William Eaker came to Eden in Concho County, Texas, after the Civil War. Y. Y. Eaker was born there two years before his father died in 1874 at the age of 60. Ira's father moved the family back to Eden—named for Fred Ede, not for the biblical garden—and bought a farm near the town when the eldest son was nine.

Schooling was important for *all* the Eaker children—Dona's father was on the school board—but Ira's mother always felt that he was the smartest one of her brood and urged him to set his sights beyond the horizon as viewed from Eden. Church was also an important part of the family routine, and as a small boy Ira had once aspired to be an apostle—until he was told that their ranks had been closed after the first 12. "I went to church enough before I was ten to do me the rest of my life," he later told his biographer, James Parton.

Ira grew up, like most boys, reading adventure stories, but an exciting reality that other boys only read about in stories was not far from his door. "My earliest heroes were cowboys and Indians," Ira later recalled. "I grew up with them. Cowboys taught me to play poker."

Jimmy Doolittle was the son of a carpenter who had left Massachusetts for California to seek his fortune. Having sailed around Cape Horn to reach the Golden State, Frank Henry Doolittle settled in Alameda. It was here that he met and married Rosa Ceremah Shepherd, and where they had their only child, a little boy. On his birth certificate, he was called simply "Doolittle." He was never to know why he was not named until later, nor why they eventually named him James Harold. He knew only that he hated his middle name.

Frank and Rosa might have remained in Alameda or thereabouts permanently, but 1896 was the year of the Klondike Gold Rush. Gold was discovered in Canada's Yukon Territory in August of that year, and news soon reached Seattle and San Francisco that a man could gather up nuggets the size of a robin's egg by the handful. A few hardy souls headed north immediately, despite the onset of winter in a harsh environment that most could not have anticipated. After the "Rush" of 1896 and the spring thaw of 1897, there came what was to be called the Klondike "Stampede."

Frank Doolittle was among the thousands who stampeded northward. He was one of many who arrived after the easy pickings had been picked, but he found his carpentry skills in high demand in boomtowns such as Dawson. His gold came in a manner that he had not expected, but in a manner more reliable than staking his fate on flecks in a gold pan. While Frank was up north, young Jimmy Doolittle spent his first three birthdays back in California without a father.

Meanwhile, stories told of golden sand along the shores of the Bering Sea fired another gold rush. In 1899, Frank Doolittle reached Nome, a little village that quickly became Alaska's largest city, and in June 1900 he sent for his family. Rosa, Jimmy, and Rosa's sister, Sarah, were among 25,000 who arrived that summer.

As he had in the Klondike, Frank Doolittle returned to carpentry. Among other things, he built a comfortable home for his family. On the plains of Texas and Oklahoma, Ira Eaker's family did not have electricity in their home until he was in his teens. In Nome, Jimmy Doolittle's family had electricity before he started to school.

Once in school, Jimmy found himself the shortest in his class, and discovered that size put him at a disadvantage. "A few of the taller boys took delight in teasing and provoking the shorter boys, and since I was the shortest one around, they tried to give me a bad time," he wrote in his memoirs. "They shoved and I shoved back. They punched and I returned their punches. . . . Since my size was against me, I decided my survival could be insured only by a speedy attack right from the start. I began to blast my opponents with a flurry of punches regardless of the consequences. The tactics worked. I found it was easy to draw blood if you were nimble on your feet, aimed at a fellow's nose, and got your licks in early. After several antagonists went home with bloody noses, I earned a certain measure of respect."

Though Frank rarely engaged in conversation with his son and remained distant and aloof, he did teach the boy how to work with tools. Jimmy wrote in his memoirs that he longed for a closer relationship with his loner father, but it never happened. In his recollections, the defining moment in their relationship came when Frank falsely accused Jimmy of lying—and then beat him up. The skinny little boy promised that one day he would do the same to his father, and Frank Doolittle just laughed.

Jimmy might have grown to manhood in Alaska, hunting and fishing and perhaps pursuing his father's trade, but in the late summer of 1908, as he was nearing his twelfth birthday, his mother decided to leave Frank, and Alaska, permanently. Taking Jimmy, she sailed for Los Angeles, where she had relatives, and where she would spend the rest of her life. Jimmy wrote in his memoirs that he assumed he would see his father again soon. It would be six years.

CHAPTER 2

MAKING THEIR WAY

In 1906, Carl Andrew Spaatz (we'll use the later double-"a" spelling for the sake of consistency) enrolled in the college prep Perkiomen School in Pennsburg, Pennsylvania, but when his father was injured in a fire in 1908, Carl was called home to run the family newspaper. By the time Charles recovered, the family's finances were stretched thin. Despite his local prominence, Charles had never become a wealthy man. Being a big fish in a 1,436-person pond had its limitations, as did the circulation of such a pond's leading newspaper. The family, which had come to include five children—plus Charles's mother—lived in the same building that contained the newspaper offices and the pressroom.

The family had always imagined higher education for Carl, though, as times were hard, this now seemed further and further from their grasp financially. Though the US Military Academy at West Point—like its naval counterpart in Annapolis—offered free education, it was considered as a higher education option even by families with no military pedigree, so competition was fierce, and it was extremely hard to gain admission.

Somehow, though, Carl got into West Point. David Mets notes that

Charles was an acquaintance of Major Thomas Rhoads, personal physician to President William Howard Taft, and that it was he who made the suggestion and facilitated the appointment. However, a June 3, 1982, article in the *Boyertown Area Times* (a descendant of Charles's newspaper, but no longer family owned) suggests that Congressman John Hoover Rothermel made a congressional appointment in exchange for Charles Spatz's not running against him for Congress.

As with many men who went on to significant military careers, Carl Andrew Spaatz's time at West Point was undistinguished academically and marred by frequent infractions of the strict rules, usually involving pranks, petty gambling, and smuggling booze into the hallowed halls. He did well academically until his later years, and graduated in the bottom half of the Class of 1914, but he did learn enough from his French course to make himself understood when he was working with French officers during the First World War.

It was at West Point that Spaatz picked up his lifelong nickname. Because of his physical resemblance to a fellow cadet, Francis Toohey of the Class of 1913, Spaatz was dubbed "Toohey," though, over time, the name somehow came to be spelled without the "h." In addition to their red hair and freckles, the two shared the same waning interest in academics. Francis Toohey reportedly graduated last in *his* class. Spaatz did a little better.

As viewed through the lens of hindsight, the most important day of Tooey's years at the academy was probably May 29, 1910. It was on this day, for a few moments, that he looked into the sky and watched the fragile biplane built by aviation pioneer Glenn Curtiss.

Curtiss was in the midst of a widely publicized and ultimately successful attempt to be the first person to pilot an airplane between Albany and New York City. He completed the flight in 171 minutes—the longest airplane flight to date—to claim a $10,000 prize that had been offered by the *New York World*. It was this moment that inspired Tooey Spaatz to become an aviator.

Having considered dropping out of West Point after the terrible hazing that he had experienced as a plebe, Spaatz decided to stay because the US Army was training an increasing number of pilots. He had been lucky to get into the academy and was betting that on the other side of West Point he would be lucky enough to get into flight school.

A graduating cadet's career track was directly linked to his place in his graduating class. Those at the top went into the Corps of Engineers. Below them were men destined for the artillery or the cavalry. The men at the bottom, like Spaatz, were assigned to the infantry. For Lieutenant Spaatz of the infantry, luck was with him so far as his first duty station assignment was concerned. In October 1914, as Europe was tumbling into World War I—then called the Great War or the World War—he was making his way to Schofield Barracks in Hawaii, where he would bide his time while waiting for an opportunity to apply for one of the small but growing number of slots within the Aviation Section of the Signal Corps. In 1914, there were only 122 men in that organization.

It was also during his time in Hawaii that Spaatz met his future wife, Ruth Harrison. Their courtship was complicated by the fact that her father, Colonel Ralph Harrison, considered it inappropriate for his teenage daughter to go on dates without a chaperone. He was also one of those old cavalry officers ruling the US Army in those days who considered military aviation to be a waste of both time and money.

In 1909, as Spaatz was preparing to enter West Point, Ira Eaker's family was on the move on the southern plains. A drought forced the Eakers out of Texas, across the Red River Valley, and into Bryan County, Oklahoma, which had been part of the autonomous Choctaw Nation until Oklahoma was formed and admitted to the Union just two years earlier. They rented a house in the tiny railroad town of Kenefic, and Y. Y. Eaker got work hauling sand for a cement works.

Ira did well enough in high school in Kenefic to gain early admission to the newly opened Southeastern State Normal School, a teachers college in Durant, Oklahoma—the closest thing to higher learning that was available to him. It was in 1912, while he was living in Durant, that Eaker saw *his* first airplane. Contrary to what might have been expected, this experience did not inspire his imagination. As he recalled in a 1961 speech at the Air University, "I was not moved at the time to consider myself a possible participant in flying."

In contrast with the underwhelming academic career of Tooey Spaatz, Ira Eaker was diligent and focused, earning consistently high scores. As James Parton points out, his only grades below A came in music and are explained by his being tone-deaf. He was an ambitious student who was described in the yearbook as "Ira Eager."

In 1915, as a freshman, he served as vice president of the Debating Club. Recalling a particularly memorable debate, the yearbook notes that "Eaker won first place by a narrow margin; his style was logic rather than oratory; his delivery was characterized by a whole-souled earnestness that won him the day."

Having spent his early years in Nome, Jimmy Doolittle experienced the culture shock of moving to Los Angeles for middle school. He later was a member of the first class to attend the Manual Arts Senior High School. Los Angeles was still young in its life as a city, and the school was only the third high school in town. Like Tooey Spaatz, but unlike Ira Eaker, Doolittle was a fair student, with a C average and a greater interest in the extracurricular than in the classroom.

As had been the case when he was in Nome, Doolittle was picked on because of his size—he was just five foot four, although he always claimed to be two inches taller. To compensate, he took up boxing, entering amateur matches at the Los Angeles Athletic Club when he was 15 and winning the flyweight division at the West Coast Amateur Championships when he was 17. He was also, much to the consternation of his mother, boxing in exhibition bouts with professionals. One Saturday night when he was still 15, he was arrested in an unsanctioned street fight. His mother bailed him out of jail on Monday morning in time to take him to school.

Neither his mother nor a weekend in jail affected his amateur boxing career, but meeting his future wife and falling under her spell did. As he later recalled, Josephine "Joe" Daniels, by his account a straight-A student, was "unimpressed" with his success as a boxer.

In 1910, the same year that Doolittle started at Manual Arts, the City of Angels hosted what was to be a watershed moment in the history of aviation in the western United States. Based on the big air show that had been held at Reims in France in 1909, the Aviation Meet held at Dominguez Field, south of downtown Los Angeles, brought many of America's leading aviators together for what turned out to be the country's first major air show. Glenn Curtiss came to demonstrate his latest machines, and Louis Paulhan came over from France to show off the airplanes designed by Louis Blériot, who had just become the first man to fly across the English Channel. Doolittle's impression was one of amazement that machines with "radical differences" in design could all fly.

Among the pilots whose demonstrations at the show Doolittle recalled in his memoirs was the great Lincoln Beachey, considered by many to be the world's greatest flyer. "An aeroplane in the hands of Lincoln Beachey is poetry," Orville Wright had said. "His mastery is a thing of beauty to watch. He is the most wonderful flyer of all."

Two years later, Doolittle, still in his teens, built his own glider—using plans that he found in *Popular Mechanics*. He tried flying it, crashed it, repaired it, and tried again. The second time, he was pulled by a friend who had borrowed his father's car in order to help Doolittle achieve a faster takeoff speed, but this attempt also failed. Undaunted, he decided to build another airplane, with a propeller driven by an engine extracted from his motorcycle, but that aircraft was destroyed in a windstorm before he could fly it.

When he graduated from high school in 1915, Doolittle headed for Alaska to seek his fortune, promising Joe Daniels that he would send for her—as his father had once promised his mother. There, Jimmy saw his father for the first time in six years. Sizing up a boy who had grown into a champion prizefighter, Frank Doolittle asked his son whether he recalled his earlier threat to get even for the beating his father had given him. Jimmy nodded, and Frank asked him whether he thought he would come out on top in a rematch. Jimmy nodded again. Frank said he probably would, and turned away.

The Jimmy Doolittle who signed up as a steward on a Seattle-bound steamer after a summer of failure with a gold pan was, by his own reckoning, "far wiser" than the one who had gone north. He enrolled at Los Angeles Junior College, and told Joe Daniels that the marriage of which they had spoken on and off would have to wait until he finished college. Her mother was relieved.

CHAPTER 3

COMING OF AGE IN A NATION AT WAR

I n 1915, as both Ira Eaker and Jimmy Doolittle were in the early days of their respective college careers, Lieutenant Tooey Spaatz had finally made the transition from infantry to aviation and was earning his wings as a US Army aviator at Rockwell Field on North Island at the mouth of San Diego Bay. With its good flying weather, North Island had become one of the most important aviation centers in the country. Glenn Curtiss opened a flight school there in 1912, and both the US Army and the US Navy maintained busy flight training operations.

Military aviation was in its infancy, and even as the men were learning to fly, they were pioneering the art and science of using aircraft tactically. The ongoing and evolving air combat tactics in the war-blackened skies of Europe were discussed and carefully dissected by the American pilots at North Island. Meanwhile, with the Germans conducting unrestricted submarine warfare against ships in the North Atlantic—including American ships—they wondered whether the United States would one day find itself in the war. None could have predicted that the first use of US Army airpower in a war would come much closer to home.

On March 9, 1916, the violent revolution and civil war that had been raging in Mexico since 1910 spilled across the border. One of the principal belligerents, the flamboyant General José Doroteo Arango Arámbula—better known by his nom de guerre, Francisco "Pancho" Villa—led a cross-border raid on the town of Columbus, New Mexico, which left ten civilians and eight members of the US Army's 13th Cavalry dead.

An outraged American public demanded retaliation, so President Woodrow Wilson ordered American troops to cross the border and hunt Pancho down. The massive intervention was under the command of General John J. "Black Jack" Pershing, who would later earn lasting notoriety as the commander of the American Expeditionary Force in Europe. The air contingent of Pershing's "Punitive Expedition" was the 1st Aero Squadron, commanded by Captain Benjamin Delahauf Foulois, who would be the US Army's top airman two decades later. Then based at Fort Sill, Oklahoma, the 1st Aero soon forward-deployed to Casas Grandes in the Mexican state of Chihuahua. This became Tooey Spaatz's first duty assignment as a combat airman. He arrived in May, shortly after he earned his wings, and was soon flying reconnaissance missions over Mexico in a Curtiss JN-3 biplane.

The Mexican Punitive Expedition was a failure. The stated objectives had been to kill or capture Pancho Villa and to halt border raids by armed Mexican gangs, but neither was met. Meanwhile, the US Army had lost many of the skirmishes that took place south of the border. For the Aviation Section, the shortcomings in their equipment choices were underscored by the poor performance of their aircraft in the high elevations of the Mexican mountains and plateaus. There was also a steep learning curve in managing logistics for an air force deployed far from its bases, but the lessons learned would be valuable later.

For the young Tooey Spaatz, the thrill of being in action so early in his aviation career overshadowed the hardships and adversity. "At that time we were all young and somewhat irresponsible, so that we enjoyed our work and we enjoyed our play at the same time," he told David Mets, comparing his Mexican adventures to his future career. "Later on, we enjoyed our work less and played less."

A year later, much had changed. Against the backdrop of unrestricted German submarine attacks on shipping, the United States declared war on Germany on April 6, 1917. Tooey Spaatz, now a first lieutenant, was assigned to the newly formed 3rd Aero Squadron at San Antonio. It was here that he reconnected with Ruth Harrison, whose father was now assigned to Fort Sam Houston. By this time, as part of the buildup for the war, the Aviation Section was undergoing a rapid expansion. Spaatz was promoted to captain and given command of the new 31st Aero Squadron.

On July 26, when Spaatz learned that the 31st was due to head overseas in two weeks, he contacted Ruth and proposed that they get married immediately—by which he meant *that day*. Ruth agreed that this seemed like the right thing to do, and so they did, much to the consternation of her parents.

Shortly after his arrival in France in September 1917, Spaatz was reassigned to the 3rd Air Instruction Center at Issoudun Aerodrome as the second in command to Lieutenant Colonel Walter Glenn Kilner of West Point's Class of 1912, with whom Spaatz had flown during the Mexican Punitive Expedition. Located about 130 miles south of Paris, the base was nothing more than a vast plot of ground that was referred to as a "mudhole." It was a forlorn collection of shacks, where the unlucky airmen were housed in tents and carted into a nearby town to take their weekly showers. Airplanes could not land because the ground was so spongy. Whipping Issoudun into shape was an uphill task, but Kilner and Spaatz leapt into the challenge.

In April 1917, as the United States went to war, Jimmy Doolittle had graduated from Los Angeles Junior College and was enrolled in the University of California in Berkeley, just a few miles from where he was born. He had studied engineering in junior college, aiming for a life as a mining engineer, and had continued in this vein at Berkeley.

After a summer working in Nevada silver mines, Doolittle returned to Cal in the fall of 1917, but took a leave of absence to sign up as a US Army Reserve flying cadet. With the war on, there was suddenly a great deal of demand for Army pilots—and Doolittle had long wanted to learn to fly. When Tooey Spaatz first applied for a slot, the total Aviation Section head count was 122. By the summer of 1917, it was up to 1,218. In 1918, that number reached 195,023, the largest number that would be seen in the service until 1942.

Doolittle and Joe Daniels had earlier agreed to wait until his college career was over to get married, but they now adjusted this pledge and were wed on Christmas Eve in 1917 in Los Angeles. His cadet pay had yet to arrive, so she paid for the license and for a short honeymoon trip to San Diego. By now, she had a good job in Los Angeles and was moving into management at Pacific Mutual Insurance.

His career as an airman began with ground school on the University of California campus, and flight training at Rockwell Field, where Tooey Spaatz had earned his wings three years before. It was an inauspicious beginning. As Doolittle was taxiing out to the runway with his instructor for his first flight in an airplane, two Curtiss JN-4s collided in the air above and crashed, tumbling to the ground in a twisted mess that missed them by only a few yards.

When Doolittle earned his wings and his second lieutenant's bars in March 1918, he expected to be sent overseas to join the US Army airmen training for combat at Issoudun. Instead, he suffered the fate of so many good military pilots on the threshold of their careers. His skill made him desirable as an instructor, and he remained behind, teaching first at Rockwell and later at Kelly Field in Texas.

Meanwhile, Ira Eaker had enlisted in April 1917 when the United States declared war. All 37 of the male students at Southeastern State Normal School raced to the nearest US Army recruiting office, which happened to be in Greenville, Texas. The seniors, including Eaker, who were about to graduate, joined as privates but were diverted to an officer training school that was being set up at Fort Roots in Arkansas.

Only a few years earlier, advancements in rank of just a single grade took years. In 1917, against the backdrop of the wartime expansion, they came quickly. Tooey Spaatz had gone from second lieutenant to captain in ten months. Ira Eaker made it from private to a Reserve Army second lieutenant in four, and earned a Regular Army commission in two.

Shortly after Lieutenant Eaker was assigned to the 64th Infantry Regiment at Fort Bliss, near El Paso, Texas, he was standing on the parade ground when an airplane flew past. He watched the pilot attempt to fly over the mountains to the west, fail to reach the proper altitude, and then circle back to land. When Eaker walked over to speak with him, the pilot explained that he was on a pilot recruiting drive and was trying to reach Deming, New Mexico. Examining the aircraft's engine, Eaker spotted a disconnected spark plug wire, reconnected it, and told the pilot to try again.

The man thanked Eaker and suggested that with his knowledge of aircraft engines—this was the first one Eaker had seen up close—he should apply for flight training. Being on a recruiting drive, he just happened to have copies of the application forms. The paperwork went up the line and back down, and in March 1918 Ira Eaker received orders to report for aviation ground school in Austin. Eight weeks later, he graduated to flight training at Kelly Field.

Four hours into his aerial education, his instructor landed, climbed out, and told Eaker, "You had better take this round by yourself."

He took off solo, executed several touch-and-goes, and by the afternoon, the instructor had him doing loops, rolls, and spins. Eaker earned his wings in July 1918, four months after Jimmy Doolittle. Though his transfer out of the infantry would not be *official* for two years, Lieutenant Ira Eaker was now in the US Army Air Service. Like Doolittle, though, Eaker never made it overseas during the war.

———

By the summer of 1918, Tooey Spaatz had been in France for ten months, having guided the transformation of muddy Issoudun into a first-class training facility. He had overseen the construction of wooden barracks with running water, and ruts had become paved roads. When he arrived, aircraft operations were essentially impossible on the rugged terrain. Within a few months, Issoudun had grown into a complex of ten modern airfields, each one earmarked for a different phase of training. In May 1918, when Kilner was relocated to Pershing's American Expeditionary Forces headquarters, Spaatz, now with the brevet rank of major, took over as base commander.

While in France, Spaatz had met the colorful General William Lendrum "Billy" Mitchell, the senior air commander for the American Expeditionary Forces. A charismatic leader and an outspoken advocate of the use of airpower in warfare, Mitchell was a larger-than-life character who greatly influenced the history of airpower in the early twentieth century, as well as the opinions and careers of most of the young officers who served under him.

In Mitchell, Spaatz found a receptive ear when he expressed his desire to get away from the training base and into combat. Mitchell liked what Spaatz had done at Issoudun and was anxious to keep him in a training role. He had even prepared orders for Spaatz to return to the United States to revamp training there with lessons that had been learned in combat.

When Spaatz complained, Mitchell sympathized with the young warrior's desire to see real combat and promised that he would get a combat tour after he spent some time in the States. Spaatz argued that he should have a combat tour *before* that, adding that he feared the war would be over before he got into action. Mitchell relented, and July 1918 found Spaatz in Toul, on the edge of the Saint-Mihiel salient, assigned— on temporary duty—to the 13th Pursuit Squadron of the 2nd Pursuit Group, where he would be flying the French-built SPAD XIII, arguably the best Allied fighter of the war and widely used by American pilots.

In his new job, Spaatz was destined to be at the center of the action for the great Allied offensive that was to take place in September. The Battle of Saint-Mihiel, in which American airpower was to play an important role in the offensive action, began on September 12, although cloud cover restricted air operations and Spaatz didn't see combat for three days.

Though the term had yet to be coined, the aerial battles of World War I truly resembled dogfights as the masses of opposing fighter planes rolled and tumbled across the sky, with each pilot intent on staying out of the sights of the opposition while attempting to place his own sights on an enemy.

Tooey Spaatz managed to place his gunsight on a German Fokker D.VII and pour a sufficient stream of lead into it to send it cartwheeling into the land battle below. His next and last tangle with German fighters came on September 26, the day that his temporary duty assignment to the 13th expired. In this engagement, Spaatz managed to down two Fokkers in quick succession, but he committed two potentially fatal errors, which were made doubly egregious by the fact that he should have known better, for they were common mistakes.

The first was his becoming so fixated on the enemy aircraft he was attacking that he forgot his own "six" (his six o'clock position, the area of sky directly behind his aircraft). In so doing, he allowed two German fighters to get on his tail. Had Charles Biddle, his squadron commander, not intervened personally, Spaatz would have been a goner. His second flub was that he lingered so long in the battle, running dangerously low on fuel, an error that was compounded by the fact that the aerial battle had drifted into the skies over enemy territory.

Fortunately, he made it as far as no-man's-land before he had to execute a crash landing—and the first troops who reached him were French. Spaatz later told a reporter that he had shot down three aircraft on that day, "two Germans and my own." Billy Mitchell awarded Spaatz the Distinguished Service Cross—despite the preventable loss of a US Army airplane.

When the Great War came to an end on "the eleventh hour of the eleventh day of the eleventh month" of 1918, Brevet Major Tooey Spaatz and his wife were on a train, passing through El Paso, Texas, en route to San Diego's Rockwell Field. When Spaatz reached his first postwar duty station, two of the first men he met were Lieutenants Ira Eaker and Jimmy Doolittle, who had arrived just a short time earlier.

On November 25, 1918, less than a week after the guns fell silent, Doolittle was part of a dramatic 212-plane flyover of San Diego. The *Los Angeles Times* reported that "they formed a ceiling over the sky that almost blotted out the struggling rays of the sun and with majestic solemnity, they patrolled the air, magnificent in the perfection of their formation, and while they framed a perfect background at 5,000 feet, the five aerobats below swooped, dived, looped and spun in as perfect unison as though they had been operated by a single hand."

Jimmy Doolittle was one of the "five aerobats." The media and the public were in love with aviation, and Doolittle, who as a boy had been part of an excited audience, was now the object of air show fascination.

In January 1919, Spaatz, Eaker, and Doolittle were on hand to greet the new commanding officer of the US Army Air Service Western District, Colonel Henry Harley "Hap" Arnold. It was an auspicious moment, as the careers of these men, especially Arnold, Spaatz, and Eaker, would be closely intertwined in a command role for more than a quarter of a century. Arnold would eventually rise through the ranks to serve as America's senior airman in World War II, but all four would play significant roles in the continuing evolution of their service, and in its triumph in that future conflict.

In the meantime, in those early days, before the wartime future we take for granted could be imagined, there was one man who *did* imagine the future of airpower. Arnold, Spaatz, Eaker, and Doolittle were to become his active disciples, and their enthusiasm for his doctrine, as well as the notion of an autonomous—or even *independent*—air force, was to define their careers.

When the First World War ended, Billy Mitchell was the public face of the Air Service. He was the kind of colorful, outspoken character that the media love, and his personality was tailor-made for the role. It had been widely assumed within the Air Service that Mitchell would be given the top job as director (the title was changed to chief after June 1920) of the Air Service. However, he was far too outspoken, and that made his bosses uneasy.

He advocated the independence of the Air Service from the US Army, citing the fact that Britain's Royal Air Force had been spun off as a separate service in 1918. Instead, in what was interpreted by the airman as a decision motivated by a desire to keep the Air Service under the thumb of the *ground* army establishment, the position went to Major General Charles Menoher, who had commanded the 42nd Infantry Division during the war. Though Mitchell was named as Menoher's assistant, for men such as Arnold, Spaatz, Eaker, Doolittle, and many others, his not getting the top job was obviously both a snub and a mistake.

This development served only to stimulate their advocacy of Mitchell's ideas, and fuel the fire that would drive them.

CHAPTER 4

LeMAY, SMITH, AND ZEMKE

The next generation of the eight included two men whose lives were touched by an awareness of World War I but who were too young to have been a part of it. They had entered a world in which powered flight existed but was still mainly a novelty. Airplanes were so rare in those early days of flight that, in most places in the United States, few people had laid eyes on one.

In Columbus, Ohio, only about 65 miles east of where the Wright brothers were inventing aviation, Curtis Emerson LeMay would later recall having seen what he always assumed was one of the Wright Flyer airplanes in the sky when he was about four years old. The sighting made a lasting impression.

Born on November 15, 1906, LeMay was the eldest child of a handyman and sometime railroad hand named Erving LeMay and a farmer's daughter named Arizona Carpenter. The family moved around a great deal during his early years, mainly within Ohio, but when Curt was nearing school age, his father's railroad career took the family, which now included Curt's younger sister, Velma, and their new brother, Lloyd, west to Montana.

The LeMays settled in at Nezperce, an obscure whistle-stop north-west of Butte. The boy who had once beheld the future in the magic of a Wright Flyer in the sky now found himself in a place as yet untouched by the technology of the twentieth century, where the "Old West" still prevailed, and where a young boy went to school on the back of a horse. He enjoyed the riding part, but cared little for the school part.

While LeMay's father was a drifter who transported his family beyond the fringes of twentieth-century civilization, Maynard Harrison Smith's father was an attorney in the Michigan "Thumb" region north of Detroit. Henry Harrison Smith was the very archetype of the establishment man, thoroughly rooted in public life. Just two years younger than Le-May, Smith was born into a solid middle-class family on May 19, 1911, in Caro, Michigan. Located about 30 miles east of Saginaw and 40 miles northeast of Flint, Caro was a town of nearly 2,000 people, founded in 1847 by a man named Curtis Emerson—who apparently was not related to the family of Curtis Emerson LeMay.

In 1928, when Maynard was 17, his father was named to the bench as presiding judge in the 40th Judicial Circuit. Of the stern and uncompromising Judge Smith, the local *Advertiser* wrote in 1934 that he "gave his undivided attention to every matter which came before his court. He had little sympathy with those who sought to involve cases with too many technicalities. Evil doers convicted in his court for major crimes . . . received little mercy, and it has been said that Tuscola County was quite free from such activities because criminals knew that they would be punished to the extent of the law, should they be captured and convicted."

The irony was that Judge Smith's only son—of four children—was as likely as anyone to get into trouble. A May 1929 article in the *Cass City Chronicle* reported: "Four people narrowly escaped fatal injuries Thurs-day evening, when the automobile driven by Maynard Smith, 18, of Caro collided with a horse and buggy two miles west of Caro on the Gilford

Road. Mr. and Mrs. Benjamin Cody of Caro were riding in the buggy. Mr. Cody received fractured ribs and Mrs. Cody suffered from shock. The horse was driven from the shafts and killed instantly."

The boy with the need for speed was not cited.

The author Allen Mikaelian wrote that "Maynard got used to getting what he wanted, and what he wanted was trouble, [and] he got away with it. By the time he was old enough to cause a serious ruckus, his father was a circuit court judge with no tolerance for the policeman or prosecutor brave enough to drag his boy into court."

In fact, the judge and Mrs. Mary Goes Smith, a busy primary school teacher, deliberately spoiled their son, rarely disciplining him at home and shielding him from the outside world. As Maynard's own son told Mikaelian many years later, "My dad was never really made to do any-thing. . . . He always had pretty much what he wanted or wished."

By the time Maynard, who was known as "Hokie" (sometimes seen spelled "Hokey")—his "Snuffy" nickname came later—was in his teens, what he "wanted or wished" came to include all manner of dangerous high jinks with cars and motorcycles, including chasing a cop up a light pole.

Hubert Zemke entered the world on March 14, 1914—his mother's twenty-fifth birthday—in Missoula, Montana, the seat and largest city in a Montana county of the same name that was nearly four times the size of Rhode Island but home to fewer than 5,000 people. Coincidentally, just 100 miles to the north, the author's father (born in 1908) was growing up on a homestead in Montana's Flathead Valley, a place that was even more remote.

For the Zemke family, being first-generation German immigrants, the outside world intruded upon their solitude in the form of the anti-German sentiment that reared its ugly head across the United States dur-ing World War I. Benno Zemke had arrived in the United States at the turn of the century, a young merchant seaman from Pomerania who jumped ship in Philadelphia. He was deported, but he tried again, and finally entered legally in 1904.

Zemke wound up with a job as a section hand with the Northern Pacific Railway and landed in Missoula, 100 miles west of where Erving LeMay later held a similar job. By 1910, he had amassed a nest egg sufficient to allow him the rare luxury of a vacation in his homeland. On his return voyage, he met Anna Maria Kutter, a Bavarian girl headed for a housemaid's job in Chicago. A long-distance correspondence led to a wedding in 1911, and the birth of their only child. Anna wanted to name him Wolfgang after Mozart, but Benno's uncle Hubert—a name that Anna always pronounced "Hoo-bart"—became the boy's namesake.

Hubert would have remembered little of the wartime anti-German bigotry, but he grew up being called "kraut" by the bullies about town. Like Jimmy Doolittle, he learned to take care of himself with his own hands, and was the state middleweight boxing champ for two years running while he was at Montana State University (now the University of Montana). In the ring, Hubert was known as "the Hub," and thereafter, the nickname stuck. He would always be known, except by his mother, as "Hub" Zemke.

It was while the LeMay family was in Montana that Erving began to take young Curt hunting, and the boy quickly developed a love of shooting and a respect for the power of firearms that would remain with him long after a horse and saddle were no longer the preferred method of travel. The family's sojourn in rural Montana was short-lived, as Erving LeMay pulled up stakes and headed west toward California and their next short-term home in Emeryville, on the marshy flats east of San Francisco Bay, a few miles from where Doolittle had spent his earliest years. It was while they were in Emeryville that the family's fourth daughter was born. She was named Methyll, a variation on the name of a cousin, Ethyllm LeMay.

The LeMays arrived in time to be present for San Francisco's great

1915 Panama-Pacific Exposition, a world's fair designed to celebrate both the promise of California's role in the world after the completion of the Panama Canal and San Francisco's own "bigger and better" rebirth after the Great Earthquake of 1906.

For Curtis LeMay, the highlight of the Panama-Pacific Exposition was becoming reacquainted with aviation. He had seen the Wright brothers a decade earlier, and now it was the Loughead brothers, who had just built an airplane in San Francisco that would be the first of many for the company that became Lockheed. In the sky above the fairgrounds were the great daredevils of whom the reigning monarch was the renowned Lincoln Beachey, considered by many to be the world's greatest aviator.

Beachey's death, which came quickly when aerodynamic stress crumpled his fragile airplane while he performed above San Francisco Bay, did not deter Curtis LeMay from his thoughts of aviation.

The LeMays were not long for the Golden State, however. Once again, Erving's wanderlust put them on the road. Erving and Arizona took the family back to Ohio by way of Pennsylvania, where their fifth child, Leonard, was born and where Curt graduated from high school in Columbus. He had wanted to go on to West Point, but this was impossible without a congressional appointment or the sort of contacts that came from putting down roots in a place longer than Erving LeMay had ever allowed himself to do. In 1924, Curt enrolled at Ohio State University in Columbus.

He worked his way through college with a swing-shift job at a steel foundry, a circumstance that allowed little time for extracurricular activities and often placed him in morning classes with his mind and body in a state of exhaustion. If his standing in other classes suffered, the Reserve Officer Training Corps (ROTC) became his focus and his top priority.

By now, LeMay had decided that he wanted to be a pilot. He had paid $2.50 to a state fair barnstormer for a five-minute jaunt, and had been seduced by the experience. Like so many members of his generation, LeMay thought the military seemed a good path to an aviation career, and he reasoned that ROTC would give him a better chance of eventually getting into US Army flight school.

In 1928, after four years at Ohio State, LeMay was still 15 credits short of the number required for graduation (he subsequently made them up), but he was an honor graduate of the ROTC program.

There were no Regular Army slots open to him in Ohio in 1928, but his ROTC honors earned him a commission in the US Army Reserve. Much to his chagrin, he discovered that Reserve officers had little chance of getting into flight school—but enlisted men in the Ohio National Guard had a better chance of becoming a pilot. He then decided to resign his new officer's commission and enlist as a private in the National Guard. When he was in the process of doing this, he crossed paths with a "nice old brigadier general" whom he had met as an ROTC cadet. The general thought LeMay was crazy until he explained his desire to learn to fly. As luck would have it, the general had the power to bring LeMay into the National Guard as a second lieutenant as a gateway to a regular commission in the US Army Air Corps—and as a flying cadet. He was ordered to report for pilot training at March Field, near Riverside, California—coincidentally the place where he lived during his final years—in November 1928.

As LeMay had done at Ohio State, Hub Zemke enrolled in the ROTC program at Montana State. With LeMay, it had been a conscious decision aimed at a career as a US Army aviator. For Zemke, two years of ROTC were required of male students, and another two opened up the option for a US Army Reserve commission. There were few airplanes in the skies over Montana in the early 1930s, and Zemke would remain unbitten by the aviation bug until after he had completed his first two years.

Among the airplanes that *were* in Montana skies were those operated by Bob Johnson, one of the state's aviation pioneers. Johnson Flying Service operated a fleet of charter aircraft out of Missoula, and was later a pioneer in the development and deployment of "smokejumpers," people who fought forest fires in places that were far from the nearest roads by parachuting into these remote areas.

One day in 1935, Zemke drove out to the airport and paid for a ride into the Big Sky of Montana aboard Johnson's Stinson biplane. His second flight would be in the skies over Texas, courtesy of the US Army.

CHAPTER 5

ROSENTHAL AND MORGAN

While the three oldest of the eight were in uniform when the United States entered the Great War, the youngest two were born during the war.

Robert Rosenthal was born on June 11, 1917, in Brooklyn, New York, the first son and second child of Samuel Rosenthal, a technician with the New York City Health Department, and his wife, Rose. Their daughter, Jeannette, was three years older than Robert, though he later recalled with a chuckle that when they were adults, she referred to him as her "older brother."

While Robert was growing up, the Rosenthal family lived on East 21st Street near Avenue X in the Sheepshead Bay neighborhood of southern Brooklyn, a few miles north of Brighton Beach and Coney Island. There was a great deal of elbow room in Sheepshead Bay while Robert and Jeannette were growing up. Indeed, there was a goat farm on East 22nd, not far from their home. "It was not bucolic," Robert said many years later of the neighborhood, "but it was a laid-back, open area."

———

Robert Knight Morgan was born into a life of privilege in Asheville, North Carolina, on July 31, 1918. He grew up in a household where he was surrounded by servants, but he triumphed over advantage the way some of the others, notably Ira Eaker, triumphed over disadvantage.

In his memoirs, he describes himself as "the first true Southerner of my family line," because his parents, David Bradley Morgan and Mabel Knight Morgan, had only just relocated to Asheville from Chicago, where their older children, David and Peggy, had been born. Bob grew up in a 4,000-square-foot home built by his father's employer, Carolina Wood Products, which manufactured furniture as well as homes. He described the house as one of his father's "perks."

Other perks flowed from the family's association with the regional high society. One of Mabel's Asheville friends was Cornelia Vanderbilt Cecil, whose father, George Washington Vanderbilt II, had built a 178,926-square-foot family home called Biltmore House, the largest private home in the United States. The two women met at the country club where both were members.

David Bradley Morgan later helped form and became president of Dimension Manufacturing Company, another furniture maker; he became even wealthier, and built another home near Biltmore when Bob was nine. During the Roaring Twenties, the country club world of fashionable soirees at Biltmore was enough to have made the "Great" Jay Gatsby feel at home, and it continued as though it would never end—until young Bob was 11.

"We never talked about it around the house when it hit, not openly anyway," Bob Morgan wrote in his memoirs of the stock market crash of 1929. "It was whispers, glances between [my parents], long silences at dinner where there had always been lively conversation. My brother and sister and I never officially learned what had happened."

Dimension Manufacturing Company struggled, then collapsed. The family home was sold, and David Morgan took a job as a night watchman at 5 percent of his Roaring Twenties salary. As Bob recalled, "The hardships we went through changed me for life, and not necessarily for the worse."

Befriended by Cornelia Vanderbilt, Mabel spent much of the next several years traveling with her in Europe, and later settled in Washington, DC, with Peggy—while David attempted to revive Dimension Manufacturing with loans from the New Deal–era Reconstruction Finance Corporation, and as their two sons worked their way through school. Eventually, both of the boys attended Episcopal High School in Alexandria, Virginia, across the Potomac from Washington, but by the time Bob arrived, David was at the University of North Carolina and Mabel had moved back to Asheville.

Bob Morgan recalled that the "hardest blow of my life" came in 1936, when he was 17. His mother, with whom he had been close as a child but who had been absent from his life for several years, was diagnosed with inoperable thyroid cancer. Realizing the futility of her situation, Mabel took Bob's old squirrel gun from the closet and turned the .410-gauge barrel upon herself.

CHAPTER 6

AT THE THRESHOLD
OF POSTWAR AVIATION

The World War I years had demonstrated the potential of aviation as
not just machines of war but machines that could bind distant
places more closely by reducing travel time between them. Just as civilians in Europe and America were beginning to implement the first airline schemes, the young aviation advocates within the Air Service were
imagining ways to demonstrate the potential of military aviation.

While Arnold, Spaatz, Eaker, and Doolittle were still at Rockwell
Field, they were on hand to witness some of the first of the numerous
long-endurance flights that proliferated in the United States in the decade
after the end of World War I. In October 1919, Spaatz himself flew in the
Transcontinental Reliability and Endurance Test—also called the Great
Transcontinental Air Race—a scheme conceived by Billy Mitchell involving 48 Air Service aircraft, half flying west from Roosevelt Field on Long
Island and half traveling east from Chrissy Field in San Francisco. Flying
an American-built de Havilland DH-4 twin-cockpit biplane, Spaatz came
in second—by 20 seconds—among the eastbound contingent. He would
have been first had he not landed at the wrong airfield and had to take
off again.

As Spaatz and the exceedingly meticulous Eaker were moving toward career paths that would find them earmarked for *responsible* command positions early in their careers, Jimmy Doolittle was developing a reputation for the *irresponsible*. As a pilot, he was a natural, one of those aviators for whom flying was second nature, and for whom the controls were like an extension of his own hands.

Like many a skilled aviator of that early generation of flight, Doolittle was also a daredevil. "I admit to being a bit of a mischief maker and am guilty of having had a little fun in an airplane," he wrote in his memoirs, describing himself as "free of spirit and a rebellious fighter pilot at heart." It was ironic that he was to achieve his greatest fame leading bombers, not fighters, but his skill and fearlessness, exhibited in fighters, would be a characteristic of his future notoriety.

In June 1919, the Air Service was in the midst of a downsizing nearly as precipitous as its growth two years before. From 311 men in 1916, it had reached a peak of 195,023 in 1918, but in 1920, it was plummeting toward 9,050. The once robust training operation at Rockwell Field was down to nine instructors by the summer of 1919, and everyone was getting his transfer papers. Hap Arnold was reassigned to the Presidio of San Francisco as air commander of the IX Corps area, the western half of the United States, and Spaatz joined him there as his assistant a month later.

Meanwhile, Ira Eaker received orders to embark for the Philippines, where he wound up with the 3rd Aero Squadron at Camp Stotsenburg, 50 miles north of Manila, where the landing field had just been renamed for Major Harold Clark, an Air Service pilot who had been killed in a crash in Panama. "We mowed a little strip out of the cavalry maneuver area and used it for a field," he later recalled in an Air Force Historical Research Center interview.

Under Eaker's command, the 3rd Aero erected the first hangar at Clark Field, which evolved into the largest US Army air base in the Far East.

Despite the technological advances that had come during the war, the state of aviation was still rather primitive. A case in point was the systems that Eaker and Lieutenant Newton Longfellow jury-rigged to help them fly through the low cloud cover that frequently blanketed the Philippines.

"We'd pull up to about cloud level and get in them briefly," Eaker explained. "By having a plumb bob hanging down the center of our brief instrument board and by putting a carpenter's level on the top longeron, you could tell . . . when you were diving and when you were climbing. And you could tell by the plumb bob when you were turning to the right and turning to the left. [We practiced until we] could climb through 5,000 feet of cloud, come out on top and then come back through safely. That was the first demonstration that I had seen of the ability to fly with instruments."

In July 1920, when Eaker's transfer from the infantry to the Air Service became official, he was promoted to captain and in September he was made executive officer of the Philippines Department Air Office, which was then commanded by General Leonard Wood, a future US Army chief of staff. Despite his decidedly junior rank, Eaker got along well with the colonels and generals at the headquarters, who recognized the value of military aviation—at least as an observation tool—and respected the new captain's opinions with regard to its practical application, in addition to appreciating his technical knowledge.

In the summer of 1921, when his tour of duty in the Philippines concluded, Eaker headed home by sailing westward. Instead of traveling east, back across the Pacific to the West Coast of the United States, many officers chose to go in the opposite direction, thus completing a circumnavigation of the globe. Indeed, Hap Arnold had done this in 1909 when his tour as an infantry officer in the Philippines had ended. It was on this trip that he saw his first airplane, this being the Type XI monoplane with which Louis Blériot had just completed the first-ever aerial crossing of the English Channel.

Eaker's odyssey took him to Indochina and a stopover in Saigon, a location that was to play an important role in American military history later in the century. He also visited Singapore, Suez, and Cairo, making landfall in Barcelona. Whereas Blériot had once made history with his international flight, Ira Eaker flew from Paris to London on a commercial airliner. So much in aviation had changed in those dozen years.

However, Eaker still had yet to decide upon aviation as his life's work. Even after he returned to his homeland and was named commanding officer of the 5th Aero Squadron at Mitchel Field on Long Island in January 1922, he still assumed that he would soon turn in his uniform for a suit, a tie, and a stint in law school. Indeed the US Army was downsizing dramatically, offering captains a year's salary as an incentive for *leaving* the service.

In life, momentous turning points often happen by chance, and such was the case with the career of Ira Eaker. He was a matter of weeks from leaving the US Army when Major General Mason Patrick landed at Mitchel Field. The second of two consecutive West Point classmates of General Pershing to serve as chief of the US Army Air Service, Patrick was on his way to the Army-Navy football game when his pilot fell ill and could not continue. When they touched down at Mitchel, it was a Saturday, and Ira Eaker happened to be the only qualified pilot on duty. He flew Patrick to West Point, and then back to Washington, DC. In the course of their time together, Eaker told his boss of his plans to get out and go to law school.

"I'm authorized to send two percent of the officers in the Army to educational institutions," Patrick told him, trying to persuade him to remain in uniform. "I'll send you to law school. Where do you want to go?"

"Columbia University, sir."

Patrick no doubt recognized that a good officer aims high, and Eaker's orders to report to New York City's Ivy League institution came through a week later.

———

In 1919, as Arnold, Spaatz, and Eaker had moved north and west from Rockwell Field, Doolittle was reassigned to the 90th Aero Squadron at Eagle Pass, Texas. He remained there until July 1920, flying DH-4s and Jennies on patrol over the same unsettled border country that had stymied Black Jack Pershing and thrilled Tooey Spaatz three years earlier.

Forbidden by their rules of engagement from firing on Mexican bandits crossing the border, Doolittle and his fellow pilots had to content themselves with harassing them. In one instance, they stampeded a herd of cattle, which chased a band of Mexican snipers into the Rio Grande. During this time, Doolittle's only incursion deep into Mexican territory involved leading a mule train into the desert 80 miles south of the border to repair a downed DH-4 so that it could be flown out.

During the early 1920s, both Doolittle and Spaatz passed through the large aviation training base at Kelly Field in Texas. Spaatz had departed from his post in San Francisco, served a few months at Mather Field near Sacramento, and landed at Kelly to serve as the air officer to the headquarters of VIII Corps.

It was while Doolittle and his wife were at Kelly Field that both of their sons were born at the US Army hospital at nearby Fort Sam Houston. James Junior was born in October 1920, and John in June 1922. In his memoirs, Doolittle questions whether he "did him any favors" by naming his elder son after himself.

Spaatz's oldest, Katharine, called "Tattie," was also born in Texas, midway between the Doolittle boys, in April 1921. Her sister Rebecca, known as "Beckie," followed in May 1923 after the family moved to Selfridge Field in Michigan. Carla, named for her father, would arrive in 1932 while the family was in California. As for Ira Eaker, though he would be married twice, he had no children.

In November 1921, Spaatz was given command of the 1st Pursuit Group, then the Air Service's only dedicated pursuit group, an assignment that would continue until 1924. It was with the 1st, initially at

Ellington Field near Houston and later at Selfridge, that Spaatz at last was able to fulfill his army pilot's dream of being in the cockpit in command of a tactical unit.

On the ground, however, Spaatz was confronted by the difficult realities of a downsizing postwar US Army. At one point, he called for a civilian motorized ambulance to take an injured pilot to the hospital. When he asked for reimbursement from VIII Corps, he was refused because the US Army had plenty of horse-drawn vehicles that might have been used. So Spaatz took up a collection from the other pilots. The pilot, John Cannon, survived to become a general and the commander of the Twelfth Air Force during World War II.

When the 1st Pursuit Group relocated to Selfridge in the summer of 1922, Spaatz found conditions scarcely better than they had been at Issoudun when he had arrived there five years earlier. The good news was that he had a few months to fix up the place before the winter snows began to blow. The bad news was that he had to do it before October, when the base would be called upon to host the third annual National Air Races, aka the Pulitzer Trophy Race.

As Ira Eaker crossed paths with General Mason Patrick in 1922, so too did Tooey Spaatz. In this case, the boss had learned that liquor was being consumed at the Selfridge Field Officers' Club in defiance of Prohibition, which had become the law of the land in 1920. Spaatz might have expressed a stunned denial, but instead he told the chief that he thought it better for the men to be drinking on base as they always had rather than poking around Detroit looking for speakeasies that might be subject to police raids that could result in embarrassment to the Air Service. Patrick let the matter slide.

Spaatz left Selfridge in September 1924 and attended the Air Corps Tactical School at Langley Field in Virginia until June 1925, when he was brought into Washington, DC, to serve in Mason Patrick's headquarters. It was here that he would serve once again alongside Hap Arnold, and get to know the charismatic Billy Mitchell. These would be exciting times in the halls of headquarters, as many friendships and alliances were formed that would later help to define the strategic direction of World War II.

In Washington, the real work of the Air Service—or at least the business of promoting airpower—was being done by Patrick's assistant. As far as the men of his service were concerned, Mitchell was its guiding spirit. While Patrick concerned himself with routine management issues, it was Mitchell who was the service's advocate and the man who had taken it upon himself to craft and institutionalize tactical and strategic doctrine. Spaatz was in the right place at the right time. When it came to writing the official manuals for pursuit tactics, Mitchell turned to the recent commander of the 1st Pursuit Group.

Even as he remained the public face of the Air Service, Billy Mitchell was becoming a controversial figure. In 1921, he incurred the wrath of the US Navy, and the embarrassment of the US Army, by asserting that he could use bombers to sink a battleship, the emblem of national military prowess around the world. The notion was considered absurd, so a demonstration was arranged with the idea that Mitchell would be humiliated and would go away quietly.

However, Mitchell's air service earned front-page notoriety by sinking the captured German battleship *Ostfriesland* in Chesapeake Bay, and with repeated success in a series of attacks on obsolete American battleships in 1924. Jimmy Doolittle, now posted to Langley Field in Virginia, piloted one of the DH-4s that sank the USS *Alabama*.

It was a turning point in the history of American airpower, but the apogee of Mitchell's own power. In March 1925, his outspokenness led to his being transferred out of Washington. Exiled to San Antonio, he continued to speak out, and in September his rhetoric mushroomed into accusations of "incompetence, criminal negligence and almost treasonable administration of the national defense by the Navy and War Departments" in the wake of the crash of the Navy airship USS *Shenandoah* during a public relations tour. Almost immediately, at the urging of

President Calvin Coolidge, court-martial proceedings were brought against Mitchell for insubordination. The young airmen in Mitchell's Air Service saw the court-martial as an assault on of the idea of an autonomous air arm and the ideals of airpower doctrine as promulgated by Mitchell.

When he was convicted and suspended from duty, they saw their hero and role model as a martyr, which served to bind them together and to fire them with a common determination to see Mitchell's vision for a powerful American air arm become a reality. Meanwhile, strong public support for Mitchell compelled Coolidge to appoint a commission to investigate Mitchell's charges of inadequacy in the US Army's treatment of the Air Service, and to study American aviation in general. To head the commission, he picked Dwight Morrow, his old Amherst College classmate, now a successful financier and the future father-in-law of the soon-to-be-famous aviator Charles Lindbergh.

Morrow's panel of military and civilian aviation experts confirmed much of what Mitchell had asserted, and recommended that the US Army elevate the status of its aviation section to a position comparable to the Quartermaster Corps or the Signal Corps. This recommendation was implemented with the Air Corps Act of July 1926 and the creation of the US Army Air Corps.

CHAPTER 7

INTO AVIATION'S GOLDEN AGE

B y the time of the Mitchell court-martial trial in late 1925, Hap Arnold and Tooey Spaatz, who both testified on Mitchell's behalf, as well as Ira Eaker, were assigned to Air Service Headquarters in the sprawling Munitions Building on Avenue B (now Constitution Avenue) in Washington, DC. This trio, who had known one another at Rockwell Field, were together again, and now at the epicenter of the action for one of airpower's defining moments.

Arnold, who had also been outspoken about airpower issues and autonomy for the Air Corps, but less so than Mitchell, was "exiled" (his own characterization) to Fort Riley, Kansas, in March 1926, but Spaatz and Eaker remained in Washington for a time. Spaatz served as chief of the Tactical Units Branch of the Air Corps, which put him in the position of selecting and equipping air bases throughout the United States.

Eaker, who had completed one semester at Columbia Law School, had been summoned to Washington by his mentor, Mason Patrick. The chief of the Army Air Corps liked what he saw in Eaker and wanted the young flyer to serve as his assistant.

"Your record shows that you are studious," Eaker later recalled him saying. "I do not require legal counsel, but I do need the assistance of a precise, legally trained mind and the expertise in preparing briefs of a trained lawyer."

"My primary duties would involve working directly with him, preparing drafts of his speeches and his reports to the War Department and Congress," Eaker noted in a June 1973 article in *Aerospace Historian*. "I learned a great deal in the three years I worked for General Patrick. Perhaps most important, he taught me to use simple words and short sentences. One day I discovered the word 'exacerbate,' and could scarcely wait to include it in his next speech. When he came to the word in his draft, he asked what it meant. I said, 'Increase, Sir.' I never forgot his response. 'We write to entertain or convince the largest number of readers. I assure you that several hundred will understand increase for everyone who relates to exacerbate. When you write for me always keep to the low road; write for the great majority, not for the sophisticates.' I never used exacerbate again, until now."

In turn, Eaker frequently served as Patrick's pilot, transporting him to locations outside Washington—before *and* after Patrick learned to fly himself in 1922. Eaker's biographer, James Parton, notes that Eaker was the only pilot with whom General Douglas MacArthur flew during the time that he was the chief of staff.

While Arnold and Spaatz were enamored with Mitchell's tone and substance, Eaker admired Patrick's more measured approach and considered him "our most respected and effective advocate of airpower," going on to say that Patrick "got more for the Army [Air] Service than anyone else could have gotten because of the high standing he had in the top echelons of the military. The Secretary of War had great confidence in him, and the men on the General Staff had great admiration for him. The War Department would have given the Army Air Service a very bad time if we hadn't had General Patrick."

———

It was in 1924, on Patrick's watch, that the US Army air arm had caught the attention of the public around the world literally by *flying* around the world. In April of that year, four Douglas World Cruisers, modified O-5 observation planes, set out from Clover Field in Santa Monica, California, and headed north and west to Asia by way of Alaska. In September, five months and numerous adventures later, three World Cruisers, including two of the original four, landed in Seattle, becoming the first aircraft to circumnavigate the globe.

Meanwhile, Jimmy Doolittle was also making a name for himself among the flurry of record-setting flights that captured both headlines and the imagination of a public newly fascinated with the feats of airmen. In so doing, he became a pioneer of instrument flying, and he also made a series of revolutionary and unanticipated discoveries about the psychology of flying.

By 1922, several unsuccessful attempts had been made to fly across the United States in less than 24 hours. Naturally, there were many who asserted that such a feat was impossible, but—also naturally—Jimmy Doolittle was not among them. He calculated how it could be done, and how the fuel tanks in a DH-4 would have to be enlarged to make it possible with just a single stop en route. He pitched the scheme to Mason Patrick personally, and it was approved.

On August 4, on his first attempt, Doolittle took off from Pablo Beach near Jacksonville, Florida, skidded in beach sand, and crashed—upside down—in the surf. One month later, he tried again, taking off after dark, planning to cross the well-lit Southeast at night, reaching Kelly Field at dawn, and flying the sparsely populated Southwest in daylight.

"From Kelly to the Arizona border, nothing happened to disturb the serenity of the voyage," he wrote in his memoirs. "The desolate appearance of the country and the constant throb of the Liberty engine began to lull me to sleep. Despite the fact that sleep meant death, my head began to nod. But good fortune perched on the cowl. A light rain began falling. The raindrops, whipped back by the propeller, began eddying over the windshield and running in a tiny stream down my back. This made me angry, but was the stimulant I needed. The rain refreshed me, woke me up, and I settled back feeling safe."

He touched down at Rockwell Field that evening, having flown 2,163 miles in less than 23 hours. For this, he was awarded the Distinguished Flying Cross, albeit seven years later.

His immediate reward, however, was an official recognition of his immense, though nascent, aptitude for practical aeronautical engineering. Doolittle was next posted as a test pilot to the headquarters of the Air Service's Engineering Division at McCook Field, adjacent to where the Wright brothers had based their original operations east of Dayton, Ohio. Superseded by the larger Wright Field in 1927, and now part of Wright-Patterson AFB, the facilities in this area have been the center of engineering for the US Air Force and its predecessors ever since. Over the ensuing years, Doolittle spent a great deal of time at McCook, being posted there between other assignments, mainly involving engineering work at other locations.

The undisciplined daredevil of only a few years earlier, now a father of two, was maturing. He graduated from the Air Service engineering school at McCook, and in July 1923 was accepted into a graduate studies program at the Massachusetts Institute of Technology, which then contained the leading aeronautical engineering school in the United States. He earned his master's degree in just one year, and a doctorate in June 1925—thanks in part to his continued access to experimental aircraft at McCook, and in part to his wife's aid in helping him review and memorize his class notes. During those years, Joe Doolittle probably learned enough to warrant an advanced engineering degree of her own. For Jimmy, his master's thesis on aircraft acceleration and stress—based on his own test flights at McCook—later earned him a second Distinguished Flying Cross.

That daredevil who matured into *Dr.* James Doolittle had neither lost his lust for the extreme nor abandoned his desire for entries in his pilot's log. His next "career" after that of a doctoral student was that of an air racer.

Today, it is largely forgotten that in the 1920s, both the US Navy and the US Army acquired aircraft explicitly as race planes, with the best known being the Curtiss R3C, a racing seaplane based on the Navy's F3C fighter. The racers had no practical function other than to fly against civilian racing planes in the numerous national and international air races that studded the aviation calendar during the Roaring Twenties.

One such event was the Schneider Cup race, a seaplane competition that had been initiated in 1913 by aviation enthusiast Jacques Schneider. Flown twice before World War I, and resumed in 1920, it took place in Europe through 1923, and was won by Europeans each year *until* 1923, when a win by the American pilot David Rittenhouse brought the competition across the Atlantic. After a cancellation of the race in 1924, the 1925 Schneider Cup race took place on a 217.5-mile course over Chesapeake Bay, near Baltimore, on October 26. The competitors included three British pilots, two Italians, two US Navy pilots, and Jimmy Doolittle. Despite having had virtually no experience in seaplanes, Doolittle won the race, setting a new world seaplane speed record of 232.57 miles per hour.

Dr. Doolittle, still possessing his lust for the extreme, was pleased with Schneider's trophy but unsatisfied with the performance that had earned it. Before the men of the Fédération Aéronautique Internationale, which authenticated aeronautical records, had packed their bags to go home, Doolittle asked them to clock him in another race, this time against his own winning speed. The result was 245.7 miles per hour, a new world record for seaplanes.

The manufacturer of the R3C, the Curtiss Aeroplane and Motor Company—no longer headed by Glenn Curtiss, its founder—was sufficiently impressed with Doolittle to ask the Army to loan him out to help them sell airplanes in South America. In the spring of 1926, a Curtiss delegation set sail with a crated P-1 Hawk pursuit plane and Doolittle as their star attractions.

On May 23 near Santiago, Chile, Doolittle's daredevil streak led him to leap from a balcony to impress some Chilean pilots with whom he was drinking, and that leap led to a pair of broken ankles. For a lesser man, this might have been the end of a promising career, and certainly the end of the sales tour—but not for Doolittle.

Though he could not walk without crutches, he slipped out of the hospital, modified his two casts with a hacksaw, pulled on his flying boots, and had himself loaded into the cockpit of the Hawk at the airfield on demonstration day.

Doolittle flew the Hawk in competition with a German Dornier aircraft demonstrated by Carl-August von Schoenebeck, an eight-victory ace while flying with the German Air Force in World War I. Despite his injuries and the clumsiness of his casts, Doolittle flew rings around von Schoenebeck. And Chile bought 16 Hawks from Curtiss.

Later in 1926, Ira Eaker also headed south toward Chile on an official Air Corps mission, inspired by the round-the-world flight of 1924. Conceived by Mason Patrick and approved by the Coolidge White House, the Pan American Good Will Flight was designed to be a political and diplomatic showcase to promote commercial aviation as well as harmony and fellowship between the United States and Latin America.

At the same time, in a geopolitical nuance that is often forgotten today, the United States itself was distrusting of the Germans, who were actively securing a foothold in the region. Even as Jimmy Doolittle's competition in Chile had been a German, the Germans were pioneering commercial air travel on the continent. This included Bogotá-based Sociedad Colombo Alemana de Transporte Aéreo (SCADTA), as well as Viäçao Aérea Rio-Grandense (predecessor of today's VARIG), airlines that were then operated by German interests and former German military airmen.

At the time, American interests offered no serious airline competition to the Germans. While most people in the United States took little interest in a potential German domination of Latin American aviation, there was a school of thought that perceived this as a strategic move that posed a threat to American national security.

The Pan American Good Will Flight consisted of five Loening OA-1A unarmed flying boat observation planes on a 23,000-mile tour that took them to the capital of nearly every country in Latin America. The airmen departed from San Antonio in December 1926, spending 59 of the next 133 days in the air and the remaining time engaged in diplomatic schmoozing.

"After a normal flight of four to six hours, we landed at primitive fields or in rivers or bays, then taxied onto beaches to facilitate mainte- nance and refueling, which normally required three to four hours," wrote Eaker in a September 1975 article in *Air Force* magazine. "We thus arrived at our lodgings, arranged by the advance officers, late in the afternoon, discarded mechanic's overalls, and prepared for social functions. . . . There was a banquet every night given by the American colony or by the officials of the country. These usually lasted, with the dancing that habitually followed, until midnight. So, to bed by midnight for four hours of sleep before the 4:00 a.m. call for a new day of flying, mechanical maintenance, and social or protocol events. The latter could not be avoided or slighted since, after all, the first priority of our mission was diplomatic. Captain McDaniel remarked near the end of our flight that we had danced more miles than we had flown."

Despite this apparently innocuous description, the mission was fraught with technical difficulties, navigational and meteorological as well as mechanical. Two of the aircraft were damaged but repaired. An- other two collided over Argentina and were lost, taking two of the four crew members aboard to their deaths.

Today it is not widely remembered that Tooey Spaatz and Hap Arnold founded Pan American Airways, but indeed they did. Early in 1927, while Ira Eaker was still in South America, it was quietly announced that SCADTA was prepared to bid on a contract to carry air mail between Bogotá and the United States by way of Panama, overflying the Panama Canal. Arnold was the information officer at Air Corps headquarters—a post later held by Eaker—when he learned of this. He phoned Postmaster General Harry New, who explained that no American airline was in a position to serve such a route.

Unconventional circumstances often call for unconventional measures. Arnold called Tooey Spaatz into his office, and together they hatched the scheme to create a competing airline. In March 1927 Pan American Airways was formed as a shell company for the sole purpose of giving New an alternative to SCADTA when awarding the contract. He exercised that option, and in June 1928 Pan American was merged into the Aviation Corporation of the Americas (ACA), founded by Juan Trippe in June 1927. The merged airline retained the Pan American name, and went on to evolve into America's international flag carrier for the ensuing half century, one of history's greatest airlines. Arnold and Spaatz, the airline's founders, returned to the relative anonymity of their day jobs at Air Corps headquarters.

When Ira Eaker and the Pan American Good Will Flight returned to Washington early in May 1927, the crews were met by a flurry of media excitement and by President Coolidge, who awarded each man a Distinguished Flying Cross.

Their glory was short-lived. On May 21, Charles Lindbergh landed in Paris, having become the first man to fly across the Atlantic Ocean solo. The place of aviation in the imagination of the American people would never be the same.

CHAPTER 8

PUSHING ENVELOPES

The 1920s and early 1930s were the time in which aviation began to define itself. It was an era of "pushing the edge of the flight envelope," of going beyond the limitations of what was considered possible. Tooey Spaatz, Ira Eaker, and Jimmy Doolittle would all be part of this. It was a time of exploring limits, not only technologically but also operationally, commercially, and politically.

The Roaring Twenties had been an era of "firsts" in the fresh new world of aviation, and it seemed as though each first was followed in rapid succession by the next. Aviators, with Charles Lindbergh atop the pantheon, had become the "rock stars" of the Roaring Twenties.

On May 25, 1927, four days after Lindbergh landed in Paris, Jimmy Doolittle earned some attention for himself. Taking off from McCook Field in a Curtiss Hawk, he became—probably—the first man in history to execute an outside loop. This maneuver creates tremendous G-force and was considered to be potentially fatal.

"My eyes were bloodshot, but I suffered no other ill effects," he reported. His feat was duly noted in the newspapers.

One of aviation's most vexing problems has always been range and endurance. Refueling an aircraft in flight was an obvious solution, though in the 1920s this was still theoretical. In 1923, Captain Lowell Smith and Lieutenant John Richter became the first to have their aircraft successfully refueled in flight, but the Air Corps allowed the aerial refueling concept to languish.

In 1928, Captain Ira Eaker and Lieutenant Elwood "Pete" Quesada were involved in an effort to rescue some German pilots stranded on an island off Labrador. After being forced down because of lack of fuel themselves, they began to discuss the idea of using aerial refueling to make a very long-duration demonstration flight.

Approved by Major General James Fechet, chief of the Air Corps since December 1927, the mission called for an Atlantic-Fokker C-2A aircraft to be refueled by a pair of Douglas C-1 transports. The flight would originate at Van Nuys, California, and take place on an elliptical track. The C-2A would carry four pilots, so that they could operate in shifts, two at a time. Eaker and Quesada were joined by Major Tooey Spaatz—as senior officer—and Captain Harry Halverson, as well as by a flight mechanic, Sergeant Roy Hooe. Their C-2A was christened *Question Mark* because no one knew how long the flight would last.

The flight was part serious experiment and part publicity stunt. In keeping with the latter objective, the flight of the *Question Mark* was scheduled to begin January 1, 1929, so that the aircraft could fly over the annual Rose Bowl Game in Pasadena.

Their fuel came from a hose that had to be manually inserted into a funnel. On one of the first refuelings, a gust of turbulence jerked the fuel hose loose, drenching Spaatz, who stripped off his clothes and conducted the next refueling naked.

On January 7, when the port engine failed, Spaatz could not restart it, so he decided to land. They touched down after 150 hours, 40 minutes aloft, and after covering about 11,000 miles. Beyond the public relations value, the flight of the *Question Mark* provided information about the effects of long-distance flights on engine components.

Before 1929 was over, Jimmy Doolittle earned another place in the record books for pushing the confines of the envelope in a different direction after having been assigned to the Full Flight Laboratory, newly established at Mitchel Field on Long Island by Harry Guggenheim and Captain Emory Land. It was here that he became part of a team that was investigating solutions to the problems of "blind flying."

As any pilot knows, finding your way on a clear day with unlimited visibility is a straightforward proposition. As your visibility is compromised by darkness, cloud cover, or ground fog, navigation becomes complicated and even dangerous. In the 1920s, resolving these problems was considered to be the prerequisite to safe and reliable scheduled air travel.

Today, a cockpit crowded with instruments makes this challenge easier, but instruments were slow in coming. While Doolittle was at Mitchel, he worked with Elmer Sperry of Sperry Gyroscope to develop an attitude indicator, or "artificial horizon," that told a pilot where the aircraft was in relation to the level horizon, as well as a directional gyroscope that was more reliable than a magnetic compass.

One aspect of blind flying that had been unanticipated and was hard for early pilots to accept was that human senses are less reliable than the instruments. Even Lindbergh admitted to ignoring instruments that his senses told him were wrong.

"When a pilot was unable to see the ground and therefore had no horizon, he often became disoriented," Doolittle recalled. "His senses were unreliable and contradicted what his instruments told him. He felt he was turning in one direction when he was actually turning the opposite way. He was confused and tended to believe his senses rather than the instruments. Many accidents where weather was a factor were dismissed simply as 'pilot error,' without further explanation. This was true, but the error was too often the pilots' refusal to believe their instruments instead of their senses."

By the summer of 1929, the Full Flight Laboratory had installed nearly a dozen flight instruments in the Consolidated NY-2 that Doolittle used as a test aircraft, including a barometric altimeter that was accurate within a few feet. On September 24 Doolittle set a milestone of aviation history with the first-ever completely blind flight, including his takeoff and landing. Had he been tempted to peek outside his enclosed cockpit, it would have done him more harm than good—the landscape was enveloped that morning in a thick layer of "pea-soup" ground fog.

After the flight of the *Question Mark* in 1929, Spaatz was given command of the 7th Bombardment Group at Rockwell Field. Two years later, he moved to the 1st Bombardment Wing at March Field, near Riverside. In February 1931, Spaatz's old friend and mentor Hap Arnold, now a lieutenant colonel, arrived at March. Having served out his self-described "exile" at Fort Riley, Arnold had moved on to the Command and General Staff School, and was now back on flying duty. With Arnold in command, their job was to expand the facilities at March to make way for its becoming the major Air Corps hub in Southern California.

Arnold and Spaatz were reunited at an auspicious moment that found the Air Corps in a position to nudge the envelope of the role of airpower in American defensive strategy. Previously, the US Navy functioned as the first line of defense against an enemy attacking the United States from across the ocean. Now, with the irony that only a few years had passed since Billy Mitchell was drummed out of the service, strategic thinkers at both the Army and the Navy had agreed that the Air Corps should have the responsibility for defending against enemy ships 300 miles out at sea.

In the years following the flight of the *Question Mark*, Ira Eaker held a number of posts unrelated to aviation. Having dropped out of Columbia Law School after a semester, he dropped into the University of Southern California School of Journalism in 1931, from which he earned his bachelor's degree in 1933. It was a change of trajectory that took him to a future job at the Information Division at Air Corps headquarters and a later role as Hap Arnold's coauthor in a series of books on airpower. During their time together at March Field, they collaborated on *This Flying Game*, the first of their three books. Published in 1936, it was essentially a primer on flying for young people interested in becoming US Army pilots. The book was well received and ultimately went through five editions.

In the meantime, Eaker had gone through a divorce and had begun a second marriage. In 1922, he married Leah Chase, the daughter of the Mitchel Field flight surgeon, but it was not a marriage made in heaven. As Ruth Harrison Spaatz told James Parton, Eaker's biographer, "I don't know what brought them together. She liked to drink and she smoked—things that Ira isn't crazy about in a woman. She just wasn't the right wife for him."

The right wife turned out to be 22-year-old Ruth Huff Apperson, a teacher at a secretarial school in Washington, DC. They married in November 1931 in the New York City apartment of the aunt of Hans Christian Adamson, a friend of Eaker's who was a wealthy newspaper publisher, aviation promoter, and friend of Charles Lindbergh.

In February 1934, with Spaatz back in Washington as head of Air Corps Training and Operations Division, and with Arnold and Eaker both at March, the Air Corps found itself embroiled in circumstances beyond its control. At the time, commercial airlines carried air mail under contract with the US Post Office. However, assertions of overcharging mushroomed into scandal. Acting impulsively, President Franklin Roosevelt abruptly canceled the air mail contracts and handed the job to the Air Corps. Secretary of War George Dern assured Roosevelt and Postmaster

General Jim Farley that this would be no problem for the airmen. However, he had not bothered to ask General Benjamin Foulois, the chief of the Air Corps.

Both Arnold and Eaker were in the midst of what was designated as the Army Air Corps Mail Operation program, Arnold as commander of the program's western geographic sector, and Eaker working under him in charge of the air mail route between Los Angeles and Salt Lake City. The service was now faced with delivering millions of pounds of correspondence on a 25,000-mile route structure—mainly at night in the dead of winter. The airlines had been using aircraft with better instrumentation for nighttime and foul-weather flying, and they had a maintenance infrastructure.

The Air Corps fleet, with its open cockpits and lack of instrumentation, was unequipped for the task. The results were worse than predicted. Ten Air Corps pilots lost their lives in crashes during the first three weeks. As the disastrous experiment failed, Roosevelt backed down and issued temporary air mail contracts to the airlines to resume service in May.

The Air Corps, which had earlier garnered positive headlines for pushing toward the edges of the technological envelope, now gathered scathing headlines for its apparent inability to master the routines of an operational envelope. In turn, this propelled the service toward the uncharted fringes of the political envelope.

Governments typically react to disastrous outcomes of their own actions by setting up commissions to study what happened. This time, the two commissions were chaired by Major General Hugh Drum and former secretary of war Newton Baker. The exercise also led to a reexamination of airpower doctrine and a serious effort to address not only technical shortcomings but tactical issues around the notion of how the US Army should *use* its Air Corps.

As the Morrow Board of 1926 had recommended the creation of the US Army Air Corps, the Baker Board sliced it in half. The Air Corps would retain responsibility for such activities as training and procurement, while operational units, the "air striking force"—which included the 1st Wing at March Field—would be under the control of a new entity called General Headquarters (GHQ) Air Force, an arrangement that became a reality in March 1935. The commanders of each, Foulois of the Air Corps (Major General Oscar Westover after December 1935) and Major General Frank Andrews of GHQ Air Force, reported *separately* to the US Army chief of staff. However, the officers within both entities wore Air Corps uniforms, and career paths would often meander through both entities.

While Tooey Spaatz, in Washington on the Air Corps side of the divide, took a dim view of the new arrangement, Hap Arnold and Ira Eaker, both of them in operational units within GHQ Air Force, took the opposite view, regarding the cup of the Baker Board report as being half full. In *This Flying Game*, Arnold and Eaker wrote: "The War Department wisely established the General Headquarters Air Force, an organization comprising the striking force elements with their supporting fighter aviation. This was the first recognition in the United States of the need for an air force designed, equipped and trained to operate beyond the sphere of influence of either armies or navies."

After the creation of GHQ Air Force, Arnold, Spaatz, and Eaker all moved on to new posts. Spaatz and Eaker both eventually did stints at the Command and General Staff School at Fort Leavenworth, while Arnold went to Air Corps headquarters in Washington.

When Oscar Westover became chief of the Air Corps at the end of 1935, he specifically requested that Hap Arnold come to Washington as his assistant. Arnold hated leaving his operational command at March Field, which he would always regard as his favorite posting, but Eaker saw Arnold's reassignment as a cup that was more than half full. As he told James Parton many years later, Arnold "saw World War II on the horizon more clearly than any of us and worked us unsparingly to be ready, and to have Army Aviation ready, to play a significant role."

Eaker took command of the 34th Pursuit Squadron at March Field in late 1934, and in 1936 he made a name for himself as the first man to fly across the entire breadth of the United States, navigating a P-12 pursuit plane solely by instruments. Shadowed by Major Bill Kepner in a second P-12, he made the entire flight from Mitchel Field to March Field with the open cockpit covered by a black canvas hood. Cockpit instrumentation had evolved considerably since Jimmy Doolittle made the first totally "blind" flight in 1929.

Eaker arrived at the Command and General Staff School in June 1936 as Tooey Spaatz was graduating and moving on to GHQ Air Force at Langley Field. At Fort Leavenworth, Eaker found himself surrounded by classmates who, like himself, would form the backbone of Hap Arnold's wartime force. There were Pete Quesada and Harry Halverson, with whom Eaker and Spaatz had crewed on the *Question Mark*. Also present were Captain John Cannon, Major Harold "Hal" George, and Major Nathan Twining, all of whom would be on Arnold's staff as the war began and would go on to important command roles during the war.

In 1937, when he graduated from the Command and General Staff School, Ira Eaker returned to Washington as assistant chief, and later chief, of the Information Division, occupying an office down the hall from Hap Arnold.

○ ★ ○

CHAPTER 9

COMING OF AGE WITH THE AIR CORPS

During the summer of 1929, the last innocent summer before the October stock market crash changed the nation and the world, and as Jimmy Doolittle was pioneering instrument flight, Curtis LeMay was watching half of his aviation cadet classmates at March Field receive the bad news that they would not be moving on to advanced training at Kelly Field in Texas.

Partly for this reason, and partly because of the nature of the work they were now doing, LeMay found himself surrounded by an entirely different group of men at Kelly. They were all serious, qualified pilots. The emphasis on cadet discipline that had prevailed earlier was gone, but in the air the men worked harder than ever. Though LeMay found the requirements of advanced flight school difficult, he was single-minded in his determination to succeed.

Throughout his career, LeMay would be admired more for what he accomplished through his dogged tenacity than for his innate adeptness. Unlike men such as Jimmy Doolittle, LeMay was not a "natural"; he learned the art and science of aviation through methodical practice. He was also the precise opposite of Doolittle in his abstinence from the kind of daredevil antics that tempted so many pilots.

"It didn't come easy. I really worked at it," LeMay later told his biographer, Thomas Coffey. "I'd wanted to have a joyride ever since that first two-dollar-and-a-half flight at Columbus; but I wasn't about to undertake it in this year of 1929. I didn't sneak off. I didn't joyride. If I was supposed to practice [figure] eights, then by God I practiced eights. I told myself, night and morning, that I must do exactly what I was ordered to do. The one thing that I wanted to do more than anything else was just to go up and take a [joy]ride in an airplane. Never did."

In October 1929, Curtis LeMay completed his advanced training at Kelly. Among those in his graduating class was Emmett "Rosie" O'Donnell, who would serve under LeMay as a general during World War II.

LeMay earned his regular Army second lieutenant's commission in January 1930 and reported to his first Air Corps posting with the 27th Pursuit Squadron at Selfridge Field in Michigan. The squadron was part of the 1st Pursuit Group, which Tooey Spaatz had commanded at Selfridge earlier in the decade. LeMay spent the better part of the next seven years flying pursuit planes with the Air Corps, especially the Boeing P-12. He remained assigned at Selfridge for five of those years, although he was allowed to go on temporary duty at Norton Field near Columbus for six months—minus one day, the requirement for temporary duty—in order to wrap up his work on the civil engineering degree at Ohio State that had previously eluded him.

While he was in Ohio during the winter of 1931–1932, LeMay found himself tasked with looking in on his teenage siblings, Leonard and Methyll, who were living with family friends while going to high school in Columbus. Erving and Arizona, with three-year-old daughter Vernice Patricia (originally spelled Patarica) in tow, were still wandering, now against the backdrop of the hardships of the Great Depression. At that moment, they were down in Portland, across the Ohio River from Kentucky.

Though they had been inveterate nomads before the Great Depression, the LeMays were now numbered among the vast slice of the population of the United States uprooted by and during it. The courses of millions of lives were changed during those years, but not that of Curtis LeMay. Being a US Army officer gave him both stability and job security—although with the US Army's budget being constrained during the Depression, there was little opportunity for advancement. Promotions in seniority and rank were dependent on someone further up the line retiring from the service. Officers remained at the same rank for years.

Down the road from Selfridge in Dearborn, the Ford Motor Company was building its famous Trimotor airliners and hiring demonstration and delivery pilots at ten times a second lieutenant's salary. LeMay was tempted—strongly—but job security, a sense of duty, and his determination to finish a career that he had started kept him in the service.

In 1931, while at Selfridge, LeMay crossed paths with Helen Maitland, a University of Michigan student from Lakewood in suburban Cleveland. She was as outgoing as he was taciturn, but opposites attract. It was an on-again, off-again relationship—it was Helen who convinced him that he should finish up at Ohio State—but they remained in touch. After she accepted a job in Akron, he took the opportunity to volunteer for flights that required traveling to that city, although things did not get really serious until Curt learned that Helen had not just one but *two* other suitors.

The wedding—a vastly larger affair than LeMay had wanted—took place at Helen's family's Episcopal church in Cleveland on June 9, 1934. With only five days of leave and no money for a honeymoon, LeMay and his bride left for Selfridge two days later. Three months after the wedding, they had barely gotten their quarters adjusted to suit them when LeMay received a transfer. He had expected to remain at Selfridge indefinitely, but the Air Corps now wanted him at Wheeler Field in Hawaii.

Soon Helen found herself moving from a comfortable brick house with modern amenities to a beachfront bungalow—there was a housing shortage on the base—where the only warm water was in the Pacific Ocean.

Operating from Wheeler, LeMay found that the navigational skills taught by the Air Corps were entirely inadequate for flying over an ocean devoid of landmarks. With this, the methodical LeMay began to demonstrate an ability to think creatively. Having convinced their boss, Colonel Delos Emmons, to think outside the box, LeMay and Lieutenant John Egan—an old Kelly Field classmate—started a full-fledged navigation school. LeMay and Egan, who were as untutored as their students in the beginning, worked hard to stay ahead, and soon they had become some of the most skilled navigators in the Air Corps.

It was during the long over-water flights in the Pacific that a change came over LeMay, setting him on a course that would define his contribution to future military aviation. He decided that he would like to transfer from fighters to bombers, to move from a system that was inherently defensive to a weapon that represented the offensive capability of the Air Corps. Having studied the Billy Mitchell doctrine, he understood that airpower could contribute decisively to winning wars by striking an enemy's ability to wage war. Long-range navigation over water or unfamiliar terrain would be essential to future strategic bomber operations, and LeMay sensed this.

When LeMay, now a first lieutenant, was rotated back to the mainland in December 1936, he applied for a transfer and was assigned to the 2nd Bombardment Group at Langley Field, near Newport News, Virginia. Commanded by Lieutenant Colonel Robert Olds, the group was the premier bombardment unit on the East Coast. It was a component of the 2nd Wing, commanded by Brigadier General Conger Pratt, which was the eastern equivalent of the 1st Wing at March Field, then commanded by Brigadier General Hap Arnold. Meanwhile, Langley Field also had the distinction of being the headquarters of GHQ Air Force, while the parallel US Army Air Corps remained based in Washington.

In February 1936, as Curtis LeMay was flying over the drifting white sands of Hawaii, Hub Zemke was making his way through Montana's drifting snow and onto the highway that would take him south to Texas. Zemke and two fellow members of the Montana State football team had decided to give it a try. Zemke was the only one of the three to pass the physical.

He reported to Randolph Field, one of the primary flight training bases that fed into the advanced school at Kelly Field, on the other side of San Antonio. Initially turned off by being thrown into close-order-drill marching, Zemke was relieved to discover that his spirits soared when he found himself in a Consolidated PT-3 biplane and soloing after less than eight hours.

By this time, his joy of flying confirmed his decision to go for a career in the US Army Air Corps. He had also decided—just the opposite of LeMay—that he wanted to pursue a career track that took him to flying fast, nimble fighters, not to what he perceived as large, lumbering bombers.

By the autumn of 1936, Hub Zemke was flying the Boeing P-12, the same biplane fighter type that Curtis LeMay had flown at 27th Pursuit Squadron at Selfridge. It had been a fairly advanced aircraft when it was introduced in 1930, but had been overtaken by technology. It was now functioning as an advanced trainer and as a demonstration aircraft. Indeed, much of Zemke's flying time as a pilot cadet over the coming months was spent making demonstrations at colleges across the South with the purpose of inspiring others to pursue a military aviation career. This, however, was mainly wishful thinking on the part of the Air Corps pursuit section. They barely had the funding to employ the pilots they already had. When Zemke graduated from flight school in February 1937, it took the Air Corps four months to grant him his second lieutenant's bars and an assignment to a pursuit squadron.

Hub Zemke's first assignment was to the 8th Pursuit Group, at Langley Field, where young pilots found agreeable working conditions, compared to the rigorous discipline of the training fields. "One of the advantages of the relaxed atmosphere at Langley was that even young Reserve second lieutenants like myself had considerable freedom in the use of aircraft," he recalled in his memoirs. "The usual form was to fly a mission given by the squadron operations officer in the morning— probably of no more than an hour or 45 minutes duration. You were then free to undertake further flying, most of us indulging in mock combat or working up team aerobatics. We were also allowed to take aircraft on personal cross-country flights every weekend, which enabled a group of fellows to take off for an airport at some resort we fancied and really go to town."

It was at Langley that Hub Zemke first crossed paths with Curtis LeMay. Both men had an interest in firearms, and both spent their Sundays skeet shooting at the officers' club, where the pursuit men and bomber men competed not only on the firing range but for allocations of ammunition as well.

"During my first weeks at Langley I noticed that practically every Sunday there were competitive events on the skeet shooting range close to the Officer's Club," Zemke wrote later, saying that this "helped develop a flier's deflection shooting. With my hunting background I wanted to participate but learned that most of the ammunition allocated for skeet shooting had been acquired for the 2nd Bomb Group whose senior officers were regular participants on the range. Prominent was a Captain Curtis LeMay, an excellent shot. Being envious and wanting to get in on the act I asked our armament Sergeant about this situation and learned that the only bar to participation on the officers' skeet was ammunition. I also discovered that pilots were authorized to draw 600 rounds per year."

Because the 8th Pursuit Group had not requested its full allotment, the 2nd Bomb Group had traditionally expropriated the lion's share. Zemke turned this around, much to the disgruntlement of the bomber crews.

As LeMay was spending his Sundays on the shooting range, he was spending his workweek at the threshold of the practical development of the strategic doctrine—which was advocated and articulated by Billy Mitchell, and to which LeMay would devote the next three decades of his career. For the application of strategic airpower, which could reach into an enemy's industrial heartland, an air force needed long-range bombers and the strategic doctrine to use them. LeMay's job, which he had gotten because of his creation of the navigation school in Hawaii, was to start developing that doctrine.

Several long-range bomber studies were conducted in the 1930s, the first of which was Project A, also known as the Experimental Bomber, Long-Range (XBLR) program, which led to the very large Boeing XB-15 and Douglas XB-19, both of which were represented by just a single prototype aircraft. By the latter part of the decade, the choice of long-range bombers focused on the more advanced, but smaller, Boeing B-17 Flying Fortress and Douglas B-18 Bolo. The specified requirements issued by the Air Corps now read that long-range bombers should be "multi-engine" aircraft. The B-17 had four and the B-18 had two. The latter was less expensive, and Douglas naturally received a much bigger initial order for the B-18 when contracts were issued in January 1936. As we now know in retrospect, the B-18 became a largely forgotten footnote, while the longer-range Flying Fortress is remembered as one of the half dozen greatest military aircraft in American aviation history. It was also destined to become the indispensable backbone of the Eighth Air Force.

In August 1937, the 2nd Bomb Group was assigned to a joint exercise over the Pacific Ocean that was designed to evaluate the ability of the airmen to locate enemy warships at sea. Unlike Billy Mitchell's demonstration in Chesapeake Bay 16 years earlier, the location of the "enemy"—the US Navy's battleship USS *Utah*—was known to the flyers only as being "somewhere" within 120,000 square miles of open sea. Curtis LeMay flew as navigator in the lead B-17, piloted by Robert Olds himself. The rules of engagement prohibited the airmen from conducting their own reconnaissance, and they were compelled to depend on imprecise coordinates transmitted by the Navy. Nevertheless, LeMay managed to locate the target, and the 2nd Bomb Group Flying Fortresses plastered the *Utah* with water bags that were carried to simulate bombs.

As with Mitchell's successes in 1921, the *Utah* interception was an embarrassment to the US Navy. It wound up stamped "Secret," though it was well-known within both services, and this classification led to a desire on the part of the airmen for a long-range flight about which they *could* brag. The plan evolved as a proposal for a well-publicized goodwill flight to South America by Flying Fortresses to celebrate the inauguration of Argentina's president Roberto Ortiz in February 1938. The War Department approved the plan, it was assigned to the 2nd Bomb Group, and Robert Olds picked LeMay as his lead navigator.

As a publicity exercise, the flight was promoted to the media and the public by the Information Division at Air Corps headquarters in Washington, the office headed by Major Ira Eaker—who had flown to Argentina himself as part of the Pan American Good Will Flight of 1926–1927.

When Eaker flew down to Langley Field to check in with Olds, whom he had known for many years, he was introduced to LeMay.

"You know, Bob, this is an important mission you're undertaking," Eaker confided to Olds when LeMay had left the room. "It's designed to demonstrate the overseas, intercontinental range of our new bomber. If you're successful, the General Staff and the Congress may give us some more of them. How can you entrust your navigation to a young lieutenant?"

As Eaker later told Tom Coffey, Olds replied, "Lieutenant LeMay happens to be the best damned navigator in the Army Air Corps."

Despite having to rely on maps from *National Geographic* magazine, LeMay successfully led all six of the B-17s down the west coast of South America, across the Andes to Buenos Aires, and safely home. The flight in turn earned the 2nd Bomb Group the Mackay Trophy, awarded annually to US Army airmen for the "flight of the year."

Inspired by this, Eaker came up with an idea for another demonstration flight designed explicitly to garner media attention. Three months after the Argentina flight, GHQ Air Force was holding its largest exercise to date in the northeastern United States. As part of this, Eaker proposed that B-17s of the 2nd Bomb Group should rendezvous with the Italian ocean liner SS *Rex*, which would reach a position approximately 1,000 miles off the eastern seaboard on May 12, 1938.

Eaker and his bosses were again betting on "young" Lieutenant Le-May, but Eaker took a further chance by agreeing to put media representatives aboard each of the three Flying Fortresses. Two would carry newspaper reporters, and the lead aircraft, flown by Major Caleb Haynes, with both Olds and LeMay aboard, would carry an NBC radio crew who would be broadcasting live.

As an Atlantic storm blew in with a blanket of low overcast, the odds of the aircraft locating the *Rex* plummeted to the needle-in-a-haystack level. Battling tremendous turbulence, LeMay did succeed in finding the liner, and in doing so at exactly the moment that he had predicted he would. The result was magnificent for the Air Corps and GHQ Air Force, and planted the seed of airpower potential in the minds of the skeptics who had been underestimating the value of airpower since the days of Billy Mitchell.

Hanson Baldwin of the *New York Times*, who was one of the reporters embedded on the flight, wrote that "valuable lessons about the aerial defense of the United States will be drawn [from the flight, which is] a striking example of the mobility and range of modern aviation."

While the 2nd Bomb Group earned the headlines and were being perceived as the elite of Langley Field, the fighter pilots across the tarmac at the 8th Pursuit Group existed in their shadow. Hub Zemke had flown Curtiss P-6 and Boeing P-12 biplanes when he first arrived, but aviation technology was making great strides—though not as great as what was occurring in Europe in the run-up to the Second World War—and the 8th was graduating to the Curtiss P-36. It was a low-wing monoplane with an enclosed cockpit and retractable landing gear, representing a quantum leap from the earlier open-cockpit biplanes. It was a hundred miles per hour faster than the earlier fighters, although it could barely keep up with the B-17s that the 2nd Bomb Group was flying.

Just as Zemke met Curtis LeMay off the field, he also got to know Tooey Spaatz, now a lieutenant colonel, though the circumstances were somewhat different than on the shooting range. In another one of those coincidences that were common when the Air Corps was like a small town, Zemke found himself in Spaatz's home—and dating his oldest daughter.

When the Spaatz family arrived at Langley in 1936 after Tooey's tenure at the Command and General Staff School, Tattie was 15 and Beckie had just turned 14. Carla, nicknamed "Boops," was still a preschooler when Tattie was dating Hub Zemke. Parenthetically, it was during the Langley years that Ruth and the older girls convinced Tooey that their surname should be spelled "Spaatz" instead of the German-seeming "Spatz."

Spaatz greeted his daughter's suitor with the taciturn sternness that fathers typically reserve for young men, especially subordinates in rank, who date their daughters. "Colonel Spaatz was a quiet, serious man," Zemke wrote in his memoirs, "while his wife was just the opposite." The relationship between Tattie and Hub faded after a few dates.

By the time Tooey and Ruth left Langley for Washington, the older girls had both left home, Tattie going to Sweet Briar College, near Lynchburg, and Beckie to a boarding high school in Norfolk. Tattie may not have been interested in a flyer, but Beckie was. In 1943, she married Emmet "Red" Gresham, a young Air Corps student pilot.

CHAPTER 10

OUTSIDE THE AIR CORPS

D uring the 1930s, as the other future Eighth Air Force leaders, men such as Tooey Spaatz, Ira Eaker, and Curtis LeMay, were moving up the ladder of command, Jimmy Doolittle was conspicuously absent from the Air Corps roster. On February 15, 1930, he resigned his commission to take a job in the private sector with the Shell Oil Company.

At the time, aviation fuel was a rapidly growing market segment—Shell was selling more than 20 million gallons annually. All the oil companies were hiring pilots with high-profile reputations to help promote their aviation products by flying in air races and touring the country in aircraft emblazoned with their logos.

The same reputation for being more of a daredevil than most Air Corps pilots, which had earned Doolittle cautionary reprimands within the service, had also earned him a higher profile with the public. It is axiomatic that companies dealing in consumer products like what the public likes. Aviators acting as spokesmen for other oil companies included such air-race-winning household names as Jimmie Mattern and Roscoe Turner. After his Schneider Trophy and his tour of South America on loan to Curtiss, Doolittle was part of the same club.

For Doolittle, it was also about the money. It was bottom of the Great Depression, and the Air Corps was still a small organization, with promotions hard to come by, and he had been getting by on a first lieutenant's salary for a decade. Shell had offered to triple his salary.

"I knew I would miss the opportunity of flying and testing every type of aircraft the Army had or anyone wanted to sell to it," he later admitted. "As chief test pilot at McCook [Field, Ohio], I was privileged to know all the aircraft manufacturers on a first-name basis. The aviation fraternity was quite small at that time and everyone knew everyone else. They were all people of substance, people of ideas, some of them geniuses. Some were good businesspeople; most were not. The creative genius is not always the chap who is best able to make a buck and run an airplane factory efficiently. But the offer from the Shell company was one that I literally couldn't afford to pass up."

As he left the service, Doolittle applied for a commission as a major in the Specialist Reserve, and to his surprise, he received it.

No sooner had he joined Shell than he became part of a joint Curtiss-Shell publicity tour of Europe. Curtiss was now Curtiss-Wright, a conglomerate formed in 1929 through a merger of various companies, especially those that traced their roots to the companies started by the Wright brothers and Glenn Curtiss—though neither Orville Wright (Wilbur died in 1912) nor Glenn Curtiss had been involved in their namesake firms for many years.

Starting in Athens and ending in Stockholm, Doolittle put on demonstration flights in a dozen countries, including Germany, where he had an opportunity to assess the growing German aircraft industry and kick the tires of a new generation of multiengine aircraft that were painted as airliners but designed to be adapted as bombers.

Naturally, no Jimmy Doolittle field trip was complete without its share of death-defying stunts of the sort that only a crazy person or an uncannily gifted pilot would dare to attempt. While in Budapest, Miklós Horthy, Jr., the son of the country's regent—and future pro-Nazi ally of Hitler—bet him that he couldn't fly under a particular bridge over the

Danube. Naturally, Doolittle could not refuse, and despite the fact that they were in the midst of a night of partying, they drove straight to the airport. In the dark, and with scant clearance, Doolittle made it.

Back home, Doolittle put in numerous appearances at air shows and air races, sometimes racing and sometimes just executing demonstration flights, but always showing off the Shell logo. In 1932 he was personally invited by the Granville Brothers of Springfield, Massachusetts, to race their Gee Bee Super Sportster for the Thompson Trophy in the National Air Races. They were in business expressly to build the fastest race planes in the world, and Lowell Bayles had won the 1931 Thompson Trophy in a Gee Bee.

"The red-and-white plane with the 7-11 dice painted on the side was fascinating to look at," Doolittle recalled. "Only 18 feet long from prop to tail, it seemed like it was all engine with a minuscule set of wings and a bomblike fuselage. The extremely small cockpit sat far back and was faired into the fuselage just in front of the vertical stabilizer. This was no doubt to counterbalance the weight of the heavy engine. . . . Recognizing that this airplane would be extremely hot to handle, I knew I had to fly it delicately. . . . It was fast, but flying it was like balancing a pencil or an ice cream cone on the tip of your finger. You couldn't let your hand off the stick for an instant."

As Doolittle notes, race officials required qualification tests, but although he was clocked at 293.19 miles per hour, it was not an official world speed record because no barograph had been installed to measure altitude. Race planes were not allowed above 1,300 feet while making speed runs. With a barograph installed, Doolittle won the race with a course record speed of 252.686 miles per hour.

With this, Doolittle announced his own retirement from air racing— he was now a mature 34—noting that "racing planes had been the guinea pigs of aviation" and this had cost many lives. He told the media that "the time had come to give attention to safety and reliability so that commercial aviation could develop."

Air race organizers took exception to Doolittle's public pronouncements, insisting that the races played a valuable role in engine development, but with or without air races, commercial airlines were starting to develop throughout the United States. As an illustration of his evolving role in the aviation world, Doolittle's next record involved commercial flight. In 1935, flying an eight-passenger Vultee monoplane on behalf of American Airlines, he became the first pilot to fly coast-to-coast with passengers in less than 12 hours, beating a record set by Eddie Rickenbacker in an Eastern Airlines Douglas DC-2 in December 1934.

In 1933, Doolittle made his first visit to Japan as part of a round-the-world tour. (He would return in 1942 as leader of the famous "Doolittle Raid.") As with his 1930 European tour, this venture was sponsored jointly by Shell and Curtiss-Wright, and designed to promote the products of both.

When their ocean liner arrived in Yokohama, en route to Shanghai, Jimmy and Joe found that his reputation had preceded him. Japanese officials studying his paperwork became deeply suspicious of a high-profile aviator traveling to China to promote warplanes. Japan had seized Manchuria from China two years earlier, and the two countries had been fighting a series of battles inside China ever since. The Doolittles disembarked and toured Japan briefly, but the Curtiss Hawk fighter was not unloaded and demonstrated until their ship reached Shanghai.

Invited to fly right seat on a China National Airlines flight during the China visit—his first-ever flight as a copilot—Doolittle had to take over the controls when the pilot got lost and had trouble reading his instruments. Aside from this and a hard landing in a Dutch-owned Curtiss Hawk in the Dutch East Indies, the trip was routine, and is barely discussed in his memoirs. He and Joe flew commercial aboard a series of KLM flights between Batavia and Europe before sailing home from England.

In 1937, Shell sent Doolittle back to Europe. In Germany, he reconnected with Ernst Udet, whom he had met on his 1930 trip, and against whom he had flown in the National Air Races. A colorful character, Udet had been the second-highest-scoring German air ace—after Manfred von Richthofen—in World War I, and had become prominent in German and global air racing and aviation circles. He had appeared in several motion pictures and was at least as well-known of a pilot in Germany as Doolittle was in the United States. The two men had become friends.

By 1937, Udet was heading the technical development division of the Reichsluftfahrtministerium, the German Air Ministry. As such, he was able to give Doolittle an inside look at the Luftwaffe—the German Air Force—which was rapidly becoming the most advanced in the world, at what was happening within the robust German aircraft industry, and at the early development of the weapons against which American pilots would be flying and fighting in World War II.

Similar in disposition, the two men were both inclined to be foolhardy and to take the types of death-defying chances during demonstration flights that thrilled observers. They were both equally unrestrained on the ground. In his memoirs, Doolittle describes a night of champagne drinking that led to target shooting with large-caliber handguns—*inside* Udet's Berlin apartment.

CHAPTER 11

CLOUDS OF WAR

Tooey Spaatz looked at Tattie, his eldest daughter, and said, "No."

She protested.

She was finishing up the year at Sweet Briar College and was making plans for a year abroad, studying at the Sorbonne in Paris—until her father vetoed the idea.

She pleaded.

"No," he repeated firmly.

By the early months of 1939, the probability—even inevitability—of a major war in Europe was apparent to most people who were paying close attention to the events unfolding on the ground. Adolf Hitler, in *Mein Kampf*, his manifesto on Germany's future, and his public pronouncements throughout the decade, had laid out a blueprint for the domination of Europe by an ever-expanding Third Reich. However, there were many who found the Führer's vision disturbing but regarded it as a bad dream, not a potential nightmare.

During 1938, the nightmare began to play out as Europe tumbled from crisis to crisis. In March, Hitler responded to pro-Nazi sentiment within Austria and absorbed that country into the Third Reich. Despite an explicit provision in the Treaty of Versailles forbidding such an annexation, no other country moved to counter the Führer's boldness. By the summer, Hitler was insisting that the Sudetenland region of Czechoslovakia, with its majority German population, should also be part of Germany. Britain's prime minister, Neville Chamberlain, and France's president, Édouard Daladier, flew to Munich, the mother city of the Nazi Party, for a summit conference with Hitler. The Führer promised them that the Sudetenland represented the limit of his territorial ambitions. Over the strenuous objections of Czechoslovakia, Chamberlain and Daladier agreed to Hitler's demand that the Sudentenland should be absorbed into Germany.

For optimists outside Czechoslovakia, it seemed after the Munich conference that the war clouds over the continent would part and the golden sunshine of peace would now warm the land. Chamberlain certainly believed this. When he flew home, he happily displayed the agreement inked with Hitler and cheerfully announced that he had helped to negotiate "peace for our time."

As these events were dominating the world stage, Tooey Spaatz, his argument with Tattie resolved, was making the move from Langley Field to Air Corps headquarters, where Major General Hap Arnold was now in command. When Air Corps Chief General Oscar Westover died in a plane crash in California in September 1938—coincidentally on the eve of the Munich summit half a world away—Arnold succeeded him. Spaatz reached Washington four months later, stepping into a job as Arnold's assistant, with a promotion to brevet brigadier general.

Ira Eaker, meanwhile, was down the hall in the offices of the Air Corps Information Division and destined soon to become Arnold's executive officer. Billy Mitchell had died in 1936 and never got to see it, but at last three of his most tenacious disciples were in the uppermost echelon of the US Army Air Corps.

"Arnold was a powerful mentor, a somewhat overpowering one at times," James Parton wrote, describing the role of the chief within the triumvirate. "With Spaatz, the other member of this trio that came to dominate army air for the next decade, Eaker enjoyed true, relaxed friendship. The trio's teamwork, like that of the three musketeers, remained constant. Arnold was always dominant, Spaatz number two and Eaker number three . . . [A]s they moved up the ladder in World War II and after, their teamwork was always in that same one-two-three order and always with mutual trust, loyalty and candor. Spaatz and Eaker were unfailingly respectful with their boss but never hesitated to speak up when they disagreed with him: The Air Corps, full of fierce individualists, had little use for yes-men. But when Arnold overruled them, he usually, they found, proved right and when he gave an order, they obeyed."

Eaker was content with this hierarchy, viewing Arnold and Spaatz as the essential element. In a 1974 interview with Richard Tobin of the Air Force Academy, Eaker compared the relationship to that described by Douglas Freeman in his Civil War book *Lee's Lieutenants*. "Whereas Lee had three Lieutenants, General Arnold had only one, relying on Spaatz more than he did on any other individual." In fact, while Eaker was correct that Spaatz was the first, these three men who had known and worked with one another for more than two decades did indeed run the Air Corps like a triumvirate.

Meanwhile, Eaker was an important lieutenant to Arnold in their continuing relationship as coauthors. After their success with *This Flying Game*, the two spent their time together in Washington on *Winged Warfare*, published in 1941, and *Army Flyer*, finally published a year later.

While the Air Corps of 1938 had achieved a unity of purpose within its ranks, those in power within its parent organization, the US Army, remained unconvinced of the potential of airpower and hostile to those in the Air Corps who advocated more autonomy. General Malin Craig, the US Army chief of staff, and Arnold's boss, had once insisted that the US

Army should not buy airplanes because they grew obsolete so quickly—but he was soon to be on the losing side of history in this regard. Craig's own boss, President Franklin D. Roosevelt, was about to become the nation's "airpower advocate in chief."

Back in 1936, Congress had authorized 2,230 aircraft as a "minimum safe peacetime strength" for the Air Corps, though when Arnold assumed command, the service had just 1,792. In a meeting at the White House on September 28, 1938, at which all the service chiefs—including Arnold, who was to take over as Air Corps chief the following day—discussed the events then unfolding at the Munich conference, Roosevelt let it be known that the number should be increased to 10,000. Over the coming months, the president floated numbers as high as twice this figure.

Arnold described Roosevelt's pronouncement as a "Magna Carta" for airpower. As he wrote in his memoirs, "It was the first time in history we had ever had a program—the first time we could shoot toward a definite goal of planes from the factories and men from the training fields. A battle was won in the White House that day which took its place with—or at least led to—the victories in combat later."

However, Craig was unconvinced. On October 24, he asserted that the "defense of the country . . . rests with ground troops. What are we going to do with 15,000 airplanes?"

He need not have worried. Congress approved only 5,500 for delivery over the next *three years*. At the time of the Munich summit, the Air Corps had fewer than two dozen four-engine bombers, and just a handful on order.

In contrast with the apparent complacency in the United States, Europe continued to tumble from crisis to crisis. In March 1939, Hitler predictably decided that the Sudetenland was not enough. Czechoslovakia, he insisted, should cease to exist entirely, its territory ceded to the Third Reich. Again Czechoslovakia protested, but again Chamberlain and

Daladier were willing to go to almost any lengths to appease Hitler and to avoid war.

Even Hitler's friendly handshakes bore the smell of preparations for war. In May, he and Fascist Italy's Benito Mussolini agreed to cooperation in time of war on an accord called the "Pact of Steel," or the "Rome-Berlin Axis." In late August 1939, Hitler sent his foreign minister, Joachim von Ribbentrop, to Moscow to sign a nonaggression pact with the Soviet Union. Because Hitler and Soviet leader Josef Stalin were at diametrically opposed extremes of the political spectrum, this move shocked and bewildered the rest of the world. What, wondered the media and the politicians, would Hitler do next?

In the summer of 1939, as this was unfolding, Jimmy Doolittle made his first trip to Europe in two years, spending three days in Germany on behalf of Shell. The changes that he noted were substantial.

"The atmosphere in the country had changed; there was an ominous air of impending catastrophe," he recalled in his memoirs. "On the streets, uniforms were everywhere; people went about their daily business with a grimness that was distressing."

He met again with his old friend Ernst Udet, who was now in uniform as the director general of equipment for the Luftwaffe. As Doolittle recalled, Udet had changed "and seemed much subdued. The old ebullience, the ever-present grin and laugh, were gone. . . . [The Germans] talked openly of war in Europe as being inevitable and wanted to know what America would do about it when it came. Their arrogance was irritating."

Udet invited Doolittle to accompany him on a vacation in Bavaria, but Doolittle declined, observing that if a war was coming, "it did not seem wise for a US Army Air Corps reserve officer to be vacationing with the top technical man in the Luftwaffe. Besides, my accompanying him might make it difficult for him to explain to Göring and Hitler why he was fraternizing with an American flyer who was probably a spy."

On August 23, a few days after Doolittle departed from Europe, von Ribbentrop signed a nonaggression pact with the Soviet Union. A week later, on the morning of September 1, 1939, German troops poured into Poland beneath a sky black with Luftwaffe aircraft. Not only did the invasion stun the world politically, but the precision of the integrated German war machine stunned the world militarily. It was the most well-trained, best-equipped, and overall superior military force in the world. Its coordinated air and ground offensive, known as blitzkrieg (lightning war), was the most rapid and efficient mode of military attack the world had yet seen. In the use of integrated tactical air operations in support of the blitzkrieg, the Luftwaffe had revolutionized tactical air warfare.

On September 3, Britain and France declared that a state of war between them and the Third Reich had existed for two days. There would be no "peace for our time" but rather a second world war.

The breathtaking spectacle of the Luftwaffe extending the tactical reach of German ground troops and laying waste to Polish cities might have been enough to change the mind of Malin Craig, but when the news came in, he was nowhere to be seen. Only the previous afternoon, he had cleaned out his desk, hung up his uniform, and retired from the US Army.

Craig's successor, General George Catlett Marshall, a longtime friend of Hap Arnold, was an officer more inclined to be supportive of Arnold's vision of airpower, and of an independent air arm, than just about any US Army officer outside the Air Corps.

As the Arnold-Spaatz-Eaker triumvirate listened to radio reports that afternoon and considered the map of central Europe, Tooey Spaatz could at least take pleasure in the fact that his instincts had kept Tattie out of Europe that fall.

CHAPTER 12

★

YOUNG MEN ON THE EVE OF WAR

B efore September 1939, most Americans regarded the events in Europe with detachment, focusing more on the lingering darkness of the Great Depression than on the ominous maelstrom of distant European politics. Hitler, with his little dark mustache, was considered almost a cartoon character through the mid-1930s.

For young men like Robert Rosenthal and Robert Morgan, who were not yet in their teens when the Great Depression had begun, the anguish that it wrought was the daily reality of their formative years. Morgan, who had grown up a child of privilege, with his mother a close friend of Cornelia Vanderbilt, had watched his father's business crash through the floor, and had wound up living for a time in a home without electricity. In his memoirs, he observed that "many Americans were routinely living that way in the 1930s. It had its cozy charm."

In an interview archived at the 100th Bomb Group Foundation, Rosenthal recalled that "things were tough during the Depression . . . [M]y family didn't have much money, but we had everything we ever needed."

Rosenthal attended James Madison High School in Brooklyn, where he was invited to join the honor society but was kicked out of the glee club. At home, music was important to the Rosenthals. Both Rose and Jeannette were accomplished pianists, and family entertainment frequently involved gathering around the piano to sing. Bob loved to sing, but, like Ira Eaker, he was tone-deaf. When his music teacher detected a "sour note here somewhere," and connected it with Rosenthal, he was out.

When he graduated in 1934, he enrolled at Brooklyn College, where he recalled being a "mediocre student who was more interested in playing football." He was captain of the team. In the meantime, he worked his way through college, putting in time at the cafeteria and the library, and working summer jobs in a hotel and as a soda jerk.

Academically, his turning point came during a course in constitutional law. As he later noted, this class "affected me, challenged me," and inspired him to go on to law school. He enrolled at Brooklyn Law School on Pearl Street in downtown Brooklyn, where he attended year-round so that he could graduate in three years. As he had at Brooklyn College, Rosenthal went to school at night, and worked during the day for the Manhattan law firm Diamond, Rabin, Botein and Mackay, which later became Poletti, Diamond, Rabin, Freidin and Mackay. Located on Madison Avenue at 57th Street, it was one of New York's most prestigious and well-connected firms. Charles Poletti was closely associated with Governor Herbert Lehman, and in 1938 he was elected as Lehman's lieutenant governor. Botein had been an assistant Manhattan district attorney and general counsel for the State Insurance Fund. Ben Rabin was later elected to Congress, and both Rabin and Botein later served on the state supreme court. Such was the environment in which Robert Rosenthal apprenticed.

Being Jewish, Rosenthal was among those in the United States who first became cognizant of Hitler as a character more sinister than one represented in a political cartoon. Long before the notorious Kristallnacht saw the vandalism of nearly 10,000 Jewish institutions across Germany in November 1938, American Jews were well aware of the institutionalized anti-Semitism that existed inside Hitler's Reich. Closer to home, the same mood was manifest in the German American Bund, a pro-Nazi organization founded in New York in 1936, which attracted thousands to its rallies during its brief heyday. Rosenthal recalled that Hitler, his mistreatment of Jews, and especially the anti-Semitism in New York affected him very deeply.

"I had a sense of frustration," he recalled. "But I couldn't do anything about it."

Down in Asheville, North Carolina, Bob Morgan was moving on with his life. He had buried his mother, Mabel Knight Morgan, and a part of himself, in 1936, but despite it all, he had graduated from the Emerson Institute, the posh Washington prep school, as the class valedictorian. Meanwhile, his father, who had hit bottom financially at the start of the Depression, had clawed his way back. David Morgan had revived his failed Dimension Manufacturing Company, and it prospered. When Bob came home to Asheville, David gave him the keys to his Buick Century at exactly the time of his young life when roaring around North Carolina mountain roads at 110 miles per hour with a "stunning brunette" named Dorothy Beattie seemed like exactly the right thing to do.

Bob Morgan had finally decided, at age 20, that he was ready for college. Thanks to his good grades and his father's money, he enrolled at the Wharton School of Finance and Commerce at the University of Pennsylvania. It was an auspicious beginning, but as Morgan recalled in his memoirs, his life soon "went into an aimless drift." Then, as now, it is axiomatic that not everyone is cut out for the Ivy League. Bob Morgan was a case in point.

In the fall of 1938, as Munich was playing out, he was working his way out of a brief, quickly annulled marriage to a girl from North Carolina named Alice Rutherford Lane whom he had met a Wharton. He was establishing a reputation for short marriages. His first, in 1931 at the age of 15, had lasted nine days. Within a few months, Morgan was dating Martha Lillian Stone, daughter of Charles E. Stone of suburban Philadelphia society, who would later be his third wife.

By the summer of 1939, as the world was on the brink of war, David Morgan had called in some favors and his playboy son was hired by Addressograph-Multigraph Corporation, one of the country's largest manufacturers of duplicating machines.

Maynard Harrison "Hokie" Smith was every bit as much of a rascal as Bob Morgan, and more so. Both had been through brief teenage marriages, leaving Alice Morgan and Arlene Smith facing the future as ex-wives before they finished high school. Of course, Arlene had the added complication of caring for young Maynard Junior. Unlike Hokie, whose father cared for his every need, the younger Maynard and his mother spent the coming years battling Hokie for child support.

Just as Morgan's father, as a prosperous business owner, pulled the necessary strings to extricate him from jams, Hokie Smith had a father, Judge Henry Harrison Smith, who could pull just about any string that could be found in Tuscola County or in the whole 40th Judicial District.

Through the well-connected friends of his father, who had worked as an attorney for Detroit automakers as a younger man, Smith managed to land a reasonably solid government job, first as a field agent with the US Treasury Department and later with the Michigan State Banking Commission.

After the judge died—ringside at a boxing match in Daytona Beach in 1934—strings could no longer be pulled. However, the elder Smith had left a tidy sum to his only son that made it possible for him to live the life of leisure that suited him—adrift in a disillusioned malaise, about which he later claimed to remember nothing. He spent his missing years wintering in Florida with his mother, going fishing, and reading books on comparative religion and a variety of pseudoscientific topics.

Like Bob Morgan and Hokie Smith, Hub Zemke had gotten himself into a spontaneous marriage after a whirlwind romance in which there hadn't even been time for the wind to whirl. The 36th Pursuit Squadron had been sent on training deployment from Langley Field down to the newly opened airport north of Sarasota, Florida. While they were in town, the pilots were invited to a dance sponsored by the local chamber of commerce, which had been instrumental in getting the airfield built.

It was at that dance that Zemke met an Italian-born girl named Maria Midulla. There followed a torrid fling reminiscent of that between Bob Morgan and Alice Lane, and at nearly the same time. As with Bob and Alice, the falling in love of Hub and Maria quickly led to an ill-considered wedding.

"I was pretty naive where girls were concerned," Zemke admitted many years later in his autobiography. "I always considered myself a pretty level-headed guy, but I really lost control here. In five days, we were married! She was nineteen and her parents, who lived in Tampa, didn't even know about it. I came to my senses pretty quickly and realized we were two incompatible people; a fit of passion wasn't going to sustain a marriage."

As with Bob Morgan, Zemke's first thought of an exit strategy was to try for an annulment. He approached a Catholic priest to ask about this option, but was told that "any such action would be morally and religiously wrong; that I had got to try and make it work. So I rented an apartment off the base and arranged to bring Maria up from Tampa. Over the years we had good and bad patches but sadly the marriage never really worked out."

Nevertheless, Hub and Maria remained together, had two children, and were not divorced until 1973.

In the months that led toward the opening days of World War II, Curtis LeMay was a lieutenant waiting for his captain's bars in an Air Corps where promotions were hard to come by. He was still with the 2nd Bomb Group at Langley Field, though in his role as perhaps the best navigator in the Air Corps, he was often on the road on demonstration flights involving the service's handful of B-17s. In August 1938, on the eve of Munich, LeMay was piloting a Flying Fortress down to South America as part of a public relations tour that took them to Bogotá, Colombia, whose 8,361-foot airport is one of the highest in the world. This was a tacit statement of the altitude capabilities of the aircraft at a time when many older aircraft still in service had trouble operating at this elevation.

In February 1939, LeMay was home at Langley when Helen gave birth to their daughter, Patricia Jane. Three months later, he was off to the Air Corps Tactical School at Maxwell Field in Alabama, which is where he was on September 1, when the Germans invaded Poland.

Most Americans reacted to the war in Europe with an appreciation of the fact that they were not involved and a determination to keep it that way. A growing number of people did feel, on principle, that the United States should and would become involved in order to keep a totalitarian regime from swallowing all of Europe, but they were still in the minority.

Those in uniform whose careers had taken them through or to Washington, notably the Arnold-Spaatz-Eaker triumvirate, saw American involvement as an eventuality for which the Air Corps needed to be prepared.

Hub Zemke spoke for a great many rank-and-file American military airmen when he observed in his autobiography, "My thinking was that in due time the US would be involved and that I'd better be prepared, educationally and psychologically, for combat. Some pilots talked eagerly about getting into combat but I rationalized there would be losses and I could be one of them. I was not looking to be a hero. That said, with the probability that one day you would be fighting for your life, the wise thing was to become as proficient as you could as a pursuit fighter pilot."

After Germany and the Soviet Union defeated, divided, and absorbed Poland in September 1939, World War II devolved into a tense standoff. Britain and France had not intervened on the ground. Nor did the expected German invasion of Western Europe materialize.

During the ensuing winter, the media started calling World War II a "phony war."

And so it was, and so it remained—until April 9, 1940.

Both Denmark and Norway were defeated and occupied more quickly than Poland, and on May 10, Hitler's legions marched on Luxembourg, Belgium, and the Netherlands, occupying them in less than three weeks before invading France. By June 14, Germany had seized control of Paris, accomplishing in five weeks what it had been unable to do in four years during World War I.

Hitler and Mussolini then expanded their Rome-Berlin Axis, formed a year earlier, to include Imperial Japan. This alliance defined the scope of the war as it was envisioned by the Axis and ensured that World War II would truly be a "world" conflict.

Although neutrality remained popular in the United States, the fall of France and Western Europe brought a growing sense of urgency about national defense. On May 16, 1940, two days after the collapse of the Netherlands and 20 months after he had mentioned the notion of 10,000 aircraft, Roosevelt proposed that Congress should authorize funding for 50,000.

On June 4, with the crisis in Europe intensifying and the president calling for a record number of aircraft, Arnold asked Ira Eaker to draft a memo to Jimmy Doolittle, inviting him to come back on active duty. Arnold had in mind using Doolittle as a technical troubleshooter, not as a pilot, although he would get plenty of both from him in the coming years. Shell granted Doolittle an indefinite leave of absence and he was back in uniform as a major.

"Coming back on active duty from an active business life presented some difficulties in dealing with my contemporaries who had remained in uniform," he admitted in his autobiography. "Many who had opted for a service life were captains and resented my return as a major. In their eyes, I appeared to be a favorite of Hap's and enjoyed special privileges.

Thus, I came back to a hostile environment, which often became noticeable in meetings and one-on-one encounters when I presented my ideas for change or improvement. But I persisted because I believed I had learned some things about management in the business world that they had missed in the military, especially when it came to dealing directly with industry, as I was now required to do."

Based at Wright Field, headquarters of the Materiel Division and the center of engineering for the Air Corps, where he had served previously, Doolittle was initially tasked with sorting out technical problems with the Allison V-1710 engine, upon which the Air Corps depended for its P-38, P-39, and P-40 fighter aircraft. He earned few friends at the General Motors subsidiary when he wrote them up for sloppiness on their assembly line, but Arnold was pleased to be getting his money's worth from having Doolittle back in uniform.

CHAPTER 13

THE VIEW FROM ACROSS THE POND

When France surrendered on June 22, 1940, Britain stood alone, facing a potential cross-Channel invasion. Instead, Luftwaffe commander Field Marshal Hermann Göring turned loose waves of bombers and the Battle of Britain was fought in the skies rather than on the beaches and fields. It was the first major campaign in history fought solely in the air.

As the Luftwaffe began a brutal, unremitting bombing assault on Britain's ports, factories, and cities, Britain's defensive line in the summer of 1940 was made up of the courageous but outnumbered pilots of the Royal Air Force. The Germans had shown the world that airpower had the potential to revolutionize a battlefield. In turn, the RAF would show the world that airpower had the potential to *save* a nation—from airpower.

As the world's two preeminent air forces were engaged in their life-or-death struggle, Hap Arnold, Tooey Spaatz, and Ira Eaker viewed the conflict from the perspective of their own small air force. In 1940, Britain's Royal Air Force took delivery of 7,940 aircraft, while the German aircraft industry turned 8,295 over to the Luftwaffe. Many of these were Messerschmitt Bf 109 fighters.

Meanwhile, despite Roosevelt's rhetorical call for airplane numbers in five digits, the Air Corps acquired only 2,141 in 1939, most of them trainers. Only 118 Flying Fortresses were ordered in 1939 and 1940, but most were for later delivery, and Roosevelt ordered that most of these should be sold to the RAF. His theory was that Britain was on the front lines in the fight against Germany, and maintaining the viability of the British defenses would provide a buffer between Hitler and the United States, thus allowing the United States to avoid direct involvement in the war. It was an election year, and public opinion still opposed involvement in "Europe's war."

For those at the Air Corps, the diversion of Flying Fortresses, around which their strategic doctrine was built, became a bone of contention. Indeed, Arnold got himself into what he described as the "dog house" for disagreeing with Roosevelt.

In May 1940, Arnold sent Spaatz to observe the war firsthand. The United States was neutral, so he was able to sail to Italy, traveling across France even as the German army was closing in. He escaped to Britain while the German jackboots first hit the cobblestones of Paris. He then spent four months in and around London as the Battle of Britain raged above and the city felt the weight of German bombs.

In Britain, Spaatz was the guest of the Royal Air Force, meeting its senior leadership, including Air Marshal Charles "Peter" Portal, who would command the RAF from October 1940 through the end of the war. Spaatz visited numerous RAF installations, flew RAF aircraft, and was greatly impressed with an integrated air defense system that used radar to track the progress of German bombers so that interceptors could be vectored to meet them. It was far more sophisticated than what the United States had in place.

Ira Eaker left Washington in November 1940 to assume command of the 20th Pursuit Group at Hamilton Field, across the new Golden Gate Bridge from San Francisco, pleased to be back in the cockpit with his first flying assignment since he entered the Command and General Staff School in 1935. He and Arnold had just finished work on *Army Flyer*, their third book collaboration, and his boss was ready to let Eaker go. As Eaker recalled in a 1962 conversation with Arthur Marmor of the Air Force Historical Research Center, the chief told him to "get out and get yourself a tactical command. There is a war coming."

Meanwhile, Roosevelt's desire to have other countries as buffers between the United States and the Axis soon cost Eaker much of his command. In April 1941, the president decided upon the creation of the American Volunteer Group, a clandestine air combat organization formed to help the Chinese battle the Japanese in the skies over their war-torn country. The pilots were all former American military pilots, and the aircraft were to be P-40s. From where would these fighter planes come? From the concentration of them nearest to the port of San Francisco—the 20th Pursuit Group!

"I knew what this would do to the morale of these pilots if they had no airplanes," Eaker told Colonel Joe Green of the US Military History Institute in 1967. "I called them in and read the telegram and told them we were going to put these planes in these crates in first class condition and in the earliest possible time."

With that, he loaded the men into trucks and drove up to southern Oregon, where they spent two weeks doing "pistol practice" and flying two AT-6 trainers "about 22 hours a day [to] complete our instrument flying [training]."

It was in November 1940, the same month that Ira Eaker reached California, that the playboy Bob Morgan reached a turning point. He was living in

Virginia, working for Addressograph and dating a series of girlfriends while still carrying on a long-distance, off-and-on relationship with Martha Stone in Pennsylvania—when he decided to trade the keys to his fast car for a rudder and a stick. As he recalled in his memoirs, it was new newsreels from the Battle of Britain and the sight of "sleek new experimental craft wheeling from the hangars at Boeing and Lockheed" that made him want to join the Air Corps. He decided that the place for him was "up in the air."

He was ordered to report to Langley Field, passing through the same gate where Spaatz, LeMay, and Zemke had gone before. Everything was routine until the eye test, when Morgan's left eye was deemed to have less than 20/20 vision. Sensing the applicant's disappointment, the optometrist handed him an ice pack to "stimulate the optic nerve," then left the room long enough for Morgan to memorize the eye chart. A short time later, he had passed his physical and was on his way.

In February 1941, at Woodward Field near Camden, South Carolina, in the open cockpit of a bright yellow Stearman PT-17 biplane primary trainer, Morgan realized that the same detached temperament that made him fearless on the highway would help make him a good pilot.

"Flying came so naturally to me that by my third or fourth hour aloft I thought I knew it all," he wrote in his memoirs. "I don't mean that I was arrogant, exactly. It was more like being so caught up in the sheer bliss of it, the pure joy and fascination of being able to 'walk around' up there in the sky, with the countryside below you looking vast and beautiful, yet somehow grayer, slower, more ordinary—so caught up in this that you couldn't help feeling almost like a god. . . . 'Gee whiz, this is flying,' I kept yelling silently to myself. 'I'm something! Boy, I'm going to be a pilot.'"

And a pilot he became, soloing after six hours. Despite being called on the carpet for buzzing the field, Morgan graduated to basic pilot training at Bush Field near Augusta, Georgia.

Meanwhile, big changes were afoot in Washington, DC, as the Air Corps in which Bob Morgan had enlisted was growing and evolving into the autonomous air arm that had been imagined by Billy Mitchell and his disciples. Effective June 20, 1941, Hap Arnold's old friend General George Marshall, the US Army's chief of staff, ordered the reorganization of the US Army into three separate and autonomous components, including Army Ground Forces and Army Service Forces. For the third component, the Air Corps and GHQ Air Force were merged into the autonomous US Army Air Forces (USAAF), with Arnold as its chief.

Lieutenant General Delos Emmons, who succeeded Frank Andrews as head of GHQ Air Force, became the commander of the new USAAF Combat Command. In turn, Arnold formed the Air Staff as an analog to the US Army General Staff, naming Tooey Spaatz, who had already spent time working with the British Air Staff, as its chief. Spaatz then set about creating the Air War Plans Division (AWPD), which would coordinate with the US Army's existing War Plans Division (WPD) but remain independent from it. Heading the AWPD was Lieutenant Colonel Hal George, Ira Eaker's classmate of a few years earlier at the Command and General Staff School. Had Eaker not been on the West Coast, this job might well have gone to him.

And had Eaker been in Washington in July 1941, he also might well have *stayed* in Washington. However, when Eaker departed from the 20th Pursuit Group in September, Arnold decided to send him overseas to Britain. The assignment was a "get acquainted" mission similar to that undertaken by Spaatz a year earlier, and by Arnold himself for three weeks in April 1941. The relationships thus formed between British and American airmen would be a valuable foundation for the cooperation between the RAF and the Eighth Air Force a few years later.

What took shape in Washington under the direction of Spaatz and George was the first USAAF war plan, appropriately designated as AWPD-1, titled *Munitions Requirements of the Army Air Forces to Defeat Our Potential Enemies*, and completed in August 1941. As the title suggests, the plan discussed numbers of airplanes, a topic on many minds, but it also included comprehensive outlines for a strategy for using airpower to win a war in which the United States had yet to become involved.

Working under Hal George in the AWPD were several young majors whose careers parallel those of Spaatz and Eaker, and whose names would be prominent in the story of the USAAF in the coming war. Haywood "Possum" Hansell and Laurence "Larry" Kuter were both fighter pilots who had become advocates of strategic airpower while they were instructors at the Air Force Tactical School. Hoyt Vandenberg was a classmate of Spaatz at the Command and General Staff School.

As the AWPD was measuring its requirements and making its plans, the need for aircraft was obviously of paramount importance. Aircraft manufacturers were increasing production and building additional factories, but there was still a substantial flow of aircraft to Britain, which had only increased after March 1941 with the passage of the Lend-Lease Act, which permitted the deferred-payment "lease" of war materiel.

Among the crated American warplanes departing from East Coast ports under Lend-Lease were Curtiss Tomahawks, export variants of the P-40 Warhawk fighters in service with the Air Corps. Along with the aircraft being shipped in the spring of 1941, the Air Corps also sent two pilots who had been flying them, Johnny Alison and Hub Zemke.

Dispatching his young wife to live with his parents in Montana, Zemke packed his bag for his first overseas trip. When they reached England, Alison and Zemke discovered that the British had earmarked their Tomahawks for use as ground attack aircraft rather than as fighters. After Zemke had a chance to fly the British Supermarine Spitfire, he understood.

"Johnny and I had taken turns in flying a Spitfire against a Tomahawk and both found that the Spit had the upper edge in maneuverability, acceleration and climb," he recalled. "We could understand why the RAF had consigned the P-40 to a ground support role."

The two Americans spent weeks touring RAF bases, flying RAF aircraft and being as impressed with the British radar network as Tooey Spaatz had been when he visited a year earlier. On June 22, two days after the Air Corps became the USAAF, they were still in England when the news came in that the Germans had launched Operation Barbarossa, a massive invasion of the Soviet Union. In this attack, the largest single coordinated offensive in history, Hitler gambled that his mighty war machine could defeat Stalin's less-sophisticated war machine in short order. For the next few months it would appear that he had bet right.

In July, Zemke was mysteriously summoned to London, where he found himself in a room with many of the highest-ranking civilians in the US government. Ambassador to Britain John Wyant was there, as were Harry Hopkins, Franklin Roosevelt's closest advisor, and Averell Harriman, Roosevelt's roving ambassador and Lend-Lease manager. Zemke was told that more than 100 Tomahawks were being rerouted to the Soviet Union, which was now, by virtue of its being at war with Germany, a British ally and an American Lend-Lease recipient.

He and Alison were to be sent to Russia "on assignment to the American Embassy in Moscow as assistant air attachés." In other words, they were to coordinate the assembly and deployment of the Tomahawks.

As the two pilots shipped out for the Russian port of Arkhangelsk, they missed crossing paths with Ira Eaker, who arrived in England on August 30 to observe the RAF, specifically with regard to coordinated air defense and fighter escort tactics—and, like Zemke, to take a turn in the cockpit of a Spitfire.

Eaker himself narrowly missed Jimmy Doolittle, who left for England on September 7, making a note in his memoirs with a hint of regret that he "might have gone to Russia" to accompany the Tomahawk shipment if Zemke and Alison had not already been assigned the task. While the focus of earlier visits to Britain by Arnold, Spaatz, and Eaker had been the RAF approach to the tactical situation, Doolittle conducted an exhaustive technical assessment of the British aircraft industry and the RAF logistical infrastructure.

From their respective visits to Britain in the summer and fall of 1941, Zemke, Eaker, and Doolittle each came away having observed and noted

Britain's remarkable, radar-enhanced air defense system and the superiority of the similarly remarkable Spitfire over the P-40.

Both observations were prophetic.

American air defense deficiencies would be made painfully evident in December, while an awareness of the P-40's deficiencies as the USAAF frontline fighter would accelerate development of better aircraft. It was the latter task to which Eaker would devote himself when he returned to the United States. Fortunately, there were a number of options then in development.

On Saturday, December 6, 1941, Eaker was in Farmingdale, Long Island, visiting the Republic Aviation Corporation. Republic's XP-47B Thunderbolt had made its first flight exactly seven months earlier, and it promised to be a quantum leap beyond the capabilities of the P-40. Eaker observed the first production model P-47B, due for completion in about two weeks, and climbed into the prototype for a two-hour evaluation flight, noting that he "took it up to maximum altitude and tried out its maneuverability."

CHAPTER 14

AMERICA AT WAR

For each generation, there seems to be a particularly momentous day, often a day of disaster, on which all those of that generation will always remember where they were and what they were doing. For some, it is Tuesday, September 11, 2001. For others, it is Friday, November 22, 1963. For that generation, or gathering of generations, which we have come to call "the Greatest Generation," the day was Sunday, December 7, 1941.

The bombs started falling on Pearl Harbor and on the USAAF's adjacent Hickam Field at 7:48 a.m. Hawaii time. In less than two hours, the US Navy suffered loss of or damage to eight battleships and a number of other vessels, the heart of the Pacific Fleet. Nearly 200 aircraft were shot down or destroyed on the ground. The next day, President Franklin Roosevelt addressed a joint session of Congress, described December 7 as "a date which will live in infamy," and asked for a declaration of war. Germany declared war on the United States three days later.

On that Sunday, Tooey Spaatz was at home in Alexandria, across the Potomac from Washington, in a house that he and Ruth were in the midst of remodeling. They heard the news from Pearl Harbor on the radio shortly after noon. He immediately dashed to USAAF headquarters. With Hap Arnold out of town, he found himself the senior officer on duty. Arnold, who had just seen a flight of B-17 Flying Fortresses off from Hamilton Field, bound for Hickam Field, had flown to Southern California to go on a quail hunt with his friend Don Douglas of the Douglas Aircraft Company. It was late in the day before Arnold would learn what had happened.

Spaatz ordered the implementation of AWPD-1, which had been integrated into the larger joint US Army–US Navy contingency plan known as Rainbow 5—though it was an *offensive* plan and the United States was still reeling from the attack and dreading more attacks, so *defensive* actions seemed more to the point. Within the next few days, Lieutenant General Delos Emmons, late of GHQ Air Force and now in charge of the USAAF Combat Command, was reassigned as the military governor of Hawaii. With a promotion to major general, Spaatz succeeded Emmons as chief of Combat Command, which was headquartered at Bolling Field, across the Anacostia River from Washington.

Ira Eaker, who had test flown the XP-47B in New York the day before, was at his mother-in-law's home in Washington, where he and Ruth were staying while they were on the East Coast. After going out for Sunday brunch, he lay down for a nap. When Ruth woke him to tell him about Pearl Harbor, he mumbled, "You'll have to think of a better story than that to get me out of bed."

She then turned up the radio so that he could hear the news reports.

He phoned Arnold's office and talked with Spaatz.

"I think I'll catch a civil airliner tonight and get back to the West Coast and join my old 20th Pursuit Group," Eaker said, wanting to be where the USAAF needed fighter pilots.

Recalling this conversation in a later interview with Donald Shaughnessy that is in the Columbia University Oral History Collection, Eaker remembered that Spaatz replied, "I think you're headed in the right direction. Get going."

Once Eaker reached California, Arnold put him in command of the air defense of the Pacific Coast against a Japanese attack that was considered imminent. In this role, he began setting up a defensive control center, tying radar sites and fighter squadrons into an integrated network such as he and Spaatz had observed in England.

Eaker also paid visits to aircraft manufacturers on the West Coast. While in Southern California, he stopped in at the North American Aviation headquarters in Inglewood, where he had an opportunity to fly the Model NA-73 Mustang fighter, the first of which had been delivered to the RAF. The USAAF had assigned the P-51 designation to the aircraft but had not ordered it in quantity.

In a later conversation, he told Tom Coffey that he "thought it was the best fighter plane I had flown. It was somewhat underpowered, but I knew it was possible to correct that with the bigger engines coming along."

Indeed, later variants were retrofitted with Rolls-Royce Merlin engines, which were also manufactured in the United States as the Packard V-1650 Merlin. The Mustang itself proved to be the best piston-engine fighter widely used in World War II. Though the USAAF was slow to acquire them initially, when they arrived in quantity, they would be a game changer for the service, especially for the Eighth Air Force.

That Sunday, Jimmy Doolittle's family was scattered to the four points of the compass and planning to converge in Southern California two weeks later for Christmas. While Joe was in California, Jimmy was at Wright Field. Their older son, James Junior, was in his second year of a mechanical engineering course at Purdue and planning to follow in his father's footsteps and begin USAAF flight training in March. Having attended Culver Military Academy, John Doolittle was at the University of Michigan and scheduled to enter West Point the following June.

Doolittle spent Sunday glued to the radio and contemplating what he should do next. On Monday morning, he penned a letter to Hap Arnold, asking that he be relieved of his duties as a technical troubleshooter and given an operational command. He reminded his boss that he had 7,730 hours of flying time, most of it in fighters.

On Monday morning, he started this letter up the chain of command to Brigadier General George Kenney, the assistant chief of the Materiel Division at Wright Field, and a former deputy to Frank Andrews at GHQ Air Force.

"The answer is no," Kenney told Doolittle, though he sent him on to see Major General Oliver Echols, the chief of the Materiel Division. Both men had already approved Doolittle's promotion to lieutenant colonel, and they both wanted him to remain as part of their organization.

"I've been expecting you," Echols told Doolittle. "Kenney just called. His answer was no. My answer is no."

However, Echols did forward the request to Washington.

The morning of December 7 found Brevet Major Curtis LeMay waking up in the home that he had rented for his family in Holyoke, Massachusetts. Though it was Sunday, it was LeMay's custom to drive over to his office at Westover Field in nearby Springfield on the weekends.

As he drove home about noon, he tuned his car radio to listen to the football game between Brooklyn and New York that was being broadcast from the Polo Grounds. The broadcast was interrupted so that a breathless announcer could inform listeners about what was happening at Pearl Harbor. To his biographer, Tom Coffey, LeMay later admitted feeling "some sense of relief" that the might of the United States could now be channeled into the defeat of the Axis.

LeMay continued home to tell Helen what he had heard, then turned the car around and drove back to Westover. After a stint as an intelligence and operations officer with the 2nd Bomb Group at Langley Field, he had been reassigned to the 34th Bomb Group at Westover. Far from being up to strength, the group had only a couple of B-17s and a few B-18s. Their mission had consisted mainly of submarine spotting in the North Atlantic. These activities could not be called "antisubmarine" operations because the American bombers carried no bombs or depth charges to drop on the German submarines that patrolled close to the Atlantic Coast.

For much of 1941, LeMay had not even been at Westover; instead he had been involved in ferrying new B-24 Liberators to Britain. The B-24, a four-engine bomber like the B-17 Flying Fortress, was developed by Consolidated Aircraft in San Diego. First flown in December 1939, it earned orders from both France and the United Kingdom. Under the policy prevailing at the time—which was supported by Roosevelt and opposed by Hap Arnold—foreign sales took precedence over Air Corps orders, and so the first production-series Liberators were earmarked to go overseas.

For LeMay, this began as a cloak-and-dagger secret mission. Early in 1941, he had been ordered to fly to Montreal in civilian clothes to visit an office occupied by a civilian entity called the Atlantic Ferry Organization. It had been quietly established on behalf of the British Ministry of Aircraft Production to facilitate transfer of aircraft from the United States to Britain. By the end of November 1941, more than 100 Liberators had gone to Britain, while the USAAF had just 11, and LeMay was one of the few pilots in the USAAF to have extensive practical experience in the aircraft.

During December 1941, LeMay's career was like a yo-yo of unrelated assignments. Suddenly at war, the USAAF was in the midst of an organizational upheaval. With his "overt" job, the 34th Bomb Group had been ordered to Pendleton Field in Oregon to prepare to develop a West Coast antisubmarine capability, so the LeMay family pulled up stakes in Massachusetts and prepared to move across the country.

Almost as soon as he reached Pendleton, however, LeMay's "covert" job resulted in orders to turn around and report to Wright Field in Ohio, where his experience with the Liberator could be put to use. This assignment, however, was also short-lived, and within weeks he found himself on his way to Wendover Field in the desolate desert of western Utah as executive officer of the newly formed 306th Bomb Group—equipped with B-17s, *not* B-24s.

On December 7, 1941, Hub Zemke was in Kuybyshev (now Samara), a city of half a million people that was serving as the temporary seat of government of the Soviet Union. At that moment, 560 miles to the northwest, German armies were encircling Moscow and preparing for their final assault on the Soviet capital. As Zemke and Johnny Alison pondered the news of the Pearl Harbor attack against the backdrop of the gloomy prospects of their Soviet hosts, the fate of the Allies seemed desperate in the extreme.

They had been in the country for three months as the Germans were slicing through Soviet defenses like the proverbial hot knife through butter. Advancing across an 1,800-mile front, they had occupied an area of the Soviet Union larger than the German Reich by the time that the two Americans and their crates of P-40s disembarked at Arkhangelsk on the last day of August.

They were graciously welcomed by their hosts, and were feted at vodka-soaked parties given by pilots of the Soviet air force, who were much more open with the American airmen than they were with their own political commissars, with whom the average Russians shared a deep mutual distrust. The two USAAF men had ample opportunity to fly a variety of Soviet aircraft. Zemke was flying a Polikarpov Po-2 biplane one day when he encountered a German Do 215 reconnaissance aircraft. Fortunately, the German pilot was not in the mood for a fight. When he saw Zemke, he banked away and disappeared into a cloud.

When Zemke and Alison learned of the Pearl Harbor attack, their first reaction was to request an immediate transfer into a combat unit back in the States. Though Alison was ordered to remain to help acquaint the Soviets with other types of aircraft that would soon be arriving as part of Lend-Lease, Zemke was granted a transfer almost immediately.

He later surmised that he was ordered back to the States because he was married and Alison was single.

By December, Bob Morgan was a pilot, but not quite a USAAF pilot. He had graduated from basic flight training in Georgia in September, and December found him at Barksdale Field near Shreveport, Louisiana, preparing to graduate from advanced flight training on December 12.

On December 7, a group of aviation cadets from Barksdale, along with a parallel group of girls, had converged on a downtown hotel room, where they were, in Morgan's recollection, "dancing to Glenn Miller records, enjoying a few drinks, laughing, and flirting." Because no one had bothered to turn on the radio, it was not until they drove back through the gate and onto the base that they learned what had happened at Pearl Harbor that morning.

As Morgan recalled in his memoirs, their reaction was not one of fear or anxiety, not of thoughts that "the fate of the world, and of our own young lives, was in the balance." Instead, he and his fellow pilots, less than a week short of being commissioned as second lieutenants, felt "a scalding surge of anger at Japan for hitting us that way. It was a sneak attack. . . . The strike at Pearl Harbor offended every virtue, every notion of honor and fair play that my generation of American boys had grown up with, handed down to us from the Western movies, from our schools, from church, from the neighborhood policemen who let us ride around in their cars, from our households. You didn't hit somebody from behind. . . . Besides, what was Japan doing messing with us anyway? We were the *good guys!*"

For those young men who were not in uniform on the day when the radio announcers interrupted the regularly scheduled programming with news from Hawaii, there was an overwhelming urge to *be* in uniform that was unlike anything before or since. On the following day, and in the following weeks, recruiting centers were mobbed by men who wanted to fight for their country.

Robert Rosenthal, who had gone to class at night in order to get through Brooklyn Law School in three years, graduated summa cum laude in 1941—achieving what Ira Eaker had hoped to accomplish two decades before—and was preparing to go to work at Poletti, Diamond, Rabin, Freidin and Mackay. His family could use the extra money. When his father, Samuel Rosenthal, had died in January 1941, his mother, Rose, had gone to work in the garment industry. Meanwhile, though, his older sister, Jeannette, was working as a designer with Bergdorf Goodman, the Fifth Avenue luxury department store, and presumably earning a good salary.

Like LeMay, Rosenthal saw Pearl Harbor as a terrible turning point that had the potential of being a *decisive* turning point in the war to defeat totalitarianism. For the past several years, he had watched the march, both real and metaphorical, of Hitler and the ideals that he represented— not to mention the strutting of the pro-Nazi German American Bund on New York's own streets. He had yearned for a mechanism to stop this dark tide. With the entry of the United States in World War II, he imagined that this had come at last.

"Suddenly [my] frustration disappeared," he recalled. "I felt now that I could *do* something, I had the ability to offer some resistance to that regime."

On Monday, December 8, the recent law school graduate went to the US Army recruiting station and volunteered for flight training with the USAAF Aviation Cadet Training Program, for which he would receive a monthly paycheck of $75, substantially less than he would have made on Madison Avenue.

"Suddenly the nation came together," Rosenthal recalled in an interview preserved by the 100th Bomb Group Foundation. "Our nation had been attacked. . . . We had been split down the middle . . . people who wanted to help England and those who . . . believed we shouldn't have been in World War I and we shouldn't be in World War II, and there were some groups who were pro-Nazi. But when the attack came on Pearl Harbor, the nation came together. The voices of dissent were silenced. I don't think our nation was ever more strongly united than after Pearl Harbor."

CHAPTER 15

THE BIRTH OF THE EIGHTH AIR FORCE

Hap Arnold's office was filled with foreign troops. Two weeks after Pearl Harbor, Washington, DC, was invaded by the British Army, as well as by the Royal Navy, the Royal Air Force, and the British prime minister.

Pearl Harbor had been a surprise—indeed, it was a *shock*—but the British invasion had been anticipated for the better part of a year. George Marshall, Hap Arnold, and Tooey Spaatz had been cooperating with their opposite numbers across the Atlantic under the assumption that the two countries would be allies—sooner or later. With the US declaration of war on Japan on December 8, 1941, and the reciprocal declarations of war between the United States and Japan's Axis partners on December 11, the two Anglophone nations that had planned to be *allied* became the *Allies*, with a capital "A."

The official, though still covert, planning for the future "when, not if" cooperation dated back to secret meetings between January and March 1941 and culminated in the Atlantic Conference, a summit between President Franklin Roosevelt and Prime Minister Winston Churchill at sea off Newfoundland in August, at which they issued the

Atlantic Charter. It assumed an imminent wartime collaboration and called for "global economic cooperation and advancement of social welfare . . . a world free of want and fear."

On December 22, Roosevelt and Churchill met again in Washington at the start of the three-week Arcadia Conference, which was intended to chart the course of Allied actions in World War II. Arcadia saw the creation of the Combined Chiefs of Staff, comprising the senior officers in each of the services of the respective Allied partners, the British Chiefs of Staff Committee, and what was to be formally constituted as the American Joint Chiefs of Staff (JCS). Along with General George Marshall and Admiral Harold Stark (replaced early in 1942 by Admiral Ernest King), the American JCS included Major General Henry Harley "Hap" Arnold. The fact that Arnold had a seat at this table spoke to the autonomy that had been achieved by the USAAF.

The key strategic decision to come out of the Arcadia Conference was summarized as "Germany first, contain Japan." When the Allies were finally able to go on the offensive, the defeat of Germany would be their first priority. Japan would be "contained" until Germany was defeated. The base of operations for "Germany first" would be the United Kingdom. Though it would not come anytime soon, this doctrine would culminate in a cross-channel invasion of northern France aimed at the defeat of Germany itself. Preparations were undertaken in 1942, but the Allies were clearly not ready to launch such an invasion in 1942. They hoped for 1943, but as we know with hindsight, the invasion, designated as Operation Overlord, took place in 1944.

With the United Kingdom as the base of operations, the Americans prepared for their own "friendly invasion" of Britain. A trickle of American officers began early in 1942, and General Dwight Eisenhower arrived to take command of the newly created European Theater of Operations, US Army (ETOUSA) in June. In the meantime, Hap Arnold assigned Tooey Spaatz the task of developing the air strategy of the still-impossible objective of defeating the Third Reich. The instrument of this strategy, based in England, would be the Eighth Air Force.

How did it come to be that it was the *Eighth* Air Force?

As the plural in the name US Army Air *Forces* implies, the USAAF comprised multiple numbered air forces. The four geographical Air Corps Air Districts became the first four. The Philippine District became the Fifth Air Force, the Panama Canal Air Force became the Sixth, and the Hawaiian Air Force became the Seventh. A total of 16 numbered USAAF air forces would be created through the end of World War II, each with subsidiary "commands" designated by roman numerals.

The fact that the Eighth Air Force was actually preceded by its VIII Bomber Command underscores the intention that the Eighth was to be an offensive strategic air force. Indeed, it was conceived from the outset by Arnold and Spaatz as a force that would strike deep at the Third Reich's ability to wage war. The VIII Bomber Command was formally constituted on January 19, 1942, and the Eighth Air Force was activated on February 1, according to the Office of Air Force History and the US Air Force's Eighth Air Force Fact Sheet, although other sources give the activation date as January 28. The former gives the place as Langley Field, with a move to Hunter Field at Savannah Army Air Base in Georgia and a consolidation of the VIII Bomber Command within the Eighth Air Force on February 10.

The mission assigned to the Eighth Air Force was enormous, but the assets available were minimal. The entire USAAF had fewer than 200 B-17 and B-24 heavy bombers, and therefore strategic operations were not yet practical. Indeed, many of the bombers assigned initially to the Eighth were B-25 and B-26 medium bombers and A-20 light bombers. Of course none of these were overseas when the Eighth was created, nor would they be for months.

Then, too, there was the practical side to operations. The Americans had been theorizing and training for two decades but had yet to fly strategic missions in combat. They were about to embark upon a steep learning curve while operating alongside the RAF Bomber Command, which had been waging the air war on its own for two years.

On January 18, 1942, Ira Eaker walked into Hap Arnold's office in Washington. He had been summoned back to Washington with a telegram that read, "Report to the Commanding General, Army Air Forces, immediately, prepared for early duty overseas."

"What's up, boss?" Eaker asked informally.

"You're going over to understudy the British and start our bombardment as soon as I can get you some planes and some crews," Arnold told him.

"Bombers, hell! I've been in fighters all my life."

"Yes, I know that," Arnold said. "That's what we want, the fighter spirit in bombardment aviation. There are only a small number of Air Force officers who can be used for Air Force command and similar responsibilities."

It had always been one of Arnold's deepest regrets that he had not gone overseas in World War I in command of a frontline tactical unit, and he was determined *not* to have that happen to officers whom he had long been grooming for leadership roles within the Air Corps and the USAAF. Arnold was planning for both Spaatz and Eaker to go overseas to be part of the Eighth, the unit earmarked for the biggest combat role in the coming war.

Spaatz was designated the first commander of the Eighth Air Force, though this was not made official until May 2, 1942. In the meantime, it was Eaker's assignment to go in February as the USAAF advance man to activate a VIII Bomber Command headquarters and to coordinate future operations with his RAF counterparts—while Spaatz remained in the States to organize the Eighth and deploy it to Britain later.

Eaker, who had just recently been promoted to colonel, was given his first star as a brigadier general. Arnold realized that when he got to Britain and started to coordinate with the RAF, he would be sitting across the table from generals and air marshals, and it would be better if the USAAF sent a general of their own.

Eaker, along with a team of a half dozen men that included Colonel Frank Armstrong, took a series of commercial flights via Lisbon, and—

after dodging a German Ju 88 over the Bay of Biscay that seemed disinclined to persist in shooting down a commercial DC-3—arrived in Britain late on February 21.

Eaker was greeted warmly by Air Marshal Sir Arthur Travers "Bomber" Harris, who assumed command of RAF Bomber Command on February 23, Eaker's second full day in Britain. Harris not only suggested that Eaker establish his VIII Bomber Command headquarters adjacent to that of Bomber Command at RAF High Wycombe, but he invited Eaker personally to move in with him and Lady Harris.

After a temporary headquarters at RAF Daws Hill, Eaker set up his VIII Bomber Command at Wycombe Abbey. Code-named Pinetree, it was an eighteenth-century former girls' school near Harris's own headquarters. The headquarters of VIII Fighter Command, meanwhile, was originally at High Wycombe, but later moved to Bushey Hall in Hertfordshire and was code-named Ajax.

Eaker and the Americans were graciously welcomed, and Eaker reciprocated. When invited to dine in British homes, he would always bring gifts of American canned goods, which were common in the United States but scarce in wartime Britain. He queued with townspeople at the village barbershop and occasionally picked up British enlisted men whom he saw hitchhiking along the roads. Of the latter, he was told that this was something a British officer would never do. At a dance in the village, he told a large crowd that "we won't do much talking until we've done more fighting. After we've gone we hope you'll be glad we came."

These modest remarks, widely quoted in the press, were welcomed by the British public. They also defined Eaker's public persona as a man of few, albeit pithy, words.

"Harris and Eaker were remarkably alike in some respects and markedly different in others," observed James Parton, Eaker's biographer. "They shared a birthday—April 13—but the air marshal was four years older and two grades higher in rank. They had arrived at directly parallel commands on virtually the same day, though the RAF had a two-year head start in operations. Both men had enlisted in World War I.

Both had been ardent pilots, flying every type of plane as they moved steadily up through the ranks."

Speaking of their respective strategic philosophies, Parton wrote that "both believed wholeheartedly in the validity of strategic air war, but differed as night from day in their ideas on how to apply it."

Indeed, the two entirely opposite approaches to strategic operations were literally as different as night and day. As the two commands entered into an agreement on the division of labor, the RAF would fly its missions at night, the USAAF by day. The RAF favored "area bombardment," or "carpet bombing," while it was USAAF policy—promulgated by Arnold and rendered by Spaatz and Eaker—to use precision targeting, which was possible only in the daylight. To execute the latter, the Americans had developed a gyroscopic wonder, the Norden bombsight, a precision instrument that was one of the true secret weapons of World War II.

The RAF had begun the war favoring precision bombing to avoid civilian casualties, but in the summer of 1940, the indiscriminate leveling of Rotterdam—for spite—and the merciless attacks on British cities during the Blitz changed and hardened British planners. It was Harris himself who captured the mood most vividly when he paraphrased Hosea 8:7 from the Old Testament to his boss, Air Marshal Portal:

"The Nazis entered this war under the rather childish delusion that they were going to bomb everyone else, and nobody was going to bomb them. At Rotterdam, London, Warsaw, and half a hundred other places, they put their rather naive theory into operation. They sowed the wind, and now they are going to reap the whirlwind."

CHAPTER 16

THE AMERICAN WHIRLWIND

Metaphorically, the "wind" that would precipitate the American whirlwind flowed from the enigmatic phrase "East Wind Rain" (*Higashi no kaze ame*). This was the secret, though probably never used, "go-code" for the Pearl Harbor attack that was designed to be inserted in a shortwave news broadcast from Japan if military communications channels were unavailable.

That which Bob Morgan had characterized as a "scalding surge of anger at Japan" was shared by millions. It was a powerful blow to American morale, especially when accompanied by the terrible news of the epidemic of defeats being suffered by the Americans in the Philippines as a dark December faded into a melancholy January. The nation that had been humiliated at Pearl Harbor was now powerless to save the brave lads who would soon be cornered at Bataan. Americans yearned to strike back at Japan, but that was impossible—or was it?

On January 17, 1942, as the Arnold-Spaatz-Eaker triumvirate was taking the first steps toward transforming the USAAF into a war machine, and creating the Eighth Air Force as the mechanism for executing the "Germany first" doctrine, a recently promoted Lieutenant Colonel Jimmy

Doolittle was walking up the front steps of the Munitions Building in Washington, DC.

The transfer that Doolittle had requested on the morning after Pearl Harbor had been denied at every rung of the chain of command—until it reached Hap Arnold. At that point, the chief of the USAAF gave Doolittle his exit from Wright Field, but instead of giving him the combat command that he sought, Arnold brought him to Washington and put him to work—*desk* work—doing technical analyses of B-25 and B-26 medium bombers.

To Doolittle, the January 17 meeting seemed to be just another part of this tedious assignment when Arnold asked him, "What airplane do we have that can take off in 500 feet, carry a 2,000-pound bomb load, and fly 2,000 miles with a full crew?"

Obviously, it would be a medium bomber, for a heavy bomber could not take off in 500 feet, and a light attack aircraft did not have that range or bomb load.

"There's only one plane that can do it," Doolittle told his boss. The North American Aviation B-25 medium bomber, named "Mitchell" for the prophet of airpower, had made its first flight in August 1940, and the first deliveries of production aircraft had begun just 11 months before this meeting. At that moment, 158 had been delivered to the USAAF.

Everyone from Franklin Roosevelt on down had wanted to examine the feasibility of bombing Japan, but it was Captain Francis Low of Admiral Ernest King's staff who had the idea to fly the mission with bombers that had a longer range than that typical of carrier-based aircraft. In turn, they met with Arnold to discuss and hatch a mission that would use an aircraft carrier to launch the bombers as close as possible to Japan. Because a carrier deck would be too short for the bombers to land, they would continue on to airfields in China.

The next time Arnold and Doolittle met, the chief briefed Doolittle and wryly asked him whether he could recommend someone to organize the mission. Both men knew whom Doolittle would recommend, although at the time it was not yet assumed that Doolittle would actually *lead* the mission.

During February, as two dozen B-25s, retrofitted with additional fuel tanks to extend their range, and crews from the 17th Bomb Group began training, including carrier takeoffs from the USS *Hornet*, Doolittle gradually decided that he *must* lead this mission personally.

"I'm sorry, Jim," Arnold told him when he conveyed his opinion to his boss. "I need you right here on my staff. I can't afford to let you go on every mission you might help to plan."

Doolittle then launched into what he described as a "rapid-fire sales pitch I had mentally prepared beforehand."

Arnold allowed himself to be coerced, and later took ownership of what ultimately proved to be a brilliant decision. He was magnanimous in his memoirs, writing that "the selection of Doolittle to lead this nearly suicidal mission was a natural one . . . [H]e was fearless, technically brilliant, a leader who not only could be counted upon to do a task himself if it were humanly possible, but could impart his spirit to others."

On April 2, with 16 B-25s on deck, the *Hornet* and its escort of cruisers and destroyers sailed beneath the Golden Gate Bridge and into the Pacific Ocean. Only then did Doolittle reveal to his men the destination of their secret mission. With that, they all sat down to briefings on their specific targets in Japan. As they sailed westward, they learned of the defeat of the Americans on Bataan, the largest defeat in US Army history since the Civil War. This naturally ratcheted up the morale value of what they were about to undertake.

Doolittle hoped to approach to within 450 miles of Japan and launch his bombers on April 19, but when a Japanese patrol boat was sighted and sunk on the previous morning, he correctly assumed that the location of the American ships was now known in Japan, and he decided not to wait. Fortunately, the Mitchells had been fueled and inspected the day before.

The *Hornet* turned into the wind, and at 8:20 a.m. Doolittle was the first to go. He jammed the throttles forward, released the brakes, and cleared the end of the flight deck as the bow pitched up. Within the next 59 minutes, all the bombers were airborne and on course toward Japan.

The heavy rain that they experienced on takeoff had cleared and visibility was good as they made their low-level approach. They made landfall about 80 miles north of Tokyo, slightly off course, but this allowed them to approach from the north instead of the east, achieving a degree of surprise. Doolittle and ten of his armada attacked the Japanese capital, while the others went south. The idea was to hit numerous targets to create the illusion that a larger force was involved. Three bombers struck in the vicinity of the Yokosuka Naval Base, while one each attacked the industrial cities of Kobe, Nagoya, and Osaka.

Despite sporadic antiaircraft fire and numerous Japanese fighters in the area, all of the American bombers completed their bomb runs and exited Japanese airspace intact. Only then did the problems arise.

The "Doolittle Raid," as it came to be known, had been planned with meticulous precision up to this point, but when it came to the landings in China, whatever *could* go wrong *did* go wrong.

Taking off earlier than intended had caused more fuel to be burned getting to Japan, leaving less fuel available to fly to China. Therefore, none of the B-25s was able to reach a Chinese airfield. In retrospect, this might not have mattered. They arrived over China after dark and a planned installation of radio beacons had not been carried out.

Miraculously, only three of the 80 men under Doolittle's command were killed during the immediate aftermath of the raid, despite the fact that 15 of the 16 Mitchells crashed in the mountains or coastal waters of China. The pilot of the remaining aircraft, which had been suffering mechanical trouble, made an emergency landing in Vladivostok.

Doolittle and his crew, like most, bailed out and survived. Doolittle and Sergeant Paul Leonard, his crew chief, managed to find the scattered wreckage of their aircraft.

"I sat down beside a wing and looked around at the thousands of pieces of shattered metal that had once been a beautiful airplane," he wrote in his memoirs. "I felt lower than a frog's posterior. This was my first combat mission. I had planned it from the beginning and led it. I was sure it was my last. As far as I was concerned, it was a failure, and I felt there could be no future for me in uniform now."

"What do you think will happen when you go home, Colonel?" Leonard asked.

"Well, I guess they'll court-martial me and send me to prison at Fort Leavenworth," he said, obsessed with his apparent failure rather than considering the "if" of getting home from this remote corner of China.

"No, sir. I'll tell you what will happen. They're going to make you a general."

Doolittle and his crew linked up with five other crews almost immediately and, traveling on foot, by boat, in motor vehicles, and by rail, managed to reach Chungking, the provisional capital of Nationalist China. Doolittle attempted to enlist Chinese support in the effort to locate the rest of his crew, but these efforts were complicated by a huge wave of Japanese reprisals throughout Chekiang Province and beyond. Of the 77 survivors of the disastrous end of the mission, a dozen were captured by Japanese. It would be months before the remainder were repatriated, but Doolittle himself received orders to return to Washington "by any means necessary."

Traveling by way of Burma, India, Egypt, and Brazil, he was finally back in the nation's capital on May 18, a month after his "visit" to Tokyo. He was whisked immediately to Hap Arnold's office, where he briefed his boss and Chief of Staff George Marshall, who greeted Doolittle in a "rare jovial mood."

Doolittle was ordered to see a tailor for a brigadier general's uniform and await further instructions. These came quickly in the form of orders to report to the White House. Here, he was reunited with his wife for the first time since they had said good-bye in San Francisco on the night before the *Hornet* sailed. They were then ushered into the Oval Office, where Franklin Roosevelt presented Doolittle with the Medal of Honor and listened intently to a recounting of the raid.

"In time, we learned that the psychological effect we had hoped to have on the Japanese had been even greater than anticipated," Doolittle recounted in his memoirs. "Our intrusion into Japanese airspace over their home island had frightened and embarrassed the Japanese war leaders as nothing else could have at that point. . . . We also learned later that our surprise bombing of Tokyo was everything President Roosevelt had wished for and what we hoped we could deliver for him. American morale soared. It showed that our country, faced with the greatest adversity we had ever experienced, had fought back."

CHAPTER 17

GROWING PAINS

W hile Jimmy Doolittle was slipping the noose of an administrative job to lead one of the most celebrated USAAF combat missions of the war, Ira Eaker and Tooey Spaatz were at the threshold of the largest overseas USAAF administrative mission of the war.

In the late spring of 1942, with Eaker in England setting up the VIII Bomber Command, Spaatz was at his headquarters organizing the other elements of the Eighth Air Force in preparation for their deployment. The VIII Fighter Command was deployed to England in May, commanded by Colonel Frank "Monk" Hunter. Considering an independent USAAF supply chain to be an integral element of maintaining their autonomy from the ground forces, Arnold and Spaatz had created and deployed the VIII Air Force Services Command. As a tactical ground support component, the VIII Air Support Command was deployed to England in July.

While the administrative work was being done, however, the practical work of getting aircraft overseas and into combat was lagging behind the hopes and projections made by Arnold and Spaatz in January. They had told Peter Portal of the RAF that two heavy bombardment groups would be sent to England "before too long." It was suggested that these would reach Britain in April, but only the advance echelon of one squadron had arrived, and without their aircraft.

Hap Arnold, who reached Britain on May 25 for a weeklong inspection tour, wired President Roosevelt, telling him, "England is the place to win the war; get planes and troops over as soon as possible."

Spaatz, now a major general and commander of the Eighth Air Force, naturally concurred with Arnold, but his best-laid plans to get to England were overtaken by unanticipated events on the opposite side of the globe. Decoded intercepts of Imperial Japanese Navy messages had revealed that a Japanese invasion fleet was en route to Midway Island, north of Hawaii, and Japanese air attacks had been ordered against Dutch Harbor in Alaska. There was suddenly a great urgency to divert air resources, including many that were earmarked for the Eighth, to the West Coast.

Larry Kuter, an AWPD veteran and now the deputy chief of the air staff, told Spaatz to halt further shipments and troop movements to England. This was in direct contradiction of Arnold's own words, but it was a perceived emergency.

As it turned out, the halted troops included Spaatz himself!

The message reached him as he was on his way to the United Kingdom.

"Kuter's relayed order threw Eighth Air Force into turmoil," wrote David Mets, Spaatz's biographer. "The C-47s of the 60th Group were fueled and loaded with cargo for the Atlantic crossing. But on the evening of [June 1], they were ordered to off-load their cargo. . . . Spaatz spent the next day at Presque Isle and flew back."

Instead of landing in England and meeting Arnold there, Spaatz was back in Washington when Arnold returned on June 4. The Battle of Midway, which began that day, was a huge American victory, but it took time for things to be turned around and for Spaatz to be heading across the Atlantic.

Spaatz reached England on June 15 and met with Eaker, and on June 25 they established a permanent overseas headquarters for the

Eighth Air Force. Code-named Widewing, it was not at High Wycombe but at Bushy Park, a closer-in suburb southwest of London.

Eisenhower reached London shortly after Spaatz's arrival to assume command of the new ETOUSA and of the buildup of American forces. So highly did Eisenhower regard Spaatz that in August, he gave him a second job as air officer for his ETOUSA command, with a place on his staff. In his wartime memoir, *Crusade in Europe*, Eisenhower wrote: "From the time of his arrival at London, [Spaatz] was never long absent from my side until the last victorious shot had been fired in Europe. On every succeeding day of almost three years of active war I had new reasons for thanking the gods of war and the War Department for giving me 'Tooey' Spaatz. He shunned the limelight and was so modest and retiring that the public probably never became fully cognizant of his value."

The role of the Eighth Air Force within ETOUSA, it was announced confidently, was to achieve "air supremacy over Western Continental Europe." At the moment, the Eighth was in no position to challenge the Luftwaffe for this crown, a fact that was painfully clear to the RAF.

As Spaatz and Eaker settled in to await the arrival of their aircraft, they were greeted by their hosts, who generously turned over the first of more than 100 airfields that would be occupied by the Eighth, as well as the Burtonwood air depot, which would be controlled exclusively by the VIII Air Force Services Command.

The RAF may have treated the Americans cordially, but at the same time, the Americans were treated very much as junior partners in the upcoming enterprise of challenging the Luftwaffe and defeating the Reich. Portal and Harris had been at it for two years—including thousand-plane raids on major German cities. The RAF had been flying planes and losing crewmen in battle, while the USAAF had merely been theorizing. Half a year after Arcadia, the Eighth Air Force had no heavy bombers ready for action.

As the Anglo-French command in World War I had urged General Pershing to give them operational command of American Expeditionary

Forces, so too did Portal and Harris desire to exercise operational control over the assets of the Eighth.

Spaatz and Eaker resisted this idea, but in June 1942, it remained theoretical. They had no air assets for anyone to operationally control. As viewed from England, the mere trickle of aircraft needed by the Eighth was slow and frustrating. From the Washington perspective, Hap Arnold grew increasingly impatient. He could see no reason why the Eighth could not be in action soon, so on June 10, in the wake of his visit with Anglo-American leaders in England a week earlier, Arnold casually promised Prime Minister Winston Churchill that the Eighth "will be fighting with you" by the Fourth of July.

More easily said than done, it was a serious miscalculation, but Spaatz and Eaker had to make good on their boss's commitment.

July 4, 1942, did, in fact, mark the first bombing mission against German-occupied Europe by Eighth Air Force crews. By that time, there were only two B-17 heavy bombers in England, so the 15th Bomb Squadron borrowed a half dozen Lend-Lease Boston light bombers from the RAF for an attack on Luftwaffe airfields in the Netherlands. At least they were American-made planes. The *New York Times* called the mission "no holiday stunt," but it was.

The few Flying Fortresses that came in during July went to building up the 97th Bomb Group, which was to become the first operational heavy bomber unit within the Eighth Air Force. This was being done against the backdrop of continual sniping from Washington.

"I am personally gravely concerned over the apparent extension of the time period which you had anticipated necessary to complete the training of our units prior to their actual entry into combat," Arnold wrote Spaatz early in August. "The strategic necessity for the immediate or early initiation of effective, aggressive American Air Force offensive operations becomes more and more apparent daily [to the leadership in Washington]."

Despite their friendship and his being Spaatz's mentor, Arnold chided the Eighth Air Force commander with references to the notoriously timid actions by General George McClellan, commander of Union forces early in the Civil War. Spaatz wrote Arnold to say that he was only awaiting a break in the weather for his first heavy bomber mission.

The weather over northern France finally cleared on August 17 for a mission against the Sotteville railroad marshaling yards near Rouen. Ira Eaker was ready to personally accompany the mission, although this plan was almost sidetracked. The day before, while on a bird-shooting outing with some fellow officers, he had stumbled into a hornets' nest and been stung repeatedly and severely. Doctors recommended 24 hours of rest, but he slipped out of the infirmary and raced to the flight line at RAF Polebrook in time for the mission.

It is sometimes reported that Eaker led the mission, but although he was the senior officer, he flew as an observer aboard the lead aircraft in the second of two flights dispatched to Sotteville. The mission commander was Colonel Frank Armstrong, Eaker's personal troubleshooter, who had taken on the task of shaping up the 97th Bomb Group to get it ready for combat.

As the bee-stung Eaker climbed into a B-17 and waved to Tooey Spaatz, the 97th launched a total of 23 bombers, 11 on a diversionary flight, and a dozen against the target.

Eaker returned with a grin on his face and greeted journalists with a cigar in his hand, pleased to report that 11 of the 12 Flying Fortresses put their ordnance within a half-mile radius, and that tracks and locomotive sheds took serious hits. He could also take pleasure in the fact that most of the bombers came through unscathed and the others received only minor damage. Three weeks later, Eaker received a Silver Star *medal* and a second silver star on his collar with a promotion to major general. Armstrong earned a Silver Star on the mission, but his brigadier general's silver star came in February 1943.

The second Eighth Air Force heavy bomber mission came just two days after Rouen, when Armstrong sent 22 B-17s against airfields near Abbeville in northern France that were the home of Jagdgeschwader 26, one of the Luftwaffe's most highly regarded fighter wings. The latter mission was coordinated to distract German attention as the Allies made a commando raid on the French coastal city of Dieppe. The former mission was a success insofar as no Flying Fortresses were lost, but the latter was a catastrophe for the Allies. The Germans quickly defeated the 6,000-man Allied force at Dieppe, killing or capturing half and forcing the remainder to beat a hasty retreat only a few hours after the landing. The Dieppe fiasco clearly showed both the Allies and the Germans that an Allied invasion of northern France was impractical, and very unlikely to take place in 1942.

Meanwhile, plans were afoot to deploy American forces in a major operation far from northern France. In late July, a month before Dieppe, the Combined Chiefs of Staff had decided that the first major ground action by the US Army forces then being marshaled in Britain would be the invasion of northwest Africa. Code-named Torch, the operation was designed to relieve pressure on the British, who were then fighting the Germans at the opposite end of North Africa, and to occupy the French colonies of Morocco, Tunisia, and Algeria, which had fallen into the German sphere of influence after the defeat of France in 1940. This move was seen as a step toward ultimately driving the Germans out of North Africa.

Torch was designed to be high on the symbolism craved by Franklin Roosevelt. If nothing else, the president understood public opinion, and he was eager for his armed forces to execute an operation of significant scale against the Germans *before* the first anniversary of Pearl Harbor. This would show the country that the United States was making some measurable progress against the Germans.

CHAPTER 18

GETTING OVERSEAS

On June 4, 1942, Curtis LeMay, recently promoted to lieutenant colonel, left the 306th Bomb Group to take command of the newly formed and under-equipped 305th.

As LeMay said in a 1986 conversation, "I had just thirty-five pilots. Of course, we were also supposed to have thirty-five airplanes, but we had only three. We had no navigators, no bombardiers, and no gunners. We had three months to get ready, three B-17s, and only a couple of people who knew how to fly them."

During LeMay's first month in command, the 305th was relocated twice, first to Geiger Field near Spokane, and later to Muroc Field (now Edwards AFB) in California's Mojave Desert. The latter is a terrible place to be, especially while living in tents in the 100-plus-degree heat of the high-desert summer.

Through July and August, as more and more men and aircraft arrived, and the 305th managed to stand up three squadrons, LeMay worked the men harder and harder, demanding the level of perfection that would make them a cohesive unit and help them survive in combat.

"By the time the [305th] had to go overseas I had worked with the navigators for only about a week or two, but I'd gotten them one training flight out of Rome, New York, in the B-17s we were going to take to England," LeMay explained. "The bombardiers came into Muroc a couple of weeks before we were due to go. They had never dropped a live bomb in their lives—because we had no airplanes to allocate to bombing training. All the training the bombardiers had was with a few sand-filled bombs dropped from a twin Beechcraft we had rigged up. The gunners were supposed to have gone through a gunnery school, but they had never shot a gun from an airplane. They would mount a gun on a truck, run it up against a bank out in the boondocks someplace, and blast away. At Muroc I gave each of the gunners one ride in an airplane, and they fired their guns as we went across the desert. That was about it."

By the end of August, the 305th began the laborious process of moving overseas. The ground echelon went first, traveling across the United States to be loaded onto transport ships with their equipment. The flight crews came next, most of them headed to Syracuse, New York, where new aircraft were supposed to be ready to be flown overseas. Some went to modification centers across the country to pick up additional new aircraft.

As LeMay had discovered in Wendover and at his succession of duty stations since, the reality was not keeping pace with the optimism of USAAF plans. When he arrived in Syracuse, none of his planes were ready, nor were the ones that were supposed to have been picked up at the modification centers.

By October, the 305th was *almost* ready to go when LeMay got word from Colonel Frederick Anderson of the Air Staff that the group was about to receive new orders to go to the Pacific. LeMay told Anderson that their ground echelon was already in England, and that without their ground crews, the group would be broken up and used as replacements. Anderson reminded him of the inexplicable meanderings of government bureaucracy.

When he was off the phone, LeMay brought his staff and commanders together and asked how many aircraft were ready for the trip across the North Atlantic. When he learned that 33 of the 305th's Flying Fortresses were ready to go and that there would be two more the next day, he told his crews to pack up. He intended to be on his way to England under existing orders before Anderson could cut new ones for the Pacific. On October 23, the 305th Bomb Group was winging its way toward Gander, Newfoundland, bound for the new Eighth Air Force base at Grafton Underwood.

Bob Morgan was about three weeks ahead of Curtis LeMay, having departed Gander on his England-bound journey on September 30. Morgan's long trip to Britain had begun five days after Pearl Harbor with his graduation from advanced flight training at Barksdale Field. After he had trained in multiengine aircraft, his career track took him into the bomber world and an assignment to the 29th Bomb Group at MacDill Field near Tampa, Florida, which was flying A-29 Hudsons on antisubmarine patrol over the Caribbean.

By now, Martha Stone from Pennsylvania had come back into his life. Shortly before his graduation, he casually proposed, she agreed, and about two weeks later, they wed in Tampa and moved into an apartment on Davis Island near MacDill. For Morgan, things went a lot more smoothly with the aircraft at the base than with the woman on Davis Island. His third marriage was not a "third time charmed." As he confided in his memoirs, "Martha was a sweet girl, and she looked up to me. But she was so young and inexperienced—and I, well, I'd had a fistful of experiences. When I realized that she was not all that worldly, I let myself get all caught up in the Army Air Forces lifestyle—up early, flying all day, staying a little too long at the officers' club at night. And meanwhile Martha was isolated, way out of her familiar world, on an island in Florida."

Soon, Bob Morgan had fallen in love again, this time with the big iron of the USAAF.

"Nothing in all my flying experience ever prepared me for the B-17," he recalled. "One look at the B-17, silver and elegant and indomitable-looking on the tarmac, bristling with [armament], that massive reassuring tailfin crowning its splendid architecture, and the world started all over again. I mean, that airplane was that stupendous to behold. . . . To me and the thousands of men who flew her, 'goddess' would not have been overdoing it."

In May 1942, after 600 hours, much of it in cross-country training missions in the Flying Fortress, Morgan was assigned to the 324th Bomb Squadron of the newly formed 91st Bomb Group at MacDill. His typical high jinks—low-level flying and an unauthorized landing in a B-17 at his hometown of Asheville—placed Morgan in a simmering kettle of hot water with his squadron commander, Major Harold Smelser. As a result, Morgan wound up having to travel by train while the rest of the pilots flew to the group's next duty station at Walla Walla Field in eastern Washington. Smelser told Morgan that he would see to it that his errant underling was never promoted beyond second lieutenant.

It was while the 91st was training at Walla Walla in July 1942 that Morgan met two of the people who would be an important part of his life, or at least in the narrative of that life as it would pertain to his career with the Eighth Air Force.

Jim Verinis, whom Morgan described as a "quiet college kid from New Haven, Connecticut," was to be his copilot and alter ego during Morgan's early career with the Eighth. Margaret Polk from Tennessee, a descendant of President James Knox Polk, would be prominent in the Bob Morgan folklore not so much for who she was but for what she came to represent.

Margaret and her sister, Elizabeth, had made a cross-country road trip from Memphis so that Elizabeth could say farewell to her husband, Dr. Edward McCarthy, the flight surgeon with the 91st.

As Morgan wrote in his memoirs, Margaret "was the kind of gal who seemed to sum up a lot of what was good about America, a lot of what our enemies never understood, or maybe even feared and were trying to crush. Margaret Polk was what we'd soon be fighting for. . . . Call me a romantic so-and-so, but I even offered Margaret the ultimate gesture of my sincerest feelings for her—I buzzed her sister's house bright and early every damn morning in my B-17, rattling the windows and shaking dishes off the shelf. It wasn't something I did for just any woman."

After a last rendezvous in Jackson, Mississippi, as the 91st was heading eastward for overseas deployment, it was now all about what Margaret Polk *represented*.

By September, the 91st Bomb Group was at Dow Field near Bangor, Maine, picking up their complement of factory-fresh Flying Fortresses. Morgan, Verinis, and their crew were assigned the one bearing the tail number 41-24485. A number is a number, but for the young men who crewed these planes, impersonal numbers did not provide an aircraft with an *identity*. Known by a number, it was just a piece of equipment. All across the USAAF, nearly every aircraft delivered to a crew that was to take it into combat *had to* have a *name*. Out came the paintbrush, and on went the lettering and artwork that personalized the noses of planes then flowing from America's factories. There were patriotic names, nostalgic names, and personal names. "Nose art" became an art form. There was quaint artwork, clever artwork, and highly skilled cartooning. And then there was the racy artwork, much of it copied from the classic pinup artists whose work graced the types of calendars that one found on the walls of garages.

Every crew member had a different idea, but Bob Morgan wanted to name 41-24485 after Margaret Polk. After seeing the movie *Lady for a Night*, Morgan fixated upon the name of a Mississippi riverboat in the movie. Gradually, Morgan lobbied the crew one by one, and finally they agreed. They contacted the famous illustrator George Petty to draw up a sketch just for them. On the eve of their deployment at the end of September, now emblazoned with Petty's pinup girl on the nose, their B-17 became the *Memphis Belle*.

Like Morgan, Robert Rosenthal was part of the generation of airmen who came into the USAAF as the United States entered World War II. Morgan graduated from advanced pilot training a week after Pearl Harbor. Rosenthal enlisted that same week and reported for preflight training at the Air Force Pilot School at Maxwell Field in Alabama three weeks later. As the Southeast Air Corps Training Center, Maxwell was nominally the headquarters for training throughout the area, but as Rosenthal and the hundreds of young men who converged on the place on the second day of January 1942 found, the facility was woefully unprepared.

"They were ill-suited to take care of us," he recalled later. "I remember eating a lot of peanut-butter-and-jelly sandwiches."

Some of the curriculum at the school was familiar to Rosenthal— math and hard science—but much of it was related to the rudiments of aeronautics and the conceptual challenge of thinking in three dimensions.

After two months at Maxwell, punctuated by a stint in the hospital for severe athlete's foot, Rosenthal moved on to Douglas, Georgia, for primary flight training. He later recalled the "sense of freedom" he felt in the open cockpit of his Stearman PT-17 primary trainer, commenting, "I never enjoyed anything more."

During the summer of 1942, as the Eighth Air Force was just beginning to form in England, Rosenthal moved on to Moody Field near Valdosta, Georgia, for advanced flight training. It was here that he got a taste for instrument flying at night. He later recalled an incident in which he was flying with a particular captain who came in for a landing without lowering the gear. He tapped the captain and indicated this situation but was ignored. They landed with the wheels up, scraping the belly of the fuselage across the pavement of the runway in a high-speed shower of sparks and embarrassment for the captain.

When Rosenthal and his class graduated in September, they were given the choice of going overseas and into combat or remaining stateside as instructor pilots. Rosenthal had signed up to fight the Nazis, so he raised his hand when they asked for volunteers to go into combat.

"What you ask for you don't get," he later said, trying to explain the counterintuitive bureaucracy. On September 6, he reported for duty as an AT-6 instructor pilot at Fort Myers Army Air Field (known earlier and later as Page Field) in Florida. "While I was very unhappy about being in the training command, the flying that I did there really helped me when I got into combat," he recalled. "It *was* a tremendous confidence-builder."

Rosenthal was finally released from the training command in February 1943 and placed onto the path that would take him to the Eighth Air Force. After 140 hours of flight time transitioning to four-engine bombers, Rosenthal moved on to Pyote Field in West Texas. Also known as the "Rattlesnake Bomber Base" after its indigenous inhabitants, Pyote was about as far from Brooklyn as Robert Rosenthal could imagine. He would later recall having two inches of dust in his quarters and having to "sweep it out with a *shovel*."

Rosenthal began coordinated crew training in June 1943 at Dyersburg Field in Tennessee, then the largest combat crew training facility in the country. As Morgan experienced at Walla Walla, these schools trained entire crews—including not just pilots and copilots but bombardiers, flight engineers, navigators, radio operators, and all the gunners—to get them working together as a team.

After Pearl Harbor, Hub Zemke, like the others, was left yearning for a chance to strike back at the Axis, but in order to get overseas to fight, he had to get home *from* overseas. He spent the weeks after Pearl Harbor pacing the floor in Kuybyshev in the Soviet Union until orders finally came for him to report to the 56th Fighter Group in South Carolina. His challenge now was to travel 5,800 miles from a remote corner of a country that was on the verge of being defeated by the Germans—in order to fight the Germans.

Fortunately for Zemke, the British and the Soviets had invaded and occupied Iran in 1941 as a warm-weather conduit for Lend-Lease supplies, and Zemke was able to hitch a ride on a British plane to Tehran. Several weeks later, after coming to believe that he might be stuck in Iran for the duration, he managed to catch a flight to Cairo by way of Baghdad. It was now March 1942, and the situation was nearly as bad for the British as it was for the Soviets. The German Afrika Korps was only about 600 miles west of the Egyptian capital and pressing British forces hard.

As would be the case for LeMay, Zemke found himself in the position of having to escape the net of USAAF bureaucracy. When he reported to the United States Embassy in Cairo, the air attaché suggested that Zemke could be useful as an observer on the battlefield in the Western Desert, and took steps to have the airman's orders amended. Zemke didn't even wait until the next day. He dashed back to the airport and grabbed a flight to Khartoum. There he caught up with a Pan American flying boat—en route to the States from delivering supplies to the beleaguered garrison in Java—that landed on the Nile to refuel. He caught the plane and made his way across Africa, heading to Natal in Brazil.

Zemke finally arrived in South Carolina, only to find that the 56th Fighter Group had moved, and he was ordered to report to Teaneck, New Jersey. In the spring of 1942, as Curtis LeMay had also discovered, just because a group had been activated didn't mean that it had a full complement of aircraft. Usually, it was just the opposite, and the handful of P-39s that were assigned to the 56th were scattered at fields throughout the Northeast, flying air defense patrols as part of the I Fighter Command of the First Air Force.

The air defense missions struck Zemke as ironic as he stared across the Hudson River at night and saw the New York City skyline ablaze with lights, utterly ignoring any notion of a wartime blackout. In fact, the patrols being flown by the group were essentially training missions.

Assigned as operations officer for the 56th, Zemke spent his time visiting the group's squadrons, the 61st at the group headquarters in

Bridgeport, Connecticut; the 62nd in New Jersey; and the 63rd at Farmingdale, Long Island. It was at the last field that he met the aircraft that was to change his career.

The P-47B Thunderbolt, the prototype of which Ira Eaker had flown on the day before Pearl Harbor, was starting to roll off the assembly line at the big Republic Aviation factory, directly across the field from the 63rd Squadron. In June 1942, the 63rd became one of the first operational units to receive the big aircraft, with the squadron mechanics getting their training directly from factory reps.

"I took the first opportunity I could to fly the Thunderbolt," Zemke recalled. "The turbo [supercharger] was an integral part of the design and supposedly gave the aircraft a top speed of over 400 miles per hour at high altitude."

By summer, as I Fighter Command was beginning to expand, its commander, Brigadier General John Cannon—Ira Eaker's former classmate at the Command and General Staff School—ordered Zemke to take over as commander of the 56th.

"There were a great many difficulties to overcome and in my determination to succeed my command became the paramount concern in my life at that time," Zemke recalled. "To find yourself elevated from a lieutenant to a lieutenant colonel in a matter of six months—as I was—and having to assume the authority of command and act the stern disciplinarian with longtime friends was a difficult transition to make. Particularly so for those of us who had been pilots in the small peacetime Air Corps, which was like a gentlemen's club where you got to know just about every other officer."

Just before Christmas 1942, the 56th received orders to trade in its air defense mission and go overseas. The personnel—from pilots to mechanics to cooks—reported to Camp Kilmer, New Jersey, to await transportation to England. Unlike the bombers, which had the range to reach Britain, the fighters had to be crated for shipment, while the crews took the slow boat. In this case, the slow boat was the Cunard luxury liner

RMS *Queen Elizabeth*, which had been pressed into service as a transatlantic troop transport.

As they were going aboard, each man was carrying his big overseas bag, crammed with his gear and worldly possessions—everyone except Dave Schilling, commander of the 62nd Fighter Squadron. Zemke noticed that he was carrying only two large jugs of whiskey. It would be an interesting voyage.

CHAPTER 19

THE TWELFTH AND TORCH

By September 1942, Tooey Spaatz and Ira Eaker could take satisfaction in seeing their bombers finally starting to strike the enemy, but they had only to look across the field at High Wycombe to know that there was still much left to do. In looking back at the story of the Eighth and of the practical application of strategic air warfare against the German war economy, there was little taking place that would inspire a sense of accomplishment. As the Eighth was mustering two or even three dozen bombers for a couple of missions weekly, RAF Bomber Command was launching missions nearly every night, including the occasional thousand-plane raid.

Gradually, more and more bombardment groups, including Morgan's 91st and LeMay's 305th, reached bases in England, became operational, and began to fly their first missions. It was on October 9 that the Eighth was finally able to launch more than 100 heavy bombers on a single day, although just 69 bombed the industrial complex around the French city of Lille, which was their primary target.

By mid-October, just as the Eighth might have been on the verge of hitting its stride, the weather began to close in, casting a blanket of overcast across northern Europe that made it difficult for precision bombing. The weather, which would only be getting worse in the coming months, meant that missions were being canceled, and more than a third of the missions that *were* launched had to turn back.

Meanwhile, in the upper echelons of the Allied Combined Chiefs of Staff, decisions were being made that would further complicate the ability of the Eighth to fulfill its potential. The strategic air campaign was about to be sidetracked by the biggest American ground campaign of 1942.

Only a few years earlier, the Air Corps had been at the mercy of US Army brass with no interest in or understanding of airpower. Now the USAAF was at the mercy of a man who understood it very well. In July 1942, General Dwight Eisenhower became commander of the North African Theater of Operations, US Army (NATOUSA), and hence of Operation Torch. He intended to fully integrate airpower into his plans, and this airpower would have to come from the Eighth.

Along with aircraft and crews, one of the most important assets that Eisenhower took from the Eighth Air Force was Tooey Spaatz himself. Having been named to Eisenhower's staff as his airpower deputy at ETOUSA, Spaatz was to be placed in that role for Torch, and for subsequent operations in North Africa. It was planned that after Operation Torch, Eisenhower would leave Britain and move his headquarters to Africa. Spaatz would accompany Eisenhower, being pulled away from his work with the Eighth Air Force just as it was about to develop its momentum.

According to David Mets, Spaatz's biographer, "The decision to move Spaatz to North Africa was Eisenhower's, but it meshed well with Arnold's thinking and concerns over preventing the demise of the strategic bombing effort against Germany. It maintained Arnold's one-theater concept in that it was a Britain–North Africa campaign against Germany. Another consideration influencing Eisenhower to transfer Spaatz was that he was expected to get along with the British."

At first, Eisenhower asked only for the temporary loan of some Eighth Air Force assets for the support of Torch, but by October he was asking for more, and plans were in motion for the creation of a new numbered air force in North Africa—using assets originally assigned to or earmarked for the Eighth. This new air force, formed in August, was the Twelfth. Unlike the strategic Eighth, the Twelfth was envisioned as a *tactical* force, with its activities closely coordinated with ground operations and controlled by ground army commanders.

To serve under Eisenhower and Spaatz in command of the new Twelfth Air Force, Hap Arnold picked Jimmy Doolittle.

Doolittle's reputation—more that of the prewar daredevil than Tokyo raider—had preceded him. As Doolittle recalled in his memoirs, Arnold had given General Douglas MacArthur, the ground commander in the Pacific, a choice of two men to serve as his deputy for air operations and commander of the Fifth Air Force. When MacArthur declined Doolittle and chose Major General George Kenney, formerly with the Materiel Division, Doolittle was clearly disappointed.

Meanwhile, the thoughtful and calculating Eisenhower was not enthusiastic about having the impulsive Doolittle in his own chain of command. "From the first moment I sensed that Eisenhower had taken an immediate dislike to me," Doolittle recalled of his first meeting with Eisenhower on August 5, 1942. "I had the uncomfortable feeling of being an illegitimate offspring at a family reunion. Ike knew of my reputation as a racing pilot through the press and had probably translated that to mean that I would be too reckless to command an air force. He knew from my military record that I had never commanded a unit larger than the Tokyo raid gang. He probably also knew that MacArthur had turned me down."

Eisenhower lobbied Arnold to send someone else, but Arnold stood fast. This may have played into Eisenhower's desire to take Spaatz with him as his deputy for air operations.

Doolittle officially stepped into his new job on September 23, with a clear understanding of the role of both the Eighth *and* the Twelfth as integrated elements of overall USAAF airpower. "The operations for North Africa, the Middle East, and the bombing offensive against Germany from the United Kingdom are inseparable and are therefore basically complementary," he observed in a memo to General George Patton, who would command the Western Task Force in Operation Torch. "That force in the United Kingdom can be no more than a token unless these diversions [from England to North Africa] are stopped. Token forces do not impress the Germans."

November 1942 was a good month for Allied ground forces in North Africa. On November 4, the British finally broke the momentum of the Afrika Korps with a victory at El Alamein in Egypt, only 60 miles from Alexandria. Of this, Winston Churchill observed wryly, noting the paucity of victories on the Allied balance sheet since September 1939, "We have a new experience. We have victory—a remarkable and definite victory. . . . Now this is not the end. It is not even the beginning of the end. But it is, perhaps, the end of the beginning."

Operation Torch came on November 8, four days later. The US Army landed 100,000 troops in Morocco and Algeria. Within two weeks, the Allies had consolidated their victories at both ends of North Africa and the Afrika Korps was on the defensive.

As planned, Eisenhower moved his NATOUSA headquarters to Algeria and sent for Tooey Spaatz. "I had left General Spaatz in England and now I called him forward," Eisenhower wrote in *Crusade in Europe*. "We merely improvised controlling machinery and gave General Spaatz the title of 'Acting Deputy Commander in Chief for Air.'"

By virtue of his place at the right hand of Eisenhower, the senior theater commander, Spaatz had a senior responsibility for coordinating the operations of both USAAF forces and RAF. David Mets later observed that the RAF's "Air Vice Marshal Sir Arthur Coningham was not particularly pleased to be serving under an American who had been in the war for less than a year [but] there is no evidence that in serving with Spaatz in North Africa, Coningham did [anything] other than continue his outstanding performance and give his complete cooperation, regardless of any personal feelings he may have had toward Spaatz."

As they took up residence in Algeria in late 1942, Spaatz and Doolittle embraced their jobs in distinctly dissimilar style. Spaatz was cast, by necessity, as a diplomat. Doolittle, by nature, was what he had always been—a man of action. As Spaatz approached his command from the vantage point of the staff meeting, Doolittle could not help but approach his from the vantage point of the cockpit.

"I saw it as my job to visit every unit I was responsible for, find out what their problems were, and seek solutions," he wrote in his memoirs. "I flew on B-26, B-25, and B-17 missions as copilot or observer. I would drop into a field and announce that I was going to fly with them that day, climb aboard one of their planes, and go. . . . I never wanted any pilot or crew member in any units I commanded to say I didn't know what I was talking about."

Meanwhile, Eisenhower gradually softened his disdain for daredevil Jimmy Doolittle.

"He was a dynamic personality and a bundle of energy," Eisenhower wrote in his wartime memoir. "It took him some time to reconcile himself to shouldering his responsibilities as the senior United States air commander to the exclusion of opportunity for going out to fly a fighter plane against the enemy. But he had the priceless quality of learning from experience. He became one of our really fine commanders."

CHAPTER 20

INTO FLAK CITY

Curtis LeMay reached Britain runways on October 26, 1942, with most of the 305th Bomb Group, pleased and greatly relieved that nearly all of the group's assigned aircraft had arrived together, and that the others were just a day or two behind. They refueled and flew on to catch up with their ground echelon, which had already set up housekeeping at their assigned base, Grafton-Underwood, 60 miles northwest of London.

True to his well-deserved reputation as a taskmaster, LeMay worked his men relentlessly to mold the 305th into a combat-ready outfit. It was a time of practice in an effort to make perfect, but in the fall of 1942 the whole Eighth Air Force was pitifully inexperienced, and nobody yet even had a concept of perfection beyond learning to maintain coherent formations while in the air. Each aircraft crew in each squadron, and each squadron within each group, had developed its own personality. These in turn needed to be tempered and molded to become part of what would be a cohesive organization.

As LeMay explained to this author in 1986, "The navigators discovered that flying over England was not like flying over Kansas, where all the section lines run north and south, east and west. In England—as in continental Europe—towns were butted up against each other, with railroads and roads running in every direction. They had a hell of a time at first. We had never flown formation until we got to England simply because we didn't have enough airplanes. The first day that we could fly over there I got the planes up and tried to assemble a formation. It was a complete debacle. We couldn't do it. During the next flight I got up into the top turret of the lead B-17 with a radio and brought the pilots as close together into formation as I could."

While the crews were honing the skills that would be required in the coming air campaign, briefings were under way for the group and squadron commanders on the all-important subject of target lists. When Ira Eaker and Tooey Spaatz had come over, it was with the mandate to conduct a strategic air campaign against targets related to the German war machine. They had come with the theories of Billy Mitchell, the leadership of Hap Arnold, and the guiding principles of AWPD-1, but they had met the realities of a complex enterprise in which the purity of the theoretical had to coexist with competing strategies. The reality was that the Eighth Air Force existed in a world of finite resources and concerns more pressing than the abstract goal of destroying the national economy of Germany.

In the fall of 1942, a war economy that was of higher priority for Allied planners than that of Germany was the United Kingdom's, which was then struggling in the face of the threat posed by the vast armada of German submarines—the U-boats—that were seriously compromising the British economy. There was pressure from all sides, especially the British government, to use the Eighth Air Force against the German U-boat pens that had been constructed in France. The U-boat "wolf packs" were sinking nearly 700,000 tons of Allied shipping every month.

The Eighth was viewed as the ideal force for this mission because attacking these targets required the precision of America's Norden bombsight rather than the area bombing practiced by the RAF.

When group commanders such as Curtis LeMay first sat down in October 1942 to be briefed by the VIII Bomber Command on target lists, they saw names of French ports such as Bordeaux, Brest, La Pallice, Lorient, and Saint-Nazaire. And so it would be that this campaign would become the primary mission of the men and aircraft of the Eighth for the next eight months.

For LeMay and the 305th, the weeks of practicing formation flying were finally put into operation on November 17 and 18 with their first two operational missions. The 305th was still a green outfit, so these were not actually "combat" missions but diversionary sorties. Eighth Air Force combat doctrine called frequently for multiple formations to be launched simultaneously and then flown in different directions. One or more of these would be a feint, designed to divide the Luftwaffe's interceptor strength, drawing at least some of the fighters away from the bombers that would actually cross into occupied Europe to attack a target.

Meanwhile, LeMay had begun to develop a series of controversial tactical ideas that revolutionized the way the entire Eighth Air Force would attack targets. First, he created the staggered formation, or "combat box," that was to be his trademark and earn him the animosity of those who claimed that it was a death trap. It was, however, designed to be just the opposite. The purpose was to put the maximum number of bombs on the target while staggering the formation so that the interlocking stream of fire from the .50-caliber defensive armament of all the Flying Fortresses could provide maximum protection for the formation as a whole.

Another, even more contentious aspect of LeMay's tactical theory brought him into direct conflict with Colonel Frank Armstrong, Ira Eaker's right-hand man. Armstrong maintained—and it was the conventional wisdom within the Eighth—that when bombers encountered flak, German antiaircraft fire, they must take evasive action.

LeMay argued that when a bomber deviated from the trajectory of its bomb run, the bombardier would lose his aim on the target, the bombs would miss, and the mission would be wasted. He further suggested that since the skies were *filled* with flak, the odds of getting hit were roughly equal with or without evasive action, and if a bomber missed its target *and* was shot down, the lives of crewmen would be wasted.

Using an old artillery field manual dating from his years in ROTC at Ohio State, LeMay looked at speed, altitude, trajectory, and a host of other factors to calculate the probability of the German 88mm antiaircraft guns scoring a direct hit on a B-17. The odds, as LeMay later recalled to Tom Coffey, were one in 372.

When the 305th was tasked with its first actual bombing mission on November 23, LeMay told his men that they would be doing it his way, with no evasive action. When they complained, he snarled that he was going to be there himself, flying the lead aircraft. The target was the U-boat base at Saint-Nazaire at the mouth of France's Loire River, which was so heavily defended that the Eighth Air Force aircrews had started calling it "Flak City."

LeMay led 15 other Flying Fortresses into a maelstrom of flak, but nobody deviated from the course as they flew their bomb runs and put their ordnance on the targets. A half dozen aircraft, including LeMay's, took hits from flying shrapnel, but they all came through the other side. Just two minutes after the first bombs fell, the bombers were in the clear. All of their bombs had hit the targets, a rarity in the Eighth at the time, especially for a crew on its first mission.

LeMay's group went on to fly five more missions through January 3, 1943, mainly against U-boat pens. Through it all, their B-17s took many hits, but only two aircraft were lost, one that experienced mechanical failure and one that simply disappeared and was presumed to have crashed. LeMay and his crews took heart in the knowledge that their loss rate was significantly lower than that of other groups. LeMay took this as a vindication of his tactical theories.

LeMay was also gaining a reputation as a commander who led from the front, who, like Jimmy Doolittle, flew the same missions as the men under his command. As he later recalled, those men needed to discern that "the Old Man knows what he's doing. . . . How can any commanding officer send his people into combat when he knows nothing about it? So I started out leading all missions personally. Not only did I feel that I ought to lead the people fighting under me, but I had to find out things."

Commenting on LeMay's leadership style, Bob Morgan of the *Memphis Belle* later observed, "LeMay was not what anyone would call an evasive action kind of guy. His style, then and for a quarter-century of military and public life afterward, was to plow straight ahead and let the bodies—both hostile and friendly—fall where they may. . . . His own pilots blanched on the morning that Curtis LeMay ordered them to go in on a fixed course, but with LeMay himself at the controls of one plane, his unit scored twice as many direct hits as anybody else. After that, every bomber in the whole Army Air Force came in straight and steady on the target. American bombing suddenly got a lot better. Unfortunately, it did not get a lot safer for American planes and crewmen."

Morgan and the 91st Bomb Group were also in the air on November 17, but while LeMay and the 305th were over the North Sea flying a diversion, the *Memphis Belle* was already flying her third combat mission.

Assigned to Kimbolton in early October, they soon discovered that it was a fighter field, where the asphalt could not stand up to waves of 30-ton Flying Fortresses, so the 91st's commander, Colonel Stanley Wray, wangled an unauthorized move to Bassingbourn. When Ira Eaker sternly told him that it was not possible to simply *take over* a British base without authorization, Wray told him that he had already moved in with his ground echelon, his aircrews, and all of his aircraft. Pleased with Wray's resourcefulness, Eaker cleared things with the RAF and the 91st remained at Bassingbourn for the duration of the war.

"As soon as we awoke, it was as though we'd all stepped onto some invisible conveyor-belt," Morgan wrote in his memoirs of the 91st's first mission, on November 7. "Every move we made now, everything we did was drawing us inexorably toward that moment when we would board the *Memphis Belle* and take off into enemy skies that held the prospect of terror, destruction, pain, and violent death. We assembled in the briefing room as soon as we were dressed. We sat in wooden chairs, our leather flight jackets zipped under fleecy collars, and watched Colonel Wray as he strode back and forth in front of a map of western Europe, brandishing a pointer, revealing to us what our mission was and what we could expect. A big, hearty man, a West Point graduate, he had a way of giving it to us straight, no sugar-coating, no under-estimations of the odds against us to make us feel good, but all leavened with a rough sense of humor."

Wray spoke with an authority that inspired confidence, but it was his first mission too. The target, they learned, was to be the U-boat pens at Brest, near the tip of the Breton Peninsula.

That much-anticipated mission, marinated in all the adrenaline and anxiety that one would expect of a first mission, was an anticlimax. The flak was heavy, but there was minimal damage to the Flying Fortresses, and minimal damage done to the enemy. Though it was not known to the crews until the post-strike photos were analyzed later, the lead bombardier failed to line up the target through the overcast and the bombs fell wide of the target.

On their second mission, Morgan and the *Memphis Belle* visited Saint-Nazaire and the same U-boat pens that would be attacked by Curtis LeMay on the 305th's first mission the following week. This time, their flight went in low, at 9,000 feet, as other decoy Flying Fortresses distracted Luftwaffe interceptors at higher altitude. The latter did, as planned, lure the fighters away from the other bombers, but several were knocked out of the sky.

The others ran into a wall of Flak City antiaircraft fire on their low-altitude bomb runs. Every aircraft was hit, and one man was killed in a hail of shrapnel, but all of the Flying Fortresses in Morgan's flight made it through. The *Memphis Belle* suffered a ruptured oil line and had to make an emergency landing at an alternate field for repairs. When Morgan was told that these would take until the following day, he took off on three engines, got the propeller windmilling so that it would cause no further damage, and headed for Bassingbourn. In his memoirs, he confided that his eagerness had to do with a "hot date" he had set up for that evening.

On November 17, the mission was once again against Saint-Nazaire. Flying into the target area at 20,000 feet, three Flying Fortresses went down and the *Memphis Belle* lost a piece of her left wing. In his memoirs, Morgan notes that other squadrons fared worse.

Five days later, one of the losses was the Flying Fortress piloted by the commander of the 324th and Morgan's old antagonist, Major Harold Smelser. His bomber, observed rapidly losing altitude, dropped into a cloud, never to be seen again.

As Morgan tells it, when Smelser's personal effects back at Bassingbourn were being packed up to go to his next of kin, it was discovered that he had long held the envelope containing Bob Morgan's promotion to first lieutenant, and a more recent one promoting him to captain. These were turned over to Colonel Wray, who shared them with Morgan. They concluded that Smelser had made good on his promise never to see Morgan promoted above second lieutenant. A week later, Morgan was a first lieutenant. A week after that, he received his captain's bars.

CHAPTER 21

VICTORY AT CASABLANCA

ra Eaker officially assumed command of the Eighth Air Force on December 1, 1942, but it was a mere formality. He had been running the show since he brought the first half dozen men of the VIII Bomber Command to England in February. When Eisenhower announced in July that he would be taking Tooey Spaatz with him to the Mediterranean, Spaatz made it clear that Eaker was his heir apparent.

Succeeding Eaker at the VIII Bomber Command was Colonel Newton Longfellow, with whom he had served in the Philippines a quarter century earlier, and who had recently arrived in England to command the 1st Bombardment Wing. In August and September 1942, in anticipation of the arrival of a significant number of groups, the Eighth Air Force had begun installing wing-level units in England. The 1st Bombardment Wing traced its lineage to the organization that was commanded by both Hap Arnold and Tooey Spaatz at March Field, while the 2nd Bombardment Wing was the same one to which Curtis LeMay had been assigned at Langley Field. The 3rd Bomb Wing existed before the war, and was assigned to the Eighth Air Force in 1942 and redesignated as the 98th Bomb

Wing in 1943. The newer 4th Bombardment Wing was briefly active in 1940 and reactivated in 1942 in England.

Other officers who were now part of the upper echelons of the Eighth Air Force team included Larry Kuter and Haywood Hansell, veterans of the AWPD of 1941 and now brigadier generals. Both of them would go on to serve briefly as Eighth Air Force wing commanders—Kuter as Longfellow's successor at the 1st and Hansell at the 3rd—and both were disappointed not to have gotten the job of commander of the VIII Bomber Command.

"Longfellow was a poor choice," Hansell complained in his memoirs, noting that Eaker had "kept him in that position too long. But one of Ira's great strengths was also an occasional weakness, and that was his loyalty to his subordinates. He had a fine loyalty both upward and downward. . . . Eaker asked me if I had any objection to subordinating myself to an officer who was junior to me. I was so anxious to be in [VIII] Bomber Command, I would work for anybody."

Later, when given command of the XX Bomber Command of the Twentieth Air Force in the Pacific, Hansell would be on the receiving end of similar criticism.

James Parton, Eaker's biographer, who was on the Eighth Air Force staff at the time, agreed, writing that "it became increasingly clear that Longfellow did not have the stuff to be a good bomber commander, and his appointment remains a clear blemish on Eaker's record—one compounded by his stubborn refusal to relieve his old friend more promptly than he finally did."

Of Kuter, Parton would write that he "distinguished himself on Spaatz's staff, particularly in helping refine AAF structure into strategic and tactical formations, and rose, following the war, to four-star rank, higher than either Eaker or Hansell. But he never proved himself in combat."

On the periphery of the team, though not yet on the Eighth Air Force staff, was Brigadier General Fred Anderson, a 1928 West Point graduate and longtime acquaintance of Spaatz and Eaker, who had served as deputy director of bombardment on the air staff at USAAF headquarters, and who had come to England as Hap Arnold's personal representative on bombardment matters in the European Theater. Anderson went on to play a key role in the coming operations of the Eighth Air Force. At the end of February, he replaced Hansell as commander of the 3rd Bomb Wing when Hansell moved to head the 1st Bomb Wing and Kuter relocated to North Africa. Two months later, Anderson moved to the 4th Bomb Wing, and in June 1943, he would replace Longfellow as commander of the VIII Bomber Command.

Frank Armstrong remained Eaker's right-hand man and one who clearly had the right stuff. A case in point came when Eaker's continuing assessment of his units turned up the fact that the 306th Bomb Group had the worst record in the Eighth. On closer inspection, he found their base at Thurleigh to be lacking in discipline. When Eaker and Armstrong drove to Thurleigh for an inspection on January 4, 1943, Eaker took the group commander aside. Typically terse, Eaker told Colonel Charles "Chip" Overacker to pack his things, as he would be riding back to High Wycombe in Eaker's car. He then told Armstrong that he was the new commander of the 306th and that he would send his luggage to Thurleigh. Within six weeks the 306th had the best record in the Eighth Air Force.

Ira Eaker could be decisive when he wanted to be.

Eaker's biggest challenge—and his biggest triumph—in the first weeks of 1943 was not operational but diplomatic. Along with the American conquest of northwestern Africa came a moment of both reassessment and celebration by the Anglo-American Allied leadership. The former came in the convening of the first summit conference between President Roosevelt and Prime Minister Churchill since the Arcadia Conference in Washington a year earlier. The celebration was in the choice of a conference venue. Beginning on January 14, the ten-day conference took place in the recently captured city of Casablanca in Morocco.

The two heads of government were accompanied by the Combined

Chiefs of Staff. Also present at Casablanca was General Dwight Eisenhower, in his dual roles as commander of NATOUSA and of the joint Anglo-American Allied Forces Headquarters (AFHQ), which was the operational command staff for the Mediterranean Theater of Operations. Eisenhower's deputy for air operations, Tooey Spaatz, was also present. US Army Chief of Staff General George Marshall brought Lieutenant General Frank Andrews, the former commander of the prewar GHQ Air Force, who had been serving as Marshall's global troubleshooter. Marshall planned to introduce him as Eisenhower's successor in command of the Britain-based ETOUSA.

The agenda at Casablanca included both organizational matters and the strategic direction of the war in Europe and the Mediterranean. The former would immediately affect Spaatz and Jimmy Doolittle in North Africa, while the latter would be directly effected *by* Ira Eaker.

The organizational matters included Spaatz's adding command of the newly created Northwest African Air Forces (NAAF) to his duties as Eisenhower's air deputy. Jimmy Doolittle, meanwhile, moved up to command the Northwest African *Strategic* Air Force (NASAF) under Spaatz's NAAF. To contribute further to the spiderweb effect of the complex chain of command in the Mediterranean, Spaatz added direct command of the Twelfth Air Force to his list of duties, although his first NAAF general called for the Twelfth to continue "in name only." Its units then were operationally divided between Doolittle's NASAF and Arthur Coningham's Northwest African *Tactical* Air Force (NATAF). Containing all of these other organizations, NAAF was by far the largest component of the Allied Mediterranean Air Command (MAC), headed by RAF Air Chief Marshal Sir Arthur Tedder. MAC also included various units in the Middle East, Malta, and Gibraltar.

With the organizational web decided, the Allied leaders at Casablanca turned to the strategic direction of the war and the question of where next to turn once the Germans were driven out of North Africa— a goal that was soon revealed to be easier said than done.

It was assumed that 1943 was the year when the Anglo-American

Allies *must* land their forces somewhere in continental Europe. The disaster at Dieppe had demonstrated that a cross-Channel invasion of France had been impossible in 1942—but what about 1943? Allied plans for a 1943 invasion, code-named Operation Roundup, had been the subject of lengthy discussions and intense planning, but these sessions were clouded by serious misgivings and concerns that the Anglo-American force levels had not yet reached the point where they could prevail decisively against the Germans.

Remembering the terrible stalemates of World War I, the British were especially hesitant. Churchill strongly favored action against what he called the "soft underbelly of Europe," calling for Allied operations in southern rather than northern Europe. At Casablanca, he was able to bring Roosevelt around to this point of view. Operation Husky, an invasion of Sicily in the summer of 1943, was to be followed quickly by Operation Avalanche, an invasion of mainland Italy.

Of equal or greater importance to airmen—especially Hap Arnold, Ira Eaker, and their opposite numbers in the RAF—was the strategic air campaign against Germany. During the last quarter of 1942, with all the focus on Operation Torch and with bad weather over Europe—not to mention the ongoing U-boat suppression operations—this had moved to the back burner of the strategic cookstove. Now the airmen were anxious to see it brought forward.

While the USAAF and RAF officers agreed on the importance of the strategic air campaign, they agreed on very little about how it should be executed. With nearly three years of experience, the British maintained that they had developed the correct approach—nocturnal area bombardment. The Americans, who had been in the game for half a year, with mixed results, held fast to their notion of precision daylight operations.

Citing the Americans' inexperience and lack of results, the British—especially Peter Portal and Arthur Harris—were insistent that the USAAF should abandon its commitment to daytime operations and join the RAF by night. They had lobbied Churchill to this end, hoping to persuade him to convince Roosevelt.

To counter this, Hap Arnold intended to use Ira Eaker.

Eaker had first learned of the still-secret Casablanca Conference on the evening of January 13 when Eisenhower ordered him to show up for a "high-level" meeting. He phoned Peter Portal to find out more, but learned that Portal had already left London. As he told James Parton, "If you didn't need to know something, then you weren't let in on it."

Eaker and Parton headed south aboard a B-17, arriving in Casablanca on January 15 in time for a formal dinner that included all the top leaders. As with most conferences, formal dinners are for toasting; the real work is done in sidebar meetings. That evening, Eaker sat down with Arnold and Averell Harriman, Roosevelt's diplomatic troubleshooter.

"The President is under pressure from the Prime Minister to abandon day bombing and put all our bomber force in England into night operations along with (and preferably under the control of) the RAF," Arnold said, according to the notes taken by Parton.

"General," Eaker replied, raising his voice, "that is absurd. It represents complete disaster. It will permit the Luftwaffe to escape. The cross-Channel operation will then fail. Our planes are not equipped for night bombing; our crews are not trained for it. We'll lose more planes landing on that fog-shrouded island in darkness than we lose now over German targets. . . . If our leaders are that stupid, count me out. I don't want any part of such nonsense!"

"I know all that as well as you do," Arnold replied with what Parton recalled as a chuckle. "As a matter of fact, I hoped you would respond that way. The only chance we have to get that disastrous decision reversed is to convince Churchill of its error. I have heard him speak favorably of you. I am going to try to get an appointment for you to see him. Stand by and be ready."

In preparation for his audience with Churchill, Eaker, the one-time journalism student, sat down on the evening of January 17 and penned a terse document titled "The Case for Day Bombing," in which he wrote:

Day bombing is the bold, the aggressive, the offensive thing to do. It is the method and the practice which will put the greatest pressure on Germany, work the greatest havoc to his war-time industry and the greatest reduction to his air force. The operations of the next 90 days will demonstrate in convincing manner the truth of these conclusions. We have built up slowly and painfully and learned our job in a new theater against a tough enemy. Then we were torn down and shipped away to Africa. Now we have just built back up again and are ready for the job we all cherish—daylight bombing of Germany. Be patient, give us our chance and your reward will be ample—a successful day bombing offensive to combine and conspire with the admirable night bombing of the RAF to wreck German industry, transportation and morale—soften the Hun for land invasion and the kill.

Knowing that Churchill liked his briefing papers concise, he kept it short.

According to the diary notations of James Parton, who was at the meeting between the prime minister and the Eighth Air Force commander, Eaker thought it a "good omen" when the prime minister, who usually wore a naval uniform, appeared in the uniform of an RAF air commodore.

Eaker's own recollection of the historic meeting was more detailed: "He came down the stairs resplendent in his Air Commodore's uniform." He goes on to recall that Churchill began by explaining that "he understood I was very unhappy about his suggestion to our President that my Eighth Air Force join the RAF Bomber Command in night bombing, abandoning daytime bomber effort."

"Young man, I am half American; my mother was a US citizen," Churchill reminded him. "The tragic losses of so many of our gallant crews tears my heart. Marshal Harris tells me that his losses average two percent while yours are at least double this and sometimes much higher."

Churchill had the numbers reversed, a point that Eaker would masterfully integrate into his verbal presentation. He began by offering Churchill a typed copy of "The Case for Day Bombing," which Churchill read aloud with great interest. With that, the two men began a conversation that went straight to the point.

"Eaker began his defense of the American tactics by maintaining that only one convincing argument had ever been advanced for night bombing over day bombing and that was that it was safer," historian Arthur Ferguson writes. "But in point of fact the Eighth Air Force rate of loss in day raids had been lower than that of the RAF on its night operations, a fact that was explained in part by the great improvement in German night fighter tactics and in part by the heavy firepower of the American bombers."

Ferguson goes on to say that Eaker estimated that the accuracy of the daylight strikes was about five times greater than "the best night bombing, thanks to the excellent [Norden] bombsight they carried. Hence day bombing tended to be more economical than night bombing, for a force only one-fifth as large would be required to destroy a given installation. Eaker of course admitted that the objective of night bombardment was not primarily the destruction of individual targets but the devastation of vital areas, and as such it could not properly be compared to precision bombing on the ground of accuracy."

Finally Churchill turned to Eaker and told him, "Young man, you have not convinced me you are right, but you have persuaded me that you should have further opportunity to prove your contention. How fortuitous it would be if we could, as you say, bomb the devils around the clock. When I see your President at lunch today, I shall tell him that I withdraw my suggestion that US bombers join the RAF in night bombing and that I now recommend that our joint effort, day and night bombing, be continued for a time."

In *The Hinge of Fate*, the fourth volume of his history of the war, Churchill wrote: "I decided to back Eaker and his theme and I turned around completely and withdrew all my opposition to the daylight bombing by the [Flying] Fortresses."

"The prime minister told me he was willing for us to give it a trial; that he would say nothing more about it," Hap Arnold wrote in his memoirs. Being in Casablanca himself, he had an opportunity to speak to the prime minister shortly after his session with Eaker. "We had won a major victory, for we would bomb in accordance with American principles, using the methods for which our planes were designed. After that I had a talk with the President and with General Marshall on the same subject and, as far as they were concerned, the matter was settled. Everyone said, 'Go ahead with your daylight precision bombing!'"

Churchill's decision that day certainly changed the course of the air war, and based on the events that flowed from it a year later, during the first half of 1944, it changed the course of World War II in Europe and assured the success of Operation Overlord, the Allied invasion of Europe on D-Day.

In the near term, it defined the evolution of the Eighth Air Force. With Churchill's decision came the approval by the Combined Chiefs of Staff of what came to be known as the Casablanca Directive. Within it, the directive brought another term into the Allied strategic lexicon by formalizing the Combined Bomber Offensive, in which RAF Bomber Command would continue to fly at night and the Eighth would continue with daylight operations.

The Casablanca Directive now officially embraced the idea of a strategic air campaign by defining the Combined Bomber Offensive as "the progressive destruction and dislocation of the German military, industrial, and economic system, and the undermining of the morale of the German people to a point where their capacity for armed resistance is fatally weakened."

Summing up the Churchill-Eaker meeting, Parton, in his retrospective role as Eaker's biographer, later observed that "persuading Churchill to change his stand (even though the PM still did not believe the Eighth Air Force could achieve its goals) ranks as Eaker's greatest single accomplishment."

CHAPTER 22

LEARNING CURVES

O n January 11, 1943, as the big brass were preparing to converge on sun-soaked Casablanca, Hub Zemke was watching the towers and shipyard cranes of Glasgow materialize out of the Scottish mist. While Curtis LeMay and Bob Morgan had come to England as part of the VIII Bomber Command, the heart of the Eighth Air Force, Zemke came as part of the VIII Fighter Command. In the first week of 1943, it was still an almost useless appendage. The current escort fighters barely had the range to accompany the bombers as far as the French coastline, but Zemke was about to become part of seeing that useless appendage become a strong right arm.

As with the bombers of the VIII Bomber Command, the VIII Fighter Command had lost a large portion of its fighter strength to Operation Torch and the Twelfth Air Force. Until Zemke's 56th Fighter Group and Colonel Arman Peterson's 78th could be stood up, the only American fighter group in England was the 4th. It had been activated in September 1942 and was built around a nucleus of American pilots who had come to England as early as 1940 to volunteer to fly with the Royal Air Force as part of the Eagle Squadrons of the RAF Fighter Command.

As the men of the 56th fought with poor-grade coal in small stoves as their main weapon in the battle against the damp chill of the English winter, Zemke, like LeMay and so many group commanders during the Eighth Air Force's first winter in Britain, improvised a training program.

"With each passing day it became more frustrating for the pilots to have no aircraft to fly," Zemke recalled in his memoirs. "We were able to send some on RAF ground courses and set up our own ground training, but this was no real substitute for aircraft. We needed to practice formations and maneuvers. Someone had the idea of simulating formations using the British bicycles which each pilot had been issued as personal transport. The spectacle of a dozen men pedaling hard around the perimeter track in echelons of four must have confirmed to the British that we Yanks were crazy. As it turned out, this trick proved a useful exercise."

As the pilots languished in this bicycle limbo, waiting for their planes, Zemke tried hard to keep them busy. As Robert "Bob" Johnson, a pilot with the 61st Fighter Group who was later one of the leading aces in the Eighth Air Force, told Eighth Air Force historian Roger Freeman, Zemke "had a mission to perform and was quite serious about it. Very stern but also very fair. He was not an easy man to get to know. He didn't socialize much at the Officers' Club and had little contact with the Lieutenants outside working hours. But somehow I got the impression there was a guy just like us imprisoned inside that disciplinarian. Despite my misdemeanors, I learned that our Colonel could and would turn a blind eye to doubtful activities if he thought they were of benefit to our combat mission."

The P-47s finally started arriving in February, and in April the 56th moved from its original post at Kings Cliffe to a base at Horsham St. Faith, on the north side of Norfolk, that had previously housed USAAF medium bombers relocated to North Africa.

On April 8, shortly after the change of station, orders came up from Ajax, the VIII Fighter Command headquarters, for the 56th to fly its first mission, joining the 4th Fighter Group in a fighter sweep over the English Channel. Zemke personally led this first mission, and another one five days later. It was an inauspicious beginning. No German fighters were encountered, and the only aircraft swept out of the sky was one of the P-47s, whose engine conked out over Dunkirk. What might have been a first loss over enemy territory ended in a crash landing on the south coast of England.

At the time, fighter sweeps were one component of a threefold role for Allied fighters based in England, with the others being bomber escort and air defense. The last was almost exclusively an RAF activity and one in which the RAF's nimble Spitfire—with its maneuverability and excellent rate of climb—truly excelled. When it came to bomber escort missions, the Spitfire's short range made it of little use beyond the French coast. American fighters, except the P-38, were no better. The arrival of the P-47 would bring the potential for change.

Fighter sweeps, which the Americans called "rodeos," were designed essentially to pick fights with the Luftwaffe. They distracted the Germans from intercepting Allied bombers, and lured them into engagements in which losses could be inflicted on Luftwaffe fighter strength.

At the time, the Luftwaffe order of battle facing the Allied air forces consisted of three *Jagdgeschwader* (fighter regiments), the equivalent of a USAAF wing. Jagdgeschwader 26 guarded Belgium, the Netherlands, and northeastern France directly opposite England; Jagdgeschwader 2 was in northwestern France and the Atlantic coast; and Jagdgeschwader 1 provided air defense for northwestern Germany.

It was Dave Schilling, not Zemke, who led the first 56th Fighter Group mission to tangle with the Luftwaffe. During a sweep over coastal Belgium and the Netherlands, three dozen Thunderbolts were interrupted by a *Staffel* of Focke-Wulf Fw 190s from Jagdgeschwader 26. They dove on the Americans from out of the sun, a favorite tactic because the glare of the sun masked the attackers, while the dive gave them added speed.

The engagement did not go well for Schilling, either personally or as the mission leader. Before the attack, his radio had malfunctioned, but he made the serious error of not relinquishing command to someone else, so when the attack came, he was unable to direct his men. As a result of this, and of general inexperience in live combat, the Americans became a swarming mass of confusion with P-47s scattered across the sky. Luckily, only two were shot down. When Schilling returned to Horsham St. Faith, he endured the wrath of Zemke.

On the May 4 mission, it was Zemke who suffered the aggravation of a failed radio, so practicing what he had preached to Schilling, he handed command over to Loren McCollom of the 61st Fighter Squadron and turned back. The Thunderbolts proceeded to escort Eighth Air Force bombers returning from an attack on the Belgian port of Antwerp. When the Luftwaffe attacked, chaos once again reigned, but this time it was the Americans who scored two victories to no losses.

Nevertheless, it was clear that the 56th Fighter Group was a mess. When the radios of the mission commanders failed twice in a row—not to mention nagging engine and oxygen system failures—it was obvious that maintenance was in disarray. When unit cohesion kept melting into a free-for-all, it was obvious that discipline was a problem. In the general morass of inexperience that was VIII Fighter Command in the spring of 1943, though, these problems were not unique to the 56th.

In the Mediterranean, Jimmy Doolittle was facing the same challenges with inexperienced aircrews as Zemke was—or LeMay or Eaker or many USAAF combat air commanders around the world in early 1943. As he wrote his wife in early March, "Have flown with each one of our bomber groups, sometimes as observer and sometimes as co-pilot. They are all exceptionally good considering the fact that many of them had absolutely no combat experience when they arrived. They had to learn their jobs while fighting."

Meanwhile, just as his men were climbing their learning curves, Doolittle had to grapple with his own. In the spring of 1943, Jimmy Doolittle was finding it profoundly difficult to accept the role into which he had been thrust by circumstance and by Hap Arnold. By his nature,

Doolittle was not a command post leader, and he used every opportunity to get into the cockpit, not just for routine flights but for combat missions. He continued to justify this—to himself and others—by insisting that he wanted his men to see him taking the same chances and facing the same dangers that they were.

He had avoided coming to grips with the reality that he was no longer just another pilot in a cockpit but rather the man at the head of an organization comprising thousands of men in cockpits. Dwight Eisenhower had called Doolittle unable to "reconcile himself to shouldering his responsibilities as the senior United States air commander to the exclusion of opportunity for going out to fly a fighter plane against the enemy." He was right and Doolittle knew it.

By April, Doolittle was finally, albeit reluctantly, letting reality sink in—although, like Zemke, he found it hard to make the transition from "one of the guys" to a commander of guys who were not his cohorts but his command responsibility. "One problem, originally, was that I argued with my superiors and, according to Army standards, wasn't severe enough with my subordinates," he admitted to his wife. "Have improved quite a bit. Now avoid inviting attention to the stupidity of my superiors but haven't yet mastered the art of bawling out my subordinates to cover up my own stupidity."

Tactically, the situation for Doolittle's NASAF, and for its parent organization, Tooey Spaatz's NAAF, was very different from that for the Eighth Air Force, where there was no parallel ground war. In North Africa and the Mediterranean, the battle in the air was inexorably intertwined with the ground war—and that ground war had gotten off to a very bad start. When the US Army began to move out from Algeria and take on the Afrika Korps, the same level of inexperience that dogged Zemke and Doolittle in the air was painfully and profoundly present on the ground. *An Army at Dawn*, the title that Rick Atkinson chose for his book about the US Army in the North African campaign, says it all. It was the same army that went on to achieve an unprecedented victory, but at the *dawn* of the campaign, the inexperience of the US Army was a prescription for disaster.

This disaster came in late February in what is known as Battle of Kasserine Pass—actually a series of battles that took place in the foothills of the Atlas Mountains of northwestern Tunisia, in and near Kasserine. In the first large-scale clash, the US Army "at dawn" was overwhelmingly defeated by one of Germany's most experienced, battle-hardened, and effective organizations. Out of this disaster at the hands of the Afrika Korps, the US Army's momentum might have led to the tumbling dominoes of future disasters, but instead, command changes engineered by Eisenhower brought an amazing reversal of fortune, and a German defeat in North Africa three months later. Nobody at Kasserine realized it in February, but the sun rose quickly after the dawn and accelerated the twilight of the Afrika Korps.

Tooey Spaatz understood the importance of how the air war was interwoven with the ground campaign, but he also kept an eye on the bigger picture and the importance of strategic airpower. As David Mets, Spaatz's biographer, points out, "Spaatz recognized from the outset that the success of the campaign hinged on gaining control of the air from the Luftwaffe. This his units gradually accomplished by destroying Axis forces in air-to-air battles over Africa and the Middle East and wrecking them at their bases in Sicily and Italy. . . . By April Tunisia was becoming untenable for the Luftwaffe, which moved its aerial armada, except its fighters, back to Sicily and beyond, This relieved some of the threat to Allied installations and permitted the use of air defense forces in more offensive operations."

As March gave way to April, Spaatz and Doolittle reached beyond the front. Having inherited the heavy bombers and many of the medium bombers of the dormant Twelfth Air Force, Doolittle's NASAF undertook a strategic campaign against transportation and port facilities, as well as airfields, in Sardinia, Sicily, and mainland Italy that were the essential links in the German logistical chain between Europe and the Afrika Korps in Tunisia.

At this point in the war, the Luftwaffe had begun using tactical airlift for resupplying ground troops in situations where surface transportation was difficult—at Stalingrad a few months earlier and in North Africa now. Meanwhile, Spaatz and Doolittle, as well as Arthur Coningham of NATAF, had begun to benefit greatly from Ultra, the high-value intelligence data coming from decryptions of the German Enigma code being made at the beyond-top-secret Government Code and Cypher School at Bletchley Park near London. Both Doolittle in his memoirs and Mets in his biography of Spaatz make specific mention of Ultra in the context of the April 1943 campaigns, especially in their campaign against the Luftwaffe airlift.

On April 5, as Mets vividly explains, "the weather was good, and the slaughter was complete. In all, the Axis lost 200 airplanes in the air and on the ground that day. Many of the crews of the Ju 52s were instructor personnel for the Luftwaffe's multi-engine and instrument training programs, and their loss had a deadly long-range effect."

A month later, the US Army from the west and the British Army from the east pinched the Afrika Korps into a narrow pocket in Tunisia from which they did not have the air or sea transportation to escape. On May 13, the Germans surrendered a quarter million troops.

Citing a memo dated May 24, Mets writes: "Spaatz was able to report to Arnold that the Allies enjoyed air 'domination' in the Mediterranean and that nothing he could foresee was likely to reverse that situation. Control of the skies permitted Spaatz's other forces to wreak havoc on the enemy. The Mediterranean gradually became safer for Allied shipping and more dangerous for that of the Axis."

* ⭐ *

CHAPTER 23

PLAYING THE ODDS

Whenn Ira Eaker had promised Winston Churchill at Casablanca that the Eighth Air Force would soon run its first mission into Germany, he did so knowing that he already had one such mission *almost* ready to launch. On January 27, the day after Eaker returned from Africa, Frank Armstrong and his 306th Bomb Group accomplished the goals of both attacking German industry and continuing the U-boat campaign— while making good on Eaker's promise to Churchill.

Though it met these objectives, the mission was not exactly textbook perfect. The original plan was to strike the shipyards at Vegesack, on the Wesel River about 20 miles inland from Bremen, where U-boats were built. However, when it was discovered that cloud cover would prohibit precision bombing there, the armada diverted to the naval yard at Wilhelmshaven, which was a bit lower on the target list.

While Eaker had promised Churchill a 100-plane raid, only 91 B-17s and B-24s could be scraped together from the assets of six bombardment groups. Of these, only 53 bombed Wilhelmshaven. Most of the remaining bombers were unable to find the target because of a navigational error, but several attacked the U-boat base at Emden as an alternate target.

Because the Luftwaffe had yet to experience a daylight raid within Germany by the Eighth, fighter opposition was less than feared, although three bombers were lost.

At Casablanca, the Combined Chiefs of Staff had authorized the Combined Bomber Offensive against the "German military, industrial, and economic system," but in the spring of 1943, Eaker still did not yet have the crews and the aircraft to effectively execute a sustained strategic air campaign.

In the meantime, the U-boat campaign continued. Bob Morgan and his crew were in the thick of the action and feeling the heat. They came close to being a statistic on their ninth mission, a visit to the U-boat pens at Lorient on the Bay of Biscay that came on January 23, just as the Casablanca Conference was winding down. Only nine of the original 13 Flying Fortresses made it to the final run into the target, and the *Memphis Belle* almost didn't make it out.

Vince Evans, the bombardier, shouted a sudden warning that an Fw 190 was making a head-on pass from straight ahead.

"I shoved the throttle forward and sent the *Belle* into a steep climb to prevent a direct hit in the front of our plane," Morgan recalled in his memoirs. "Standard procedure would have been to dive, but that would have smashed us into the bomber group right below us. So I took us upstairs."

Most of the cannon shells that the German had intended for the front of the *Memphis Belle* instead impacted the tail.

"Chief, the tail is hit, the whole back end is shot off!" Sergeant Johnny Quinlan, the tail gunner, reported over the intercom. "The whole tail is leaving the plane!"

Those were words that no crew ever wanted to hear, and no doubt there were many odds calculations going on in the aircraft that afternoon. Morgan could feel in the controls that the tail had been damaged, although it had not fallen off, and Quinlan reported that the fire in the tail had gone out. Going to investigate himself, Morgan could see from the navigator's compartment that the tail, while badly damaged, was still there. Upon returning to the cockpit, however, he could feel by the rudder pedals that the rudder was no longer functioning. Added to this problem was the fact that Luftwaffe cannon fire had blown off part of the nose and a subzero wind was howling through the *Memphis Belle* with a speed matching the *Belle*'s airspeed, and the fear that the Luftwaffe would see that they were having trouble and finish them off.

Morgan decided that even without a rudder he could still turn the aircraft by applying throttle to the engines on one side or the other. A left turn could be made by applying more power to the engines on the right wing and vice versa.

"Guys, listen," Morgan announced over the intercom. "She's hurt. She's hurt pretty bad. She's hard to maneuver. I have enough alternate methods that I can fly this airplane, and that's what I intend to do. So let's all get back to our jobs. Fend off those fighter planes. Do the same things you've always done, and I'm gonna take you home."

Fortunately, the Luftwaffe had turned away and Morgan finally managed to get the Flying Fortress back over Bassingbourn.

"The approach I made just happened to be tailored to my freewheeling style—fast and hot," he recalled. "The more velocity, the less chance of drift. I knew I still had brakes, and brakes were my friend. We came barreling down on that runway, hit the tarmac with twin sharp puffs of smoke from our wheels, skidded like a taxicab that had just missed its fare, and screeched to a halt as [crew chief] Joe Giambrone's crew came at us on the dead run. They were about to encounter their most challenging repair job of the war thus far."

It was a wonder that the crew had survived, and a bigger wonder that the *Memphis Belle* had survived.

She was back in action on February 14 for her first mission into Germany. It was, as Morgan himself called it, anticlimactic. Both the primary target at Emden and the secondary one at Hamm were clouded over, so they came home with a full bomb bay. Two days later, *Memphis Belle* had her number four engine and part of a wing shot off over Flak City. Morgan called it a "bad day at the office."

Indeed, it was merely typical of the days at the office for most men of the Eighth, when the office was a Flying Fortress.

Early 1943, after his triumph at Casablanca, was a dark time for Ira Eaker, not only operationally but personally as well. After his moment of triumph in sun-splashed Casablanca, he had returned to gray and gloomy England in a gray and gloomy mood, feeling that even his closest friends were turning on him.

The first blow came from the one man whom Eaker would have thought would sympathize most with the goals of the Eighth Air Force—Tooey Spaatz. What irritated Eaker most was that Spaatz had chosen to send a memo, dated January 26, as Eaker was on his way back to England, rather than to discuss the matter face-to-face while the two were both in Casablanca.

"When I reached the office," Eaker wrote back on January 29, two days after Wilhelmshaven, "I received the sad blow that you had decided to take all of our P-38s. We had the 78th Group ready to accompany our bombers by about February 1, if this had not happened. Obviously, our bombers will have to go alone for at least another six weeks."

Eaker went on to say that Spaatz's denying the Eighth the long-range P-38s was "the most serious blunder we have made in a long time," adding that "I have a sneaking hunch that you agree. However, when we get a bad order, we carry it out with the same diligence we would a good order. The other blow I received on return was an order from ETOUSA to ship the 91st and 303rd [Bomb] Groups at an early date. Since you had not mentioned this in conversations I had had with you, I was led to believe you had no such intention . . . I am still hoping that you can avoid a further depletion of our little Air Force here."

A few days later, on February 4, when Frank Andrews arrived in England to assume his post as Eisenhower's successor at ETOUSA, Eaker thought that he had found an ally to make up for Spaatz's having become a fair-weather friend of the Eighth Air Force. Instead, Eaker found that Andrews's loyalty was to George Marshall in Washington.

After being briefed by Eaker, Andrews wired Marshall, asking him to send Hap Arnold to England for "discussion on build-up of Eighth Air Force," adding: "Bomber strength deteriorating rapidly to point where raids cannot be made in sufficient strength to disperse antiaircraft strength of enemy. Unless better results can be obtained US Air Forces adversely involved."

The reply was not what either Eaker or Andrews expected. Arnold was out of town, having traveled eastward from Casablanca to visit the China-Burma-India Theater, so the message was received by George Stratemeyer, his chief of staff, who drafted a reply for Marshall's signature. Instead of giving the Eighth Air Force what it needed to accomplish its strategic mission, Marshall decided to let Eaker off the hook and allow him to *postpone* it!

"We concur fully with your viewpoint to employ present insufficient forces on daylight missions deep into enemy territory is too costly and accomplishes too little," came the reply. "Any decision either to postpone effort until adequate forces become available or to use present force against targets in France and low countries or to try out night bombing will be supported here."

In other words, despite the Casablanca Directive and Eaker's apparent coup with Churchill, the Eighth Air Force was back where it had been half a year earlier, hemorrhaging assets to support the North Africa campaign while using what it had to continue the campaign against submarine pens instead of the strategic mission in Germany.

Eaker was anxious to press forward with missions into Germany, but he decided to limit these missions to the northwestern corner of the country until he could build up the fleet.

In 1972, Eaker told Colonel Joe Green of the US Military History Institute that "it became my duty to make certain that we did not, through any unwise or careless or hasty action, sacrifice our whole force. We could have taken, say, our first 100 bombers out at such a rate and against such distant targets that we would have lost them all in ten days, because on some of those targets we lost 10 percent on a mission. But I always said and reported to General Arnold that I would never operate that force at a rate of loss which we could not replace."

These calculations, balancing the risks and rewards, were not confined to the upper levels of command. The crews could figure the odds as well as anyone, but Eaker felt these numbers were not fully appreciated in Washington.

During that cold and foggy winter, Eaker could feel the confidence ebbing away.

"Morale sagged in late January and early February," Curtis LeMay told his biographer, MacKinlay Kantor. "All the combat crews had been sitting around, figuring out what their chances were. And the chances weren't very good. They got their statistics together, crudely but with terrible effect, and discovered that we were averaging an 8 percent loss on each mission. The tour of duty [in early 1943] was 25 [missions]. Taking it from there, a 4 percent loss would still leave any theoretical crew completely shot down—or shot up—with the completion of their specified 25 missions. If there were a 2 percent loss on every mission, a crew at the start would have a 50-50 chance of finishing their tour and going home. Beyond that, the ratio declined speedily. . . . Someone sat down there at Widewing, General Eaker's headquarters, and told him that it was on the graph: the last B-17 would take off for its last mission early in March."

Reportedly, Eaker replied, "Okay, I'll be on it."

As gloomy and alone as Eaker may have felt at Widewing, he had to have known that a great many men had confidence in him and believed that he understood them and had their best interests at heart.

Bob Morgan, one of those bomber pilots who knew and considered the odds, wrote in his memoirs: "Against [the] tide of pressure, public opinion, strategic-level skepticism and plunging morale, the VIII Bomber Command drew on a weapon even more devastating than the Norden bombsight. This weapon was our Commander, General Ira Clarence Eaker. The strapping, dark-browed, purse-lipped Ira Eaker believed in the mission, and he had the stature, nerve, and credentials to blow cigar smoke in the face of anybody who believed otherwise—including the noted cigar-smoker who ran the British government from 10 Downing Street. . . . [I]t was Ira Eaker, more than any other single force, that kept our American bombers flying in those uncertain months of late 1942 and early 1943."

By most accounts, the morale issue began to turn around by March 1943. In his memoirs, LeMay observed that "people shook themselves as if they'd been a little tired or groggy, and were properly ashamed; and then they got up and said, 'Let's get cracking. It might as well be this mission as the next mission. So—what the hell?' Thus it didn't make any difference any more. Everybody stopped worrying and everybody got back into the act."

On March 18, the act for the Eighth was Vegesack, the target that had been intended as their first inside Germany nearly two months earlier. This time, 73 Flying Fortresses and two dozen Liberators came over the target, dropping 268 tons of ordnance while losing only two aircraft.

As was beginning to be routine, reconnaissance aircraft photographed the target area after the raid and photo interpreters calculated that 76 percent of the bombs had been dropped within 1,000 feet of the aiming point, hitting seven U-boats as well as other facilities. Air Chief Marshal Peter Portal, commander of the RAF, generously called the results "the complete answer to criticism of high altitude, daylight, precision bombing."

Eaker even heard from Churchill personally, who extended "all my compliments to you and your officers and men on your brilliant exploit."

"To my mind the Vegesack raid is the climax; it concludes the experiment," Eaker said in a March 24 message to everyone in the VIII Bomber Command, trying to put to rest the debate about American tactics. "There should no longer be the slightest vestige of doubt that our heavy bombers with their trained crews can overcome any enemy op-position and destroy their targets. . . . All of us can now, I feel, look forward confidently to the next chapter in the air war, wherein we shall employ the lessons we have learned in the experiment, in an air offensive with forces of sufficient size."

CHAPTER 24

★

A STAR IS BORN

B ob Morgan spent only about two months with William Wyler during the spring of 1943, but it changed his life and transformed the *Memphis Belle* into one of the most famous American aircraft of World War II. Morgan may have given Flying Fortress 41-24485 the name *Memphis Belle*, but Wyler made her a *star*.

Wyler stood out around Bassingbourn because of his confident manner and commanding presence. Although he wore a major's uniform, he seemed to be very much in charge, and he was usually surrounded by cameramen. Gradually, Morgan learned that this self-assured stranger was an Oscar-nominated Hollywood director who had come to England with the blessing and encouragement of the USAAF brass to make a documentary about the Eighth Air Force.

The original idea was to focus not on the *Memphis Belle* but rather on the first Eighth Air Force bomber crew to complete—*as a crew*—the 25 missions that were the ticket for them to go home. Unbeknownst to the men who were actually flying the missions, a public relations plan was already taking shape.

———

Born Willy Wyler in Alsace when it was part of the German Empire, the director was the son of a Swiss father and a German mother whose cousin was Carl Laemmle, the founder of Universal Pictures. In 1921, while Laemmle was on a visit to Europe, he met Willy and invited him to come to America and work for Universal Studios. Wyler landed in Hollywood two years later and directed his first picture in 1925. By 1943, he'd had five Academy Award nominations, which included *Mrs. Miniver*, for which he would win the Oscar in March 1943 while he was working out of Bassingbourn. He went on to earn a dozen other nominations, making him the most nominated director in Academy history. He won four times.

"You can imagine my surprise when William Wyler bought me a drink one night and said he wanted to make me a star," Morgan recalled in his memoirs.

"What he said to me in his slight European accent in the officers' lounge one evening, between puffs of smoke from that straight-jutting cigarette, was that he wanted to bring his camera on board the *Memphis Belle* and fly some missions with the crew," Morgan explained. "He squinted at me—he had a very intense movie director-type of squint—and I looked back at him. I was trying to buy a few seconds to think that one over. Oh, if mother could only see me now. The idea was kind of irresistible [but] one thing I didn't need during a bombing run was for some guy to be crashing around the plane with a camera in one hand and his oxygen bottle in the other, bumping into my gunners and asking my navigator for a close-up. I sure as hell wasn't about to go back and do any retakes for anybody."

When Morgan asked Wyler why he had picked him and his crew, the director replied, "That name of your plane. *Memphis Belle*. It has a mystique. Don't you think? Also, I have asked around, and I've heard that you're a magnificent pilot. How many missions now? Eight? And haven't you led most of those missions? If I flew with you, I'd be right in the center of the action, Captain Morgan. And I'd have a pretty good chance of coming back."

"You know, Major," Morgan said, taking a "good belt" of the Scotch that Wyler had bought him, "we'd have no problem with an eleventh man on the airplane, as long as he stays out of the way. It's crowded in there."

"I assure you, Captain," Wyler said calmly, without Morgan detecting a trace of sarcasm, "I will not get in anybody's way."

The "mystique" of the *Memphis Belle* notwithstanding, Wyler had the same conversation with Captain Oscar O'Neill of the Flying Fortress *Invasion II*, with the 401st Bomb Squadron, also part of the 91st at Bassingbourn. Both crews were nearing the ten-mission mark when Wyler began his conversations with their pilots. Wyler put Morgan and O'Neill, who had been friends since flight school, into a countdown race. In fact, Wyler would assign cameramen to fly missions aboard a number of other bombers as well, including *Hell's Angels* of the 303rd Bomb Group.

Wyler's first mission with Morgan and his crew, on February 26, was not aboard the *Memphis Belle*. They were in another Flying Fortress, the *Jersey Bounce*, while the *Belle* was laid up for repairs after a mission to Saint-Nazaire ten days earlier.

The mission was to Bremen, but most of the bombers diverted to Wilhelmshaven because of overcast. Here, they were intercepted by what Morgan estimated as 100 Luftwaffe fighters, and lost seven of their own.

Back at Bassingbourn, when Morgan asked the apparently unflappable Wyler how he enjoyed the mission, his comment was, "A lot of action, I see."

The next mission, with the *Memphis Belle* herself back in the action, took the 91st Bomb Group to Lorient on March 6, where the skies were clear, the precision bombing accurate, and enemy opposition surprisingly light. Things were even better the following week, when the *Memphis Belle* visited the Sotteville railroad marshaling yards, the target near Rouen in northern France that was the first one attacked by Eighth Air Force heavy bombers seven months earlier.

After an aborted mission on St. Patrick's Day, the seventeenth mission for the crew of the *Memphis Belle* unfolded five days later as part of a strike against Wilhelmshaven's U-boat yards in the company of 75 other Flying Fortresses and 26 Liberators.

"More than fifty fighters attacked us, and once again we saw Ju 88s trying to bomb us from above," Morgan recalled, noting that Wyler was hovering behind the flight deck at the time. "The Nazis shot down three planes from our squadron, including one piloted by my close friend Captain H.C. McClellan. I watched as McClellan's young wife became a widow. Wyler saw it too. He even captured McClellan's spinout on film. He also caught the image of a fighter that sliced in from above and knifed right through our formation. . . . The Focke-Wulfs damaged nine other of our ships. One of these was piloted by the superb Red Claiborne, who had been flying as my left wing man from the very beginning. Two of Red's engines were shot out as we left the bombing run, and his oxygen supply was hit, too. He had no choice but to descend to about 10,000 feet so that his crew could breathe. Everyone in the squadron went down with him. It was against the rules, strictly speaking, to go down and cover a plane that had been disabled—you were just letting yourself in for some Luftwaffe target practice—but Red and his crew were too good to just get sacrificed to the wolves. . . . So we dropped along with him, a protective shield of firepower. [Wyler] got plenty of hot footage."

By March, as the crews of the *Memphis Belle* and *Invasion II* were nearing the twenty-fifth mission that would take them home, clearer skies prevailed over the continent, and the pace of the missions increased. With this came a higher casualty rate and, as Morgan recalled, "exhaustion among the fliers and the support people on the ground. . . . [P]ilots began to break down under the accumulated strain [and] mid-air collisions of friendly bombers, while never commonplace, began to add to the high rate of attrition."

With April 17 came one of the deepest penetrations into the Third Reich by the 91st Bomb Group thus far. The target was the Focke-Wulf factory complex in the great German port city of Bremen—the factory that made the fighter aircraft that had proven to be the scourge of the Eighth Air Force bomber crews.

The Bremen mission was also the largest to date by the Eighth Air Force. Both the *Memphis Belle* of the 324th Bomb Squadron and *Invasion II* of the 401st would be among the 115 Flying Fortresses that took off that morning. It was the twenty-first mission for Bob Morgan's crew, but the twenty-fourth for Oscar O'Neill and his men. One more, and they would be the first Eighth Air Force crew to complete their tour. Wyler had cameramen aboard both aircraft that day, but he himself chose to fly with the *Memphis Belle*.

The B-17s entered their bomb run on a black carpet of flak that hurled shrapnel through the formation. The aircraft were bouncing and pitching all over the sky, not from evasive action but from the concussion of thousands of exploding 88mm shells. When this abruptly stopped, it was merely the calm before the storm. The Luftwaffe piled on with hundreds of interceptors. Johnny Quinlan, the *Memphis Belle*'s tail gunner, reported over the intercom that one of his guns had jammed, and Morgan yelled at him to get it fixed. A moment later, Vince Evans, the bombardier, warned the pilot that a Luftwaffe fighter was closing on them from straight ahead. Morgan pulled back on the yoke, and the German flew beneath, barely missing the *Belle*.

The strike force lost 15 Flying Fortresses that day, six of them from the 91st. One of these was Oscar O'Neill's *Invasion II*, and William Wyler lost a cameraman. O'Neill, who survived the war in a German POW camp, never had his Hollywood moment, but his daughter, Jennifer O'Neill, went on to become an actress of considerable prominence in the 1970s.

With *Invasion II* gone on her twenty-fourth, all eyes were on the *Memphis Belle*. The crew was ordered to stand down for the next ten days, and Morgan—along with navigator Chuck Leighton, radio operator Bob

Hanson, and tail gunner Johnny Quinlan—were ordered to go down to the BBC radio studios at Bush House in London to record a program for broadcast in the United States at the end of the month. They would appear on *Stars and Stripes in Britain*, a regular program on the Mutual Network that featured American troops overseas.

With there being popular interest in the *Memphis Belle*, Morgan was naturally asked about the actual "Memphis Belle," Margaret Polk. A lot of women had come and gone in his life since he had reached England—and in his memoirs he mentioned "Mary Ann," who worked for British Intelligence—but he still had a snapshot of the Memphis Belle pinned on the flight deck of the *Memphis Belle*.

"I have to admit that I laid it on a little thick," Morgan recalled of his comments about her during the taping for the program. "I wanted her to hear it and feel flattered, of course, but it never occurred to me that I was also adding fuel to America's fascination over this storybook romance of ours."

On May 13, while the crew was standing down and Morgan was in London, the distinction of being the first Eighth Air Force bomber to complete its twenty-fifth mission slipped through their fingers. On that day, in a mission against the former Avions Potez aircraft factory at Méaulte in France, *Hell's Angels* of the 303rd Bomb Group became the first. Though he also had crews assigned to *Hell's Angels*, Wyler made the decision to follow the *Memphis Belle* crew to the end because so much publicity had now grown up surrounding her, and because he liked the name. Of course, the name "Hells Angels"—which, like "Memphis Belle," had originated in a prewar Hollywood movie—would also become an indelible part of postwar folklore as that of the infamous outlaw motorcycle club.

The twenty-fourth mission for the *Memphis Belle* and her crew came on May 15. She was one of 113 bombers sent by the Eighth against Wilhelmshaven and the naval facilities on the North Sea island of Helgoland. In Morgan's recollection, the primary target for the entire mission was Wilhelmshaven, and Helgoland was suggested by someone—"I never learned exactly who"—after Wilhelmshaven was reported to be overcast. The official record, however, notes that both Wilhelmshaven and Helgoland were planned targets. In any case, the *Memphis Belle* flew back to Bassingbourn with one mission left to fly.

That night, a contemplative Bob Morgan sat down and penned a letter—one of many—to the Memphis Belle.

"The *Belle* finished her twenty-fourth today and after one more she will be retired from Capt. Robert K. Morgan's hands and given to some other person to carry on with," he wrote. "I am going to have the name painted off though, for I feel that she has done her part. . . . I know now that I would never be able to finish my tour of duty over here if it hadn't been for the fact that you were behind me at all times. . . . You must realize that the young kid full of hell and stuff isn't the one who is coming back. The war has done many things to me, but I am sure one of them is to make a better man out of me."

Having had to wait two days for the final mission to be scheduled, the *Belle*'s crew assembled earlier than usual for their briefing on the morning of May 17. If they had the feeling that everyone was watching them— and they *did*—it was because everyone *was*. Wyler showed up with his 16mm camera, ready to film. There was no way that he was going to miss *this* mission.

Major Eddie Aycock, the commander of the 324th Bomb Squadron, decided to invite himself aboard to fly as Morgan's copilot. Meanwhile, Jim Verinis, the *Memphis Belle*'s original copilot, stopped by to say hello. Though Verinis had moved on to the *Connecticut Yankee* as pilot in January, Morgan had always considered him to be the *Belle*'s "second pilot" and never brought a permanent replacement copilot aboard. In Wyler's film, he would be listed as "copilot." Ironically, Verinis had already finished his own twenty-fifth mission a short time before, but as an individual, not part of a crew, as would be the case with the men of the *Memphis Belle*.

Hearts missed a beat when Vince Evans, the bombardier, arrived out of breath to say that he could not find his Norden bombsight. The bomb-sights were the most highly classified pieces of equipment in the Eighth Air Force. They were entrusted to bombardiers personally, who were expected to guard them with their lives. They were not kept in the bomb-ers between missions but stored in vaults. Evans had looked, and his was not there. He ran back to keep looking and finally he found it. He had put it in the wrong vault after the last mission. Everyone exhaled.

The *Memphis Belle* flew lead for the two dozen Flying Fortresses from the 91st Bomb Group out of a total of 159 bombers headed for Lorient that day. The skies were clear and the flak was heavy, but the crews noted that the Luftwaffe threw "only" about 50 interceptors at them. One of these never made it home. Blown out of the sky by waist gunner Bill Winchell, this Fw 190 was the eighth German fighter confirmed to have been shot down by gunners aboard the *Memphis Belle*.

Morgan noted that one of Vince Evans's bombs hit the aiming point squarely, meaning that the whole load hit the target. Because he was the lead bombardier, all of the other bombardiers followed him, and the whole group was on the mark. A few minutes later, they were out of the fire, and the Luftwaffe fighters dropped away. By Eighth Air Force records, the Luftwaffe lost eight fighters that day, while the Eighth lost six of its own. The *Memphis Belle* survived.

Back at Bassingbourn, Colonel Stanley Wray ordered Morgan to hold in the pattern while everyone else landed so that the *Memphis Belle* could make a grand entrance. Morgan called it a "little bit of show-biz" on his part.

By the time Morgan buzzed the field, touched down, and watched the *Belle*'s four Hamilton Standard propellers spin to a halt, a substantial crowd had gathered to greet the crew. When Morgan asked Wyler what would have happened if the *Memphis Belle* had gone down on her last mission, Wyler calmly told him that he did have a cameraman aboard *Hell's Angels*.

The following day, the king and queen of England visited Bassing-bourn to meet the crew. Morgan recalled that Queen Mary was cheerful and talkative, but that George VI remained quite taciturn. Haywood Hansell, commander of the 1st Bomb Wing, came up later to award each man the Distinguished Flying Cross.

The *Memphis Belle* was not yet finished. She flew a mission to the German port of Kiel the following day with a different crew, but the USAAF then decided to send the airplane back to the States along with the crew for a publicity and war-bond-selling tour.

On June 13, they climbed aboard the aircraft at Bassingbourn and headed west toward the United States via Greenland. For half a year, they had been through everything that the German flak batteries and the Luftwaffe could throw at them. Yet none of them could imagine what was in store for them during the next ten months until Wyler's film, *Memphis Belle: A Story of a Flying Fortress*, was released in April 1944—nor in the years that were to follow.

CHAPTER 25

THE BALLAD OF SNUFFY SMITH

While the other seven of the eight men profiled in this book were contributing to aviation history, building careers, or volunteering to fight for their country, Maynard Harrison "Hokie" Smith was living with his mother in Caro, Michigan, spending his winters in Florida, and digesting tomes on pop philosophy and pseudoscience. The only work that he was doing as Hitler was marching across Europe was working his way through the money he had inherited from his father.

Like every man in the United States between the ages of 18 and 36, he had registered for the draft in September 1940, but they were taking younger men first, so he had imagined himself as essentially immune. After Pearl Harbor, everything changed. The draft age was extended to 45, so 30-year-olds like Smith were suddenly in the vulnerable range. All around him, men were volunteering, but this selflessness did not suit Hokie Smith. He had grown accustomed to the leisurely lifestyle that his inheritance provided him.

It was not the draft that finally caught up to him but one of his earlier indiscretions. Arlene, his ex-wife, whom he had married and divorced when she was still a teenager, continued to darken his otherwise blithe existence with demands for child support.

Hokie felt that her remarriage took him off the hook, but the law did not agree, and in August 1942 he was arrested for nonpayment. The judge sitting on the same bench once warmed by Smith's father gave the errant deadbeat two choices: go to jail or join the US Army. As Jim Sparling, later a columnist for the *Tuscola County Advertiser*, wrote in 2000, "When I went into the army, a group of 30 of us assembled on the courthouse steps [in Caro, Michigan] for a picture. While we were lining up, the sheriff came down the steps with Maynard 'Hokie' Smith beside him in handcuffs."

Inducted on September 1, Smith was assigned to the USAAF and was off to Sheppard Field in Wichita Falls, Texas, where he developed a deep resentment to taking orders from drill sergeants a decade younger than he was. Having learned that all gunners were sergeants, he volunteered for Aerial Gunnery School down at Harlingen Field, near Brownsville.

It was around the same time that Hokie Smith became "Snuffy" Smith, *possibly* a reference to the cartoon character of the same name who was a mainstay of Billy DeBeck's popular *Barney Google* comic strip. More likely, it was one step removed. A popular B movie in 1942 was *Private Snuffy Smith*, based on the strip, in which Snuffy, played by Bud Duncan, joined the army to escape the federal agents sniffing around his moonshine. The story line and the character's quirky disposition clearly parallel those of Maynard Smith.

Smith qualified as a B-17 ball gunner, picked for this duty in part because of his slight stature. In this job, he was the man who curled up into the unimaginably cramped confines of the spherical Bendix ball turret on the belly of the Flying Fortress. A large man simply would not *fit* into a ball turret.

Snuffy went overseas in March 1943, assigned to the replacement pool, but he was in England for six weeks before he finally got his first mission. There was a reason.

Andy Rooney, later a well-known commentator for the CBS television program *60 Minutes*, was then a young reporter with the GI newspaper *Stars and Stripes* in England. Having met Smith, he described him as "known to everyone as a moderately pompous little fellow with the belligerent attitude of a man trying to make up with attitude what his five-foot-four, 130-pound body left him wanting."

This cantankerous nature led crews who needed a replacement gunner to shy away from him, but he was finally picked up by the 423rd Bomb Group, the most recent addition to the 306th Bomb Group. Known as the "Reich Wreckers," they were based at Thurleigh in Bedfordshire, about 50 miles north of London, and had flown their first mission back on October 9, 1942. Most of the original crews were gone by now, either shot down or sent home after completing their magic 25 missions.

The cranky replacement was assigned to Lieutenant Lewis Johnson, the pilot of the B-17 with tail number 42-29649. His twenty-fifth and last combat mission would be Snuffy Smith's first.

On the first day of May, the Eighth Air Force sent 78 B-17s to the U-boat pens at Saint-Nazaire. The Flying Fortresses of the 423rd Bomb Squadron of the 306th were part of the strike package that day, and so were those of the 324th Bomb Squadron of the 91st Bomb Group. Snuffy Smith was sharing the same patch of sky over western France with Bob Morgan and the *Memphis Belle*.

Morgan described it as a "bad mission from the start," adding that "there were clouds over the target, and they gave us a bad time. We never really knew whether we hit the target or not."

The 306th Bomb Group's official report echoed Morgan's recollections, noting that "bombing was bad due to heavy overcast. . . . Target visible only when directly overhead when such hits as could be seen were mainly in water or on point of land short and to the right of aiming point."

Flak was officially described as "ineffective and behind the formation," but Snuffy Smith found it unnerving. "First you hear a tremendous whoosh," he recalled, "then the bits of shrapnel patter against the sides of the turret, then you see the smoke."

In moments, it was over and they were on their way home.

This might have—indeed *should* have—marked the end of Smith's first mission and Johnson's last.

"I ought to ditch this plane just off the coast to make a dramatic story I can tell my children someday," Johnson joked to his copilot, Lieutenant Robert McCallum.

The usual plan was to fly a northwesterly path until opposite Land's End in Cornwall, the southwest tip of Britain, then turn east. However, the lead navigator made a serious error and led the formation of 91st and 306th Bomb Group B-17s into an eastward turn 200 miles too far south. As they sighted land, the bombers began their usual descent to 2,000 feet. Instead of Cornwall, though, the land was Brittany, and they were bearing down on the heavily fortified port of Brest!

When the skies were suddenly filled with a black carpet of flak, the bombers descended with the idea of slipping beneath the altitude at which the antiaircraft shells were fused to explode. The official report of the 306th stated that they flew over Brest at 800 feet, adding that the flak was intense and "very accurate." The Flying Fortress piloted by Lieutenant Robert Rand of the 91st was the first to go down, and the *Memphis Belle* lost an engine to the flak. The 91st lost four planes in what came to be called the "May Day Massacre."

As many as 20 Luftwaffe fighters jumped the bombers as soon as they cleared the flak. The official report mentions that interceptors attacked from below. From inside his cramped ball turret, Smith returned fire.

As he was watching the tracers scurrying past the airplane, he suddenly felt the jolt of a huge explosion as the fuel tanks amidships exploded into a fireball. The explosion knocked out the electrical power, which was needed to move the ball turret, so Smith slid open the hatch and squeezed out.

Meanwhile, Johnson ordered Sergeant William Fahrenhold, the flight engineer, to go aft to assess damage. Both he and Smith discovered the same thing from opposite sides. Along with the electrical lines, the intercom lines had been severed, so neither man knew what was happening on the opposite side of the impenetrable wall of flame that had engulfed the radio compartment and central fuselage.

As Smith watched, Sergeant Henry Bean, the radio operator, pushed past him with his uniform on fire. In one swift motion, he hurled himself through one of the waist gun ports and was gone. Smith watched as his burning body hit the horizontal stabilizer, bounced, and fell toward the English Channel.

One of the waist gunners had already jumped, and the other one was halfway out, his flight suit or his parachute harness snagged on the waist gun hatch. Smith pulled him inside and asked if the heat was too much for him. He stared back and replied, "I'm getting out of here."

Smith helped him open the aft escape hatch, and he too was gone. Being the new man, Smith didn't know the gunners, and it was not clear whether it was Joseph Bukacek or Robert Folliard whom he helped that day. Neither of them, nor Henry Bean, was ever seen again.

Deciding to stay with the stricken Flying Fortress, Smith grabbed a fire extinguisher and went to work on the fire. As he was beating down the flames, he noticed something out of the corner of his eye. He turned to see Staff Sergeant Roy Gibson crawling forward from his position as the tail gunner. He was drenched in blood, but Smith rolled him over. He finally ascertained by looking at the wound in his back, and by the way Gibson was having difficulty breathing, that his left lung had been punctured. Rolling him on his left side to keep the blood from pouring into his right lung, Smith stabbed him with a morphine syringe and returned to firefighting.

Smith saw an Fw 190 closing in and grabbed one of the .50-caliber waist guns. As the fighter flashed past, he lurched toward the gun on the opposite side of the Flying Fortress and continued firing.

As that Focke-Wulf disappeared into the distance, Smith went back into the radio compartment, where the radio, camera, and gun mounts were melting. He started grabbing anything that was loose and on fire and throwing it through a hole that had been burned in the fuselage. As he was doing this, .50-caliber rounds in the burning ammunition cases started to explode and he jettisoned these as well.

For more than an hour, Smith alternated between fighting the fire, tending to Gibson, and shooting back at the attacking German fighters. When the fire extinguishers ran out, he unzipped his fly and emptied his bladder into the flames. When that ran out, he beat on the smoldering wreckage until his own flight suit started to smolder.

Through the years, most of the credit for fighting the fire has gone to Smith, but reports published immediately afterward in the *New York Herald Tribune* and repeated in Smith's own hometown *Tuscola County Advertiser* stress that Fahrenhold and Joseph Melaun, the navigator, were also armed with fire extinguishers and working on the blaze from the opposite side.

Meanwhile, Lewis Johnson was guiding the bomber toward the nearest friendly field, which turned out to be at Predannack in Cornwall. He lined up in the runway and brought the damaged aircraft down.

Johnson landed separately from Snuffy Smith and Roy Gibson. Just as the aircraft touched the runway, it broke into two pieces, each of which careened down the runway, skidding to a halt in clouds of dust and sparks.

Had the blaze not been beaten down as it was, the Flying Fortress would have burned into two pieces an hour earlier and these would have dropped like rocks into the English Channel. No one would have survived. Incredulous ground crews inspecting the damage stopped counting bullet and shrapnel holes when they reached 3,500.

If it hadn't been for Andy Rooney and Lewis Johnson, Snuffy Smith might have slipped from his brilliantly shining moment of heroism back into ignominious obscurity. The first journalist to interview Smith after the mission, Rooney wrote the *Stars and Stripes* article heard round the world, and Johnson wrote the Medal of Honor recommendation that was heard loud and clear in Washington.

The story of the ill-tempered little man who fought the odds and saved lives was just the kind of story that played well in the media and in American households. Snuffy Smith was gradually becoming a larger-than-life figure.

In Washington, it was discovered that if a Medal of Honor, the nation's highest award for bravery in action, was awarded to Smith, he would be the first enlisted airman to receive it, and the first *living* airman since Jimmy Doolittle to receive it. The Medal of Honor recommendation caught the attention of President Franklin Roosevelt, who agreed that it should be awarded. Even the awarding of the medal would be larger-than-life. It was decided that Secretary of War Henry Stimson, who was due to be traveling to Britain in July, would go up to Thurleigh to award it personally.

When it was discovered that no Medals of Honor were available in England, someone rushed to find one and handed it to Stimson just as he embarked. Almost no one knew it at the time, but Stimson was not merely on a routine inspection tour, although that was his cover story. He was actually traveling to England specifically to make arrangements with Winston Churchill for future Anglo-American collaboration on the atomic bomb program.

When Stimson arrived at Thurleigh on July 15 for the carefully choreographed ceremony, he was greeted by Ira Eaker and a half dozen other generals. The band played, and 18 Flying Fortresses were ready for a low-level flyby. Everything was in place for a perfect media event. Everything, that is, except Snuffy Smith.

The call went out. "Where is Sergeant Maynard Harrison Smith?"

It is probably fitting that Snuffy was the only snafu at his own award ceremony. In the air, he was ten feet tall, a man of gallantry. On the ground, he was still five foot four, and the best that could be said was that he was an antihero. The man who seemed unable to ever do anything right was on KP duty that morning, as he was so often for sloughing off here, oversleeping there, or not bothering to attend required briefings.

"Where is Sergeant Maynard Harrison Smith?"

He was scraping breakfast trays in the mess hall.

Did he not know that this was his big day? Did the officer who exiled him to KP not know?

Brushed off and poured into a clean uniform, Sergeant Maynard Harrison Smith took the field, stood at attention, and uttered a meek "thank you" when Stimson draped the starry blue ribbon around his neck.

CHAPTER 26

FOCUSING THE AIR CAMPAIGN

F ive months after the Casablanca Directive had laid out a blueprint
for the Combined Bomber Offensive against the Third Reich, executing "the progressive destruction and dislocation of the German military,
industrial, and economic system," the idea was off to a slow start for the
Eighth Air Force.

Indeed, this offensive did not really get off the ground until the
weather cleared and the bombers could routinely get off the ground.
Meanwhile, in the spring of 1943, there were still too few aircraft and
crews and too many competing interests. The diversion of resources that
had begun with the ramp-up for Operation Torch continued, and Eighth
Air Force mission planning was still dominated by the U-boat campaign,
either the pens in France or the shipyards in northwestern Germany.

Ira Eaker was caught between this rock and the hard place of his
boss's impatience. Hap Arnold did not see the low, leaden overcast that
canceled missions, nor feel the pressure of the demands being made on
too few men and aircraft.

In February, when Frank Andrews, the ETOUSA commander, had
alerted Chief of Staff George Marshall to the Eighth's lack of resources

and the detrimental effect on operations, Arnold was out of town. Perhaps George Stratemeyer, Arnold's chief of staff, thought he was doing Eaker a favor when he suggested that Marshall postpone strategic operations. Hap Arnold would never have agreed to such a suggestion in February and he certainly would not sanction such blasphemy in April.

Far from letting Eaker off the hook, Arnold was growing impatient with him. In July 1942, he had goaded Tooey Spaatz, comparing him to George McClellan. Now he lashed out at Eaker's inaction, though he saved the sharpest edges of his tongue for Eaker's senior commanders, Newton Longfellow of the VIII Bomber Command and Monk Hunter of the VIII Fighter Command.

"I am rapidly coming to the conclusion that our bombing outfit in the Eighth Air Force is assuming a state of routine repetition of performance and perhaps finding many excuses and alibis for not going on missions, which with more aggressive leaders might be accomplished," Arnold complained to Frank Andrews in an April 26 memo. "Information I received from England is . . . that our fighter pilots are looking for excuses to go to the Savoy. . . . May this not be the result of having a leader who is not sufficiently aggressive? Has Monk Hunter lost his spirit—his dash? I know he is not the Monk Hunter I used to know. He seems to be playing safe on most of his missions. . . . Is not the same thing true of the Bomber Command? Does it not lack an aggressive leader?"

Historians usually focus on Eaker's performance in Casablanca—and certainly his face-to-face meeting with Churchill possessed the shimmer of high drama—but his April visit to Washington was no less important in the timeline of keeping the Combined Bomber Offensive on track. Not only was he able to convince Arnold that the Eighth was on the right track, but he was able to convince his boss that he possessed sufficient aggressiveness to *keep* it on track. Eaker also was able to plant a seed in Arnold's mind that would eventually blossom into the conclusion that the target of the long-delayed strategic campaign ought to be the Luftwaffe itself.

"His presentation was superb," Hap Arnold wrote in a memo that he handed to Eaker on May 2 to carry back to Andrews in England. "As far as I can see, everyone on the Joint Chiefs of Staff is convinced that the idea is sound. Of course there are certain individuals asking questions as to where the airplanes will come from."

The latter item—a dig at Eaker, with whom Arnold was otherwise now pleased—underscored the same problem that the Eighth Air Force had grappled with for the past year.

How Andrews might have reacted to the memo and how he would have integrated the Combined Bomber Offensive into the grand plan for coming ground operations will never be known. The following day, as Eaker was preparing to board his own aircraft to return to England, the B-24 carrying Frank Andrews westward from England slammed into Mount Fagradalsfjall in Iceland. He was dead at the scene. He was replaced by Lieutenant General Jacob Devers—a USAAF man replaced by a ground army man—and Devers was succeeded by Dwight Eisenhower.

It took another summit conference to finally focus Allied strategic thinking on the air offensive that had been called for at Casablanca. Convened in Washington on May 12, 1943, the Trident Conference considered the details of the Operation Husky invasion of Sicily, scheduled for July, and the objective of invading mainland Italy and taking one of the three major Axis powers out of the war. The other element of the Allied grand strategy decided at Trident was the decision to launch the long-awaited Anglo-American invasion of northern France, now designated as Operation Overlord, in May 1944.

Two important changes in the direction of the strategic air campaign flowed from Trident. The first was the recognition that the U-boat pens could not be destroyed with existing high-explosive bombs *and* that the Battle of the Atlantic against the U-boats was being won *at sea* through improved radar, better convoy organization, and support from Allied warships and antisubmarine patrol aircraft. While missions against the U-boat pens continued, their importance relative to the broader mission of the Eighth Air Force was downgraded. Parenthetically, the U-boat pens on the French coast were so well made that they were *never* destroyed, even after the war, and remain in place to this day. Those at Lorient were used by submarines of the French Navy until 1997.

Another result of Trident was the realization by Roosevelt and Churchill that Eaker was right about the Luftwaffe. A key prerequisite to the success of Operation Overlord would be a serious air campaign against the German air arm—one that was undertaken with the same persistence as the U-boat campaign.

Though Eaker had returned to England and did not attend Trident, the Combined Chiefs of Staff solidly approved what was being called "the Eaker Plan" as the basis for what became the Pointblank Directive. Said Portal, who was there, the British Air Ministry "was convinced that, if given the resources asked for, General Eaker would achieve the results he claimed."

Calling for a strategic campaign against the Luftwaffe, the Pointblank Directive was formalized on June 10 and issued on June 13. It was a document more important to the fulfillment of the potential of the Eighth Air Force than the Casablanca Directive.

In the meantime, Eaker also responded to Arnold's continued criticism of his immediate subordinates. In a frank memo written on June 12 in the midst of finalizing plans for Pointblank, Eaker told his boss that none of his officers "has yet had any experience in this theater or a command and combat experience in any other theater to justify his immediate assignment as [VIII] Bomber Commander with the exception of Hansell and the possible exception of Anderson."

Eaker went on to explain that Hansell was "nervous and highly strung, and it is very doubtful whether he would physically stand the trials and responsibilities," and promised that he would replace Longfellow with Fred Anderson by July 1. Eaker signed off by adding that "you are not satisfied with conditions here. Neither am I, and I am not satisfied with the support I have had."

"I am willing to do anything possible to build up your forces but you must play your part," Arnold wrote back on June 15, scolding his old friend and onetime coauthor, and underscoring the need to "can these fellows who cannot produce—to put in youngsters who can carry the ball. . . . In any event, a definite change seems to be in order but you have to be tough to handle the situation. . . . You have performed an excellent job but there are times when you will have to be tough."

As promised, Fred Anderson assumed command of the VIII Bomber Command on July 1, while Hansell was replaced at the 1st Bomb Wing by Frank Armstrong, Eaker's right-hand man. Though his combat experience was limited, especially in comparison with LeMay's, Anderson would prove to be an ideal choice, notably for the effective working relationship that he had developed with the Enemy Objectives Unit, the secret organization that conducted target planning for the Eighth.

Curtis LeMay, in turn, was given command of the 4th Bomb Wing at Elveden Hall (aka Camp Blainey) in Suffolk, from which Anderson had just departed. When he arrived at his new assignment and discovered what Elveden Hall really was, he was overwhelmed. The man used to Nissen huts found himself living and working in a vast manor house remodeled in the nineteenth century by Maharajah Duleep Singh, the ruler of the Sikh Empire and owner of the celebrated Kohinoor Diamond. Owned by the Guinness family since it was purchased in 1894 by Edward Cecil Guinness, the 1st Earl of Iveagh, the huge estate was taken over by the Eighth Air Force during World War II, and has more recently been taken over by motion picture companies for the filming of such features as the James Bond film *The Living Daylights*, Stanley Kubrick's *Eyes Wide Shut*, and *Lara Croft: Tomb Raider*.

"I found myself with a copper dome over my head and God knows how much 'richly veined marble' staring me in the face," LeMay complained in his memoirs. His mind was on operational matters and on his new job. In the space of a few months, he had been "kicked upstairs" from a group command to a wing, and then to a division.

As Tom Coffey, LeMay's biographer, later observed, "Each time he was assigned a new job, throughout his career, he was convinced he wasn't up to it. And he was further convinced that the only way he would ever bring himself up to it was through hard work. . . . Success meant work, which is why he considered work so essential for himself and why he demanded so much of it from the people around him."

As he had done the day that he arrived in England with the 305th Bomb Group, LeMay put his crews—he had four groups under his command within the 4th Bomb Wing—in the air immediately, often to practice formation flying and mutual air defense tactics. He began a relentless training schedule for the crews to practice instrument takeoffs in order to get past the ground fog so common in England, which had caused so many missions to be delayed or canceled.

LeMay also sent his crews to school, initiating a meticulous study of targets that had been attacked by groups throughout the Eighth Air Force over the preceding year, deconstructing previous missions, examining prestrike photos and poststrike photos, and studying factors from weather to enemy opposition that affected the results. The idea, as LeMay saw it, was to learn from past mistakes as well as past successes. He put together a loose-leaf binder called the 4th Wing Tactical Doctrine File, which contained the best information available on how to run a successful mission.

LeMay theorized that the Eighth Air Force crews knew more about daylight precision bombing "than anyone else in the world. The experts were right here and what they had to say was worth listening to. We gathered all that information together. We discussed it, thrashed it out, discarded some of it, kept what was good, then put it in writing in the form of a tactical document. It's in looseleaf form [so that] if something changes we throw away the old [page] and put in our new one."

It was intended that the groups of the 4th Bomb Wing—the 94th, 95th, 96th, and 100th—would operate as a unit. The debut of this arrangement came on July 4, which was both Independence Day and the first anniversary of the Eighth Air Force's own debut mission. This time, 83

B-17s were sent to the U-boat pens at La Pallice, while 192 Flying Fortresses were launched against aircraft factories in Le Mans and Nantes, in France. It is now generally overlooked that the French aircraft industry made a substantial contribution to the German war machine during World War II. Under the terms of a July 1941 agreement, plane manufacturers in France were allowed to continue operating so long as two-thirds of their production was for Germany. A substantial proportion of the transport aircraft used by the Luftwaffe, while of German design, were manufactured by French factories.

After a mission to Hamburg on July 17 was aborted because of overcast, the 4th Bomb Wing was dispatched on July 24 on what was then the largest and longest Eighth Air Force mission to date. The plan called for a three-part assault on port facilities and industrial sites in German-occupied Norway, targets that were as far as a thousand miles from the Eighth Air Force bases. LeMay sent 45 Flying Fortresses to Trondheim, 84 to Bergen, and 179 to Heroya. While the Bergen contingent found the target obscured by overcast, the other two achieved results deemed "excellent." Indeed, the Germans had to permanently abandon construction work on massive aluminum and magnesium plants that they were building in Heroya.

In late July, as the Eighth Air Force undertook a sustained campaign against industrial targets in Germany, including those related to Operation Pointblank—specifically the aircraft factories that manufactured the same aircraft that were the antagonists of the Eighth's heavy bombers—one man was conspicuously absent from the air.

Curtis LeMay had been ordered out of the sky by Fred Anderson and brought back to Widewing to help plan what was to be the largest mass strategic air operation yet imagined by the leaders of the Eighth Air Force.

CHAPTER 27

REGENSBURG AND SCHWEINFURT

D uring the last week of July 1943, under the mandate of the Point-blank Directive, the Eighth Air Force launched a series of maximum-effort missions against German aircraft factories. In planning these attacks, Ira Eaker and Fred Anderson concentrated on targets in northern Germany that were within the range of operations routinely flown by the Eighth.

These included Heinkel Flugzeugwerke at Warnemünde and Appa-ratebau GmbH Oschersleben (AGO) Flugzeugwerke in Oschersleben, as well as various Fieseler Flugzeugbau plants in the Kassel metropolitan area. While Fieseler is best remembered for light observation aircraft and AGO is a mere footnote in German aviation history, it should be recalled that both companies manufactured Messerschmitt Bf 109 and Focke-Wulf Fw 190 fighters under license.

Meanwhile, as Eaker, Anderson, and LeMay looked at the big map of German industry that was mounted on the Widewing wall, their eyes invariably fell on the largest concentration of fighter aircraft production in Germany. The city of Regensburg was home to the massive Messerschmitt GmbH facility that topped the Eighth's Pointblank Directive wish list.

Also on the minds of the Eighth Air Force leadership and those of the economists turned strategic planners at the Enemy Objectives Unit were other targets whose factories contributed to the effectiveness of the Luftwaffe. In the lexicon of strategic war plans they spoke of "bottleneck industries." On the flowchart of the German industrial economy, these were places where the lines intersected. They were the junctions that, if removed, affected myriad other industries downstream in many directions.

The glittering bottleneck that caught the eye of the Eighth Air Force and its planners in the summer of 1943 was a product so simple that it had but a single part—antifriction bearings, especially ball bearings. They were elementary but essential, not only to fighter aircraft and aircraft engine production, but to a broad spectrum of industrial products from military vehicles to factory machine tools. As the planners began to research the German bearing industry, they discovered that the majority of Germany's ball-bearing factories, or *Kugellager*, were located in or near the city of Schweinfurt. It was *almost* too good to be true.

Regensburg and Schweinfurt had the makings of ideal Pointblank targets.

However, they both lay in Bavaria, Germany's southernmost state and deeper inside the Reich than the Eighth Air Force had yet flown. They were at the limit of the range of the bombers and far beyond the range of the Eighth's escorting fighters. The airmen who had been advocating for strategic airpower since Billy Mitchell's time had a challenge laid before them.

In the history of USAAF strategic air operations, August 1943 is remembered for two very long, extremely ambitious, maximum-effort, and ultimately very costly missions. These adverbs and adjectives made them milestones. One was to the vast oil refinery complex at Ploesti, Romania.

The other was to *both* Regensburg and Schweinfurt. The former was a Ninth Air Force operation to which the Eighth contributed aircraft and crews. The latter was completely an Eighth Air Force show.

Ploesti was important for being the largest petroleum refinery complex in continental Europe. Having allied itself with Germany as a junior member of the Axis in November 1940, Romania had contributed troops to fight alongside the Germans in the Soviet Union and was providing the German war machine with around 60 percent of its refined petroleum. Ploesti had been bombed once before, in June 1942, by a strike force led by Colonel Harry "Hurry-Up" Halverson—who had crewed with Tooey Spaatz and Ira Eaker aboard the *Question Mark* back in 1929. As with Jimmy Doolittle's Tokyo raid, it was high on symbolism but low on actual damage done to the target.

Now, 14 months later, more-substantial results were expected from the second Ploesti strike as 177 Liberators took off from Benghazi, Libya, and crossed the Mediterranean as part of Operation Tidal Wave. It was here that the adjective "costly" came into play. The strike cost the USAAF 53 aircraft shot down and more than 300 crewmen killed. The damage to the petrochemical facilities at Ploesti was considerable, but reparable. August 1 became known as "Black Sunday," casting its shadow across the ongoing planning for the Regensburg-Schweinfurt mission.

The idea that Regensburg and Schweinfurt should be attacked simultaneously evolved directly from Hap Arnold's earlier criticism of Eaker for his lack of toughness, and Arnold's demands that Eaker and his commanders be more aggressive.

When Secretary of War Henry Stimson visited England in July, Eaker—who had not been briefed on Stimson's secret nuclear weapons discussions with Churchill—decided on a large-map briefing that would show him something dramatic relative to Operation Pointblank. As Eaker explained to Stimson, the rationale behind the simultaneous attacks was to use two attacking armadas to divide Luftwaffe air defenses, which would already be caught off guard by an Eighth Air Force attack in a part of the Reich that had heretofore been untouched by the bombers. The date picked was August 17, the first anniversary of the first mission into occupied Europe by Eighth Air Force heavy bombers.

It was decided that, as 4th Bomb Wing commander, LeMay would lead the Regensburg mission personally, flying in the right seat of the lead Flying Fortress, piloted by Captain Thomas Kenny of the 96th Bomb Group. Brigadier General Robert B. Williams would lead a larger force on the Schweinfurt mission. Frank Armstrong, commander of the 1st Bomb Wing, had been on Eaker's mind for this assignment. However, when he was injured in a fire in his quarters at the end of July, he was sent home and replaced as 1st Wing commander by the inexperienced Williams, who had been commanding the 16th Operational Training Wing at Biggs Field in Texas. Williams had known Hap Arnold at Rockwell Field in the 1920s and, like LeMay, had been assigned to the 2nd Bomb Wing at Langley Field in the early days of the B-17. Though he had seen little action, Williams wore the scar of having lost an eye during the Blitz of 1940, when he was serving as an Air Corps observer in London.

Because of the distance to Bavaria, it was decided that the bombers would not return to England after the mission but continue south across the Alps, landing at USAAF fields in North Africa. With this in mind, Eaker sent LeMay on an advance trip to North Africa to brief Tooey Spaatz and Air Marshal Arthur Tedder, the senior air commanders in the Mediterranean, who readily agreed to "cooperate in every possible way."

On the morning of August 17, as the crews prepared to climb into their bombers, a heavy overcast that had darkened the south of England descended in the form of pea-soup ground fog. The crews had been briefed that the takeoff roll would begin at 5:45 a.m., but Fred Anderson called from Pinetree to order a one-hour hold, which was soon expanded to 90 minutes.

LeMay paced the ground, worrying that every delay made it more likely that his crews would have to land in Algeria in the dark. Finally, he decided that ground crews could lead the bombers to the end of the runway using flashlights. Once there, having been drilled relentlessly by LeMay for instrument takeoffs, they would be on their way. LeMay called Anderson, who was with Eaker at VIII Bomber Command headquarters. When the two officers atop the Eighth Air Force chain of command okayed the plan, LeMay raced to the flight line, climbed into Kenny's B-17, and was off.

Once above the overcast, the 146 Flying Fortresses of the 4th Bomb Wing assembled into formation and prepared to head south and east to Regensburg. Assuming that the 1st Bomb Wing was also in the air, LeMay contacted Anderson for the final "go." The VIII Bomber Command boss explained that Williams and more than 200 Flying Fortresses were still on the ground, and asked LeMay to circle in the blue skies above and wait.

After burning fuel for a half hour, LeMay began leading his force across the English Channel. A short time later, Anderson discovered that the radio link between Pinetree and LeMay was down.

"I might have done the same thing myself," Eaker recalled, having assumed that LeMay shut off his radio to avoid being recalled. "And so would Anderson. It's such a job to get the bombers assembled, it's destructive of morale to cancel because then you've got to do it again the next day."

LeMay saved his own wrath for the 1st Wing, recalling in his memoirs that if they "had been concentrating on the same sort of bad-weather-instrument-takeoff procedure which we had been developing for a solid month, they might have been able to get off the ground. A few minutes late, perhaps, but still part of the originally planned show. And we couldn't horse around about this—return to our bases, sit on the ground, [and] take off once more."

LeMay and his men soon discovered that the 1st Wing's planes were not the only Eighth Air Force aircraft that were still grounded by the fog. The fighters that were supposed to escort them as far as the continent never got off the ground.

Williams was delayed for another three hours, and did not get the 1st Bomb Wing and its 230 bombers on their way to Schweinfurt until LeMay was practically to Regensburg.

Having taken off in fog, the 4th Bomb Wing arrived over Regensburg at 11:48 a.m. to find the skies sparkling clear, a textbook example of the ideal weather for precision bombardment. As it turned out, it was one of the most precise attacks to date. The lead bombardier, manning his Norden bombsight a few feet ahead of where LeMay sat, put his bombs directly on the target and the rest of the bomber stream followed.

That, for the 4th Bomb Wing, was the good news—the *only* good news. The Luftwaffe attacks, which were typically furious but brief, went on for hours as the Flying Fortresses lumbered across Germany. In his book *Decision Over Schweinfurt*, Tom Coffey observed that so many bombers were shot down so quickly that some of the crews thought their whole wing would be obliterated before they even reached Regensburg.

By the time the 1st Bomb Wing reached Schweinfurt at 2:59 p.m., the Luftwaffe interceptors had had the opportunity to land, refuel, and rearm. To complicate matters, Williams had previously briefed the crews to approach Schweinfurt from the east with the sun at their backs. When they arrived in the afternoon instead of the morning, he decided that having the sun at their backs was more important than flying the compass coordinates as planned, and he led the 1st Bomb Wing in from the opposite direction.

Despite this, the results were reasonably good. The two largest factory complexes, Kugelfischer and Vereinigte Kugellagerfabriken, took 80 direct hits, and German sources accessed after the war reported a 34 percent loss of production capacity, with output falling from 140 tons in July to 50 in September.

The punishment meted out to the Eighth Air Force by the Luftwaffe, however, was staggering. LeMay's force lost 24 aircraft, 15 of them before they reached the target, while Williams lost 36, 22 before reaching the target. The total amounted to 60 aircraft and nearly 600 men.

The first 4th Wing aircraft reached Algeria around 6:00 p.m., short of fuel after the circling delay of England that morning. Some landed in open patches of desert, but only two had to ditch in the Mediterranean—and the crews were picked up by Allied ships.

On the ground, maintenance facilities were sparse or nonexistent, and the crews had to do most of the hands-on work of patching up their Flying Fortresses for the trip home. This infuriated LeMay, who rolled up his own sleeves and went to work. Back when he was first assigned to command a B-17 group, he had made it a point to develop a complete understanding of all the aircraft's structural and mechanical systems. The 4th Bomb Wing had few crew chiefs more knowledgeable than their commander.

They managed to get about 80 of the 122 Flying Fortresses that survived Regensburg ready to fly back to England—by way of the Atlantic—on August 24. Of these, 57 were in good enough shape to carry out a raid on Bordeaux on the return trip.

When Ira Eaker, Fred Anderson, and their staffs first learned of the losses suffered over Regensburg and Schweinfurt, they were stunned. It is one thing to do the calculations and run the odds, but another thing to come to grips with the thought of 600 empty bunks after just one day.

Eaker worried that the losses would cause a reappraisal of the daylight bombing portion of the Combined Bomber Offensive. Had the Eighth Air Force lost 60 bombers in one mission a year earlier, it would have.

Coincidentally, during the third week of August, at the same moment as the Regensburg-Schweinfurt mission, Churchill and Roosevelt were meeting in Quebec with their Combined Chiefs of Staff for the Quadrant Conference. At this conclave, the attention of the leaders was directed first and foremost to the war against Germany, and the biggest milestone on the timeline was Operation Overlord, the invasion of northern France.

Maurice Matloff of the Center of Military History wrote that at Quadrant "all agreed that the Combined Bomber Offensive (Operation Pointblank) was to remain in the 'highest strategic priority' and was to be extended from all suitable bases—particularly from Italy and the Mediterranean—as a *prerequisite* for Overlord."

After August 17, Ira Eaker had many new concerns, but those that had furrowed his brow in the spring were gone. His worry about an adequate number of bombers was fading fast as new bomb groups were arriving almost weekly to flesh out the original wings and add new ones.

Having shaken up his command structure and undertaken a mission as daring as August 17, Eaker hoped to have demonstrated to Hap Arnold that he could be the "aggressive leader" that his boss wanted. It was not to be, however.

Two weeks later, they came face-to-face again as Arnold flew into England, fresh from the Quadrant Conference, for a six-day visit to the Eighth Air Force. According to Major General John Huston, who edited Arnold's wartime diaries for publication, Eaker later observed that his boss "was jolly and upbeat during the visit. . . . However, it did not take long for relations between these two men to return to their tense chill. Arnold's main problem with the Eighth was his inability or unwillingness to accept weather, limited aircraft and crews, lack of long-range fighter escort, or the need to rest as valid impediments. Hap expected the maximum effort for every mission on every day that weather permitted. Hap's correspondence with Eaker reflected his impression that Eaker and the Eighth were not doing their best under the circumstances."

Nevertheless, Arnold praised Eaker publicly on his return to Washington and recommended him for promotion to lieutenant general, and Eaker received his third star by the end of September 1943. As Huston points out, though, Arnold was soon "criticizing Eaker and attempting to cajole the Eighth's commander into greater efforts."

Conversely, Huston went on to say that in his own "postwar comments, Eaker was much more gracious than Arnold. He understood the pressures operating on Hap and hence took no offense at Arnold's comments, some of them fairly strong in view of their more than 20 years of close personal relationship. Evidence of the paradox in their relations was Eaker's editing and revising their coauthored volume *Winged Warfare* while Hap was in England. Eaker continued the task during any few moments he could spare from leading the Eighth and answering communications, often angry, from the Pentagon."

In England, Eaker also accompanied Arnold on most of his inspection tour. He visited Bury St. Edmunds, home of the 94th Bomb Group, on September 3 to meet some of the men who had flown on the Regensburg-Schweinfurt operation. In his autobiography, Arnold recalled that it was here that he first met LeMay as a commander, a meeting that LeMay did not recall in his own memoirs.

Meanwhile, it continued to be a sore point for LeMay that he was still a colonel, especially after Regensburg and two months after becoming a wing commander, which warranted a promotion to brigadier general.

As the number of wings increased, bombardment divisions (later known as air divisions) were being formed. On September 13, the 4th Bomb Wing, along with the new 14th and 45th Bomb Wings, were brought under the newly activated 3rd Bombardment Division, and LeMay, still a colonel, was moved up to command this organization.

On September 28, two weeks later, and three weeks after Arnold's visit, LeMay finally got his brigadier general's star.

CHAPTER 28

ON POINTBLANK'S FRONT LINE

On the morning of June 13, Hub Zemke was flying lead with the 56th Fighter Group's 61st Fighter Squadron in a fighter sweep over Belgium as the group's other two squadrons were stacked above to back them up.

The arrival and wide deployment of the P-47 Thunderbolt extended the reach of the VIII Fighter Command over portions of occupied Europe where few Allied fighter types had been able to operate routinely before. Spitfires and P-40s were effective barely as far as the coast of France. Curtis LeMay had famously quipped that the only fighters he saw over the targets inside Germany were the ones with black crosses. The P-47s could accompany Eighth Air Force bombers into France, Belgium, and as far as Aachen in Germany.

With this added measure of safety for the bombers, their crews had started referring to the fighters as their "Little Friends." Meanwhile, the fighter pilots had started to refer to their big P-47s as "Jugs" rather than Thunderbolts. Both nicknames became a ubiquitous part of Eighth Air Force lore.

At about 9:37 a.m. that morning, Zemke spotted as many as 20 suspected Luftwaffe fighters closing on the 61st from straight ahead and about 4,000 feet below the Americans.

After flying more than two dozen missions over the course of two months, the 56th had yet to down a single Luftwaffe fighter, and the men were eager to prove themselves in combat—especially when the rival 4th and 78th Fighter Groups were reaching into double digits of combat victories.

Leading an eight-ship section, Zemke dove on the Germans, who apparently had not spotted the Jugs. Hesitating until he had a positive identification of the other aircraft, he opened fire inside 200 yards and watched the Fw 190's right wing come off. He fired again at a second plane, hitting its wingtip before its pilot rolled out of the way.

In his after-action report, Zemke wrote that this put him behind another Fw 190, "which sat in the gunsight as one would expect for the ideal shot. Again, when the trigger was pulled this aircraft exploded with a long sheet of flame and smoke."

Lieutenant Robert Johnson also scored a kill that day, the first of his eventual 27, and the young 56th Fighter Group had its first three victories.

The Luftwaffe took its revenge on the last day of the month during a bomber escort mission over France, as the 56th lost four of its pilots in combat. Bob Johnson was nearly a fifth casualty, but he managed to ditch in the North Sea and was rescued.

That night, Zemke and his men held a long and somber debriefing of the day's actions. Out of this came a reappraisal of escort tactics that would revolutionize 56th Fighter Group operations.

"There were some pretty shaken pilots around the base that night," Zemke later confided in his memoirs. "I was fast coming to the conclusion that the close escort we were ordered to perform by high command was not the best way to protect the bombers. What we needed to do was to range ahead of the Big Friends and break up the enemy concentrations before they got into a position to launch attacks."

The summer of 1943 was the summer of Operation Pointblank, and the Eighth Air Force bombers were running missions deeper inside

Germany—and the deeper they went, the more vigorously they were opposed by the Luftwaffe and the more desirable it was to have escort
fighters available to counter the German interceptors. Though the P-47
had been a significant improvement over earlier fighters, its operational
range was limited.

After July, the Jugs started using the cardboard laminate "bathtub"
tanks for ferrying the aircraft, but these compromised the aircraft's aerodynamic characteristics and slowed them down. On August 17, during
the infamous Regensburg and Schweinfurt missions, the P-47s could not
go "all the way," but, as Zemke recalled, "I wanted [the 56th] to penetrate
as deeply as [we] could safely go."

The 56th "skinned" their tanks over Antwerp and engaged a *Staffel*
of Bf 110 twin-engine fighters, which was later joined by Fw 190s of
the Luftwaffe's Jagdgeschwader 26. In the ensuing fracas, the 56th lost
three of its own, but managed to down 17 German fighters, plus one
"probable."

Two days later, the VIII Bomber Command was too exhausted to run
another major attack against the German heartland, but the Luftwaffe
did not know this. When a modest mission against occupied France went
out, the Germans hit them as soon as they crossed the coastline. The
presence of the Jugs, loitering at 27,000 feet, high above the bombers,
made it a fair fight. The Luftwaffe lost nine, including a Bf 109 that fell to
the guns of Lieutenant Gerry Johnson. This being his fifth victory, the
milestone that defined "ace" status, he was now the first ace in the 56th
Fighter Group.

In the weeks following Regensburg and Schweinfurt, as the VIII
Bomber Command was licking its wounds and Ira Eaker was being tor-
mented by Hap Arnold for more maximum efforts, things were gradually looking up for the men of the 56th. They had moved to new quarters
at Halesworth and were coming to appreciate the paved runways at their
new home after the grass fields at Horsham St. Faith.

The unwieldy bathtub fuel tanks were disappearing from the flight
lines, gradually replaced by more aerodynamic 80-gallon metal "tear-

drop" tanks. At the same time, the ground crews had developed a system to use the aircraft's vacuum pump to pressurize the tanks so that they could be used at higher altitudes.

At Ajax, the VIII Fighter Command headquarters at Bushey Hall, Monk Hunter finally packed his bags on August 29, replaced by Brigadier General William Kepner, a prewar wingman of Ira Eaker's at the 34th Pursuit Squadron. In his impatient assessment of the Eighth Air Force in April, Hap Arnold had specifically told Eaker to replace Hunter, and now he was gone.

Hub Zemke agreed with Arnold, recalling, "I had never considered General Hunter to have what was needed to head VIII Fighter Command," although Hunter had authorized a Distinguished Flying Cross for Zemke in late July. Zemke considered Kepner, whom he had first met at Langley Field before the war, to be a competent replacement, though he stopped short of high praise. As he wrote in his memoirs, he saw Kepner as "an able commander. Mustached, angular featured, and small in stature, he had a reputation for verbosity, but behind his wordy dictates there was a razor-sharp mind."

At the same time, Kepner also had an eye on Zemke, who was rapidly gaining a reputation as one of the better fighter group commanders in the Eighth Air Force. So too was Ira Eaker keeping tabs on Zemke and the 56th Fighter Group. On September 17, Eaker came to Halesworth for a short visit and to congratulate the group on its "recent showing." In his memoirs, Zemke recalled that Eaker was "affable and interested," but adds that the Eighth Air Force chief was critical of the "unkempt and varied clothing our people were wearing, which made it difficult for him to distinguish between officers and [enlisted] men."

Zemke "took the hint" and ordered his men to wear clean uniforms to group meetings and in the officers club. As for Eaker, future events would reveal that he was more favorably disposed toward Zemke than he seemed.

Across the world, at Dyersburg Field in Tennessee, Robert Rosenthal and his crew were assigned the B-17 with the tail number 42-30758 and promptly named it for their pilot. As Bob Morgan and his crew had devoted a great deal of time to the decision to name their B-17 *Memphis Belle*, most crews sat down on the eve of their deployment to argue about and agree upon a name for the bomber they were taking overseas. Now it was the turn of the men who would soon depart Tennessee in Flying Fortress number 42-30758.

By this time, Robert Rosenthal had become "Rosie" Rosenthal. He later observed that a great many men whose surname began with those same four letters wound up with that nickname. Meanwhile, everyone was aware of the popular 1942 song "Rosie the Riveter," which had been recorded by numerous artists. The term would soon become a generic term for the thousands of women working in wartime American factories, but at the time it was simply the title of a song that people knew. Against the backdrop of all this, the B-17—as well as its crew—became known as *Rosie's Riveters*. She would, however, be just one of several B-17s that Rosenthal would pilot during his time with the Eighth, and the Riveters were destined not to fly the plane on several of their most significant missions.

Rosie and his crew finally departed from Dyersburg Field on September 1, 1943, and headed for England. Less than two weeks had passed since Regensburg, Schweinfurt, and the realization of the difficulties that lay ahead for crews executing the Pointblank Directive.

Following the great stream of eastbound men and aircraft through Presque Isle, Maine, and Prestwick, Scotland, Morgan's men reached England on September 6. Unlike Curtis LeMay and Bob Morgan a year earlier, Rosenthal and his men arrived not as part of a squadron or group but as an individual crew. They awaited assignment to a squadron that had lost one of its crews over one of those German cities visited by the Eighth Air Force on August 17.

After nine days in the replacement pool, they were assigned to the 418th Bomb Squadron of the 100th Bomb Group, based at Thorpe Abbotts in Norfolk, about 100 miles east of London. The group was part of Curtis LeMay's 3rd Bomb Division.

Neil Bosworth "Chick" Harding had taken command of the 100th Bomb Group in July and had led it to Regensburg in August. Before the war, Harding, along with LeMay and Robert Olds, had been an important figure in Air Corps bomber aviation. Indeed, the three of them had been part of the 1938 goodwill flight that took a group of B-17s down to Argentina, and they had remained friends.

A 1927 graduate of the US Military Academy who had been a star player on the West Point football team, Harding was also a rising star in the US Army. He had outranked LeMay with seniority until LeMay was promoted to brigadier general. Harding was well liked by his men, but he was also known for being lax on discipline, something that LeMay ignored—and later wished he hadn't.

As Rosenthal related in an interview now preserved in the collection of the 100th Bomb Group Foundation, when he arrived, the 100th was "not a well-disciplined group . . . [F]ormation flying was loose."

He remembered Harding as "the nicest person you'd ever meet. He couldn't do enough for you . . . just a wonderful person. But he didn't enforce any rules and people who served under him took advantage of him and didn't perform properly."

Rosenthal and the Riveters had joined the 100th on the eve of what Ira Eaker and Fred Anderson had planned as a week of 300-plane maximum efforts, the most intense operations since August 17. They flew their first mission with a 118-plane strike force sent against Bremen on October 8. The crew came through, but *Rosie's Riveters* was so badly shot up that she was out of commission for many months and her crew went on to a series of other aircraft.

The following day, Rosenthal and his men were back in the air as part of an exhausting nine-hour mission to Marienburg in East Prussia. On this mission, they flew *Royal Flush*, a bomber that had just come back from being patched up after an earlier mission.

With the weather over Germany still favoring precision attacks, the

Riveters suited up to fly the third of three days in a row on October 10, again aboard *Royal Flush*. Rosenthal recalled that, having been "banged up" in the earlier missions that week, the 100th could contribute only 13 Flying Fortresses to a strike force of 274 that the Eighth sent to targets across Germany, most of them in the vicinity of Münster.

It would be a bad day.

As the group approached the target, they were intercepted by a huge cloud of Luftwaffe fighters attacking in waves, raking the B-17s with their guns and slamming them with rockets. One by one, Rosenthal watched the planes of the 100th being blown out of the sky around him. *Royal Flush* reached the target alone, and the Luftwaffe hammered them all through their bomb run.

Once the bombs were gone, Rosenthal was able to begin evasive action to give the interceptors a run for their money.

"I did some crazy maneuvers that I had picked up in the Training Command," he recalled. "I was all over the sky, so we were not a good target for the Germans. After maybe five or ten minutes, they abandoned us and went after easier targets. My crew complained that I didn't give them a 'stable platform' so they could shoot down the German planes, but I think they would have shot *us* down. They outnumbered us terribly. There was a rocket hole through our wing. Two engines were out. Our two waist gunners [Loren Darling and John Schaefer] were seriously wounded."

In this condition, the *Royal Flush* staggered back to England, where poor weather added insult to injury by delaying their landing at Thorpe Abbotts.

"We were the only ones back at the base after that mission," Rosenthal continued. "The place was eerily quiet. We went to the officers club and there was nobody there."

At the post-mission debriefing the next day, LeMay asked the pilots to report their experiences by group. When he called for the 100th, the only man who stood up was Rosie Rosenthal. He was the only pilot left from the group who had flown the mission.

This is a moment that has been mentioned in countless accounts of the Eighth Air Force in World War II—and it was the moment at which the group earned its nickname "Bloody Hundredth."

When Rosie had finished his verbal report, LeMay responded with a terse, "Good work."

To Rosenthal, the term "good work" had always meant merely "mediocre work," but after the debriefing, another group commander told him that he had never heard such "lavish praise" from LeMay.

Of LeMay, Rosenthal was also lavish in his praise, observing many years later that "in my mind, he was the greatest air commander in the history of aviation, a very tough man, brilliant, determined. . . . He wanted perfection. He demanded it and he got it."

In the annals of the 3rd Division, that day over Münster is recalled, as Rosenthal put it, as "the most intense air battle of the war."

If not, it was close.

In his own after-action teletype message, LeMay called it "a catastrophe." He always blamed Chick Harding and his failure to demand more discipline of his crews. As LeMay told Tom Coffey in 1984, "He wasn't doing very well. I knew I had to fire him but I just couldn't. I thought he'd snap out of it. Anyway, I should've fired him but I didn't. Then fate stepped in. He had a gall bladder problem or something. Had to go home for an operation [albeit not for several months]. That taught me a lesson. It took time to get the 100th back in shape."

CHAPTER 29

THE TRIALS OF SIR IRA

E ffective September 7, 1943, as the senior USAAF officer in England, Ira Eaker found himself with the command responsibility of *two* numbered air forces. In addition to the Eighth Air Force, Hap Arnold and Chief of Staff General George Marshall placed the Ninth Air Force, which was being relocated to England, under Eaker's chain of command.

A year earlier, the Ninth had been a mixed bag of units assembled in the eastern Mediterranean. Now, having grown in size, it was being reinvented as the tactical complement to the strategic Eighth Air Force. The Ninth continued under the direct command of General Lewis Brereton, but he would now answer to Eaker.

It seemed only natural that Ira Eaker should be given this job. For anyone in England, British or American, in the media or across the sprawling archipelago of American air bases, he was *the* face of American airpower. He had been the first senior airman to arrive during the dark, early days of 1942, and everyone adhered to the not entirely unfounded perception that he had built the Eighth Air Force from scratch with his own bare hands.

In the fall of 1943, King George VI invited America's senior airman in Britain to Buckingham Palace for a long chat, which included bedecking him with official laurels. As James Parton pointed out, foreigners are typically honored with the Order of the British Empire, but Eaker was made a *Knight Commander* of the British Empire, two steps higher in the pecking order of the hierarchy of British nobility. Parton, who was there, recalled that some on the Eighth Air Force staff referred to Eaker as "Sir Ira," which he discouraged.

In the media at home, he had become the very symbol of growing American airpower. On August 30, 1943, "Eaker of the Eighth" graced the cover of *Time* magazine. On November 29, a life-size portrait on the cover of *Life*, then the apogee of popular culture, stared from newsstands. The caption read, "Lieut. General Ira Eaker Eighth Air Force," as though the two were one and the same.

So larger-than-life had Eaker become that he and his stalwart second, Frank Armstrong, were inspiring the creators of a future dramatic franchise that would include a bestselling novel, an Oscar-nominated motion picture, and a Golden Globe–nominated television series. Even as William Wyler was turning the *Memphis Belle* into a star, Lieutenant Colonel Beirne Lay, Jr., and Captain Sy Bartlett were laying the groundwork for placing a fictionalized Ira Eaker into the pantheon of World War II legend.

Lay, who joined the Air Corps in 1932, earned his wings a year later, and went on reserve duty in 1936, had been writing for magazines such as *Esquire, Harper's,* and the *Saturday Evening Post.* His big break came when Paramount Pictures turned his 1937 autobiography, *I Wanted Wings,* into a 1941 motion picture. Back on active duty, Lay had been one of the original six Eighth Air Force staffers to come over with Eaker in 1942 and was handpicked by him to head the Eighth Air Force film unit. As such, he was William Wyler's senior officer. He also flew in combat, including the Regensburg mission, with the 100th Bomb Group.

Bartlett, meanwhile, started his career in 1933 as a screenwriter at RKO Pictures and was a well-known part of the Hollywood social scene before joining the USAAF. Assigned as an intelligence officer with the

Eighth, he got to know Eaker and Armstrong very well, and soon he and Lay agreed to collaborate on the project that became *Twelve O'Clock High*, the 1948 bestseller and the 1949 20th Century Fox film of the same name.

In the movie, Major General Patrick Pritchard, a barely concealed portrait of Eaker, was played by Millard Mitchell, while Armstrong was the inspiration for Brigadier General Frank Savage, portrayed by Gregory Peck.

Even as Eaker was finding himself institutionalized as an icon, his hours were consumed with planning the Eighth Air Force's long-overdue return to Germany's ball-bearing capital. Schweinfurt, with its glittering river of ball bearings flowing into the mobility of the German war machine, remained the signature nemesis of the Eighth.

From the intercepts and decryptions of the Ultra-coded radio traffic, Eaker and Fred Anderson knew that the damage done in August could be compounded, but nearly two months passed before the Eighth returned. This passage of time illustrated that, despite the steadily increasing influx of new aircraft and crews, the Eighth Air Force was still a fragile organization.

No one knew this better than Ira Eaker, who labored under a furrowed brow and the burden of balancing the Eighth's potential with its capabilities. He knew what he could do with his force, but he yearned to do more, and from Washington came the insistence of Hap Arnold and his staff that the Eighth *should* do more. Indeed, in a September 28 memo, Larry Kuter of the Air Staff had spoken in terms of "building a fire under General Eaker."

Yet the fire under him had been built by Eaker himself. No one was more impatient than he.

The second Battle of Schweinfurt came on October 14, capping the week of 300-plane maximum-effort missions that included Rosie Rosenthal's sobering baptism of fire. Eaker and Anderson had waited to launch against Schweinfurt until clear weather over the target could be assured. In August's Regensburg-Schweinfurt mission, the plan had been for multiple waves striking in coordinated, parallel attacks, but weather had put the bombers over the targets five hours apart. *This time*, there was a great deal of attention to precise timing, although once again, it was easier said than done. On the appointed morning, 149 Flying Fortresses of the 1st Bombardment Division and 142 of the 3rd launched from their fields in England, formed up, and headed southeast. However, 60 Liberators from the 2nd Division that were supposed to form a third wave were dispersed by the overcast over England, failed to get into formation, and either aborted or were rerouted to alternate targets.

The Flying Fortresses headed into Germany as planned, and their coordination was textbook perfect. The 2nd entered its bomb run at nine minutes to 3:00 p.m., only six minutes after the 1st Division had exited the target area. The results were good, although everyone—at the time and in hindsight—agreed that an earlier follow-up attack would have been far more decisive.

On both sides, they were aware that if the Eighth Air Force could have mounted a second mission close on the heels of its August Schweinfurt mission, it would have completed the damage done before repairs could be made and before this highly concentrated industry could be disbursed to other locations within Germany. The Germans expected an immediate follow-up mission, and Albert Speer, the Reich's armaments minister, wrote in his memoirs that such an attack could have been catastrophic for his war machine.

Nevertheless, the postwar US Strategic Bombing Survey observed "a high concentration of bombs in all the target areas . . . on and about all three of the big bearing plants. . . . Strategically it was the most important of the sixteen raids made during the war on the Schweinfurt plants. It caused the most damage and the greatest interference with production."

Speer later confirmed that Germany had "lost 67 percent of our ball bearing production."

However, for the men of the Eighth Air Force the damage done to their own organization loomed far larger than any consolation they could take in the ruin they had wrought.

On that day, thereafter known as "Black Thursday" in every account of the Eighth Air Force, the crews encountered Luftwaffe resistance on an unprecedented scale. As the Eighth attacked in waves, so did the Luftwaffe. The Luftwaffe hit the Eighth coming and going. The Germans shot down 28 Flying Fortresses on their way into Schweinfurt and 32 on the way out. Many others made it home but were written off as total losses. The 60 bombers shot down matched the losses from both Schweinfurt and Regensburg in August, and did not include those that were damaged beyond repair. When the sun set on Black Thursday, there were once again 600 empty bunks at Eighth Air Force bases across England.

Eaker and Anderson were up all night at Pinetree, waiting for news of and from the returning crews. It was not a happy time. It was one of the hardest nights of Eaker's career.

"Yesterday the Hun sprang his trap," Eaker wrote sadly in a wire that he sent to Arnold on the morning after his sleepless night. "The whole operation was perfectly timed and coordinated and skillfully executed. More than 300 enemy fighters participated in attack; more than 700 attacks made on our formations during the principal battle. One of our combat wings was practically wiped out. . . . This does not represent disaster; it does indicate that the air battle has reached its climax."

He asked Arnold to "rush" a minimum of 250 replacement aircraft and crews each month, telling him that the Eighth "must grow bigger, not smaller." He asked his boss for more fighters—especially long-range P-51 Mustangs—and for 8,000 external fuel tanks for his fighters.

Arnold replied to Eaker's message by complimenting the crews and by quickly taking steps to supply Mustangs to the Eighth, going so far as to redirect shipments of them that had been earmarked for George Kenney's Fifth Air Force in the Pacific, as well as for Tooey Spaatz in the western Mediterranean. The P-51s, unlike the P-47s that Eaker had on

In the spring of 1942, Major General Tooey Spaatz and Brigadier General Ira Eaker traveled to England to set up the Eighth Air Force for operations against the Third Reich. When Spaatz left for the Mediterranean, Eaker guided the Eighth through its difficult early years. ✪ *Library of Congress*

In January 1929, the C-2A known as *Question Mark* made history by using aerial refueling to stay aloft for 150 hours. The crew included (*left to right*): Lieutenant Harry Halverson, Captain Ira Eaker, Sergeant Roy Hooe, Major Tooey Spaatz, and Lieutenant Pete Quesada. ✪ *US Air Force*

Robert Knight Morgan grew up in Asheville, North Carolina, and was part of a generation of twentysomethings who joined the USAAF for adventure and to strike back at the Axis. ✪ *USAAF*

Bob Morgan and the crew of the B-17 known as *Memphis Belle* were the first in the Eighth Air Force to complete twenty-five missions as a crew. Seen here in England after their last combat mission are (*left to right*): Sergeant Harold Loch, top turret gunner; Sergeant Cecil Scott, ball turret gunner; Sergeant Robert Hanson, radio operator; Captain Jim Verinis, copilot; Captain Bob Morgan, pilot; Captain Chuck Leighton, navigator; Sergeant Johnny Quinlan, tail gunner; Sergeant Casimer "Tony" Nastal, waist gunner; Captain Vince Evans, bombardier; and Sergeant Clarence "Bill" Winchell, waist gunner. ✪ *USAAF*

Sergeant Snuffy Smith received his Medal of Honor from Secretary of War Henry Stimson personally in a ceremony at the Eighth Air Force base at Thurleigh on July 15, 1943. When the ceremony began, Smith was in the mess hall on KP duty, and was rushed to the podium. ⭐ *USAAF*

Jimmy Doolittle in the pilot's seat of a B-25 medium bomber. He flew a B-25 in his famous Tokyo raid in 1942, and both flew and commanded many B-25s in 1942 and 1943 before taking command of the Eighth Air Force in 1944. ✪ *USAAF*

Robert "Rosie" Rosenthal (*right*) and David "Handlebar Hank" Lyster (*left*) congratulate Gail "Bucky" Cleven (*center*) on his escape from German captivity. All three men served with the 350th Bomb Squadron of the 100th Bomb Group. ✪ *USAAF*

Colonel Hub Zemke shortly after his release from the German prison camp
Stalag Luft I in May 1945. ✪ *USAAF*

Curtis Emerson LeMay (*right*) worked his way up the Eighth Air Force chain of command from the 305th Bomb Group to the 3rd Bomb Division. Haywood Hansell (*left*) was a veteran of the USAAF Air Staff who commanded the 1st Bomb Wing of the Eighth. ✪ *USAAF*

hand, could escort the bombers deep into the Reich as far as Schweinfurt, but only a handful had arrived in Britain so far.

"Your commendations have been placed in the hands of the air combat crew members and have done untold good," Eaker told his boss in his October 15 reply. "It is amazing what a pat on the back will do for a hard-fighting, battle-weary fellow."

Despite Arnold's congratulations in the aftermath of October 14, he remained as eager as ever to see Eaker continue to mount maximum-effort missions, and he was displeased when Eaker was unable to do so, even though mainly for reasons outside his control.

In a 1984 conversation with James Parton, Haywood Hansell, who was back on Arnold's staff by October 1943, explained that Arnold "was terribly impatient. He just did not understand [that] air combat [Eighth Air Force] crews, led by Ira, were doing a simply astonishing job. I marveled at their willingness to keep on fighting. I think Ira probably did too. [The second Schweinfurt mission] took tremendous courage and willpower and an unswerving adherence to the objective."

Throughout the wartime narrative of the relationship of Eaker and Spaatz to their boss, there would continue to be countless examples of Arnold's impatient insensitivity. However, each of these must be qualified with the understanding that sensitivity was not in Arnold's job description. His responsibility was to win a difficult global conflict against a resilient foe, and to do so as quickly as possible.

Indeed, in his June 15, 1943, memo to Eaker, he had explained that he was scolding Eaker expressly to get him "to toughen up." Like drill sergeants, commanding generals must be dynamic in their manner. Eaker understood this more than he liked it. His being removed from the action by the breadth of oceans exacerbated Arnold's frustration more than it compromised his understanding of the conditions on the ground.

By late October, bad weather closed in on northern Europe, limiting the ability of the Eighth to conduct precision bombing operations. With few exceptions, this prevailed through the end of the year, curtailing the types of missions that both Arnold and Eaker would have liked to see. From his Washington perspective Hansell recalled Arnold's daily meetings with George Marshall. The chief of staff would ask, "What did the Eighth Air Force do yesterday?" Arnold would say, "Nothing."

It added insult to injury for Eaker to reflect that Arnold was now obsessed with the Eighth flying the strategic missions that Eaker had practically been begging to fly a year earlier when he was watching his resources being shunted off to Africa or sidetracked on the fruitless campaign against the U-boat pens.

It added further insult that Arnold and Marshall now went ahead with plans to activate *another* numbered air force to share the strategic mission of Operation Pointblank, which had heretofore been within the sphere of the Eighth Air Force.

The idea of the new Fifteenth Air Force was to concentrate USAAF heavy bombers then scattered throughout the Mediterranean Theater into a single new command with a strategic mission. According to James Parton, Eaker registered serious objections, seeing the Fifteenth as he had seen the Twelfth a year earlier, as an organization that would drain resources away from the Eighth Air Force and its mission.

For most of its time in combat, the Fifteenth would be commanded by Major General Nathan Twining, late of the Thirteenth Air Force in the South Pacific—but as its first commander, Hap Arnold picked Jimmy Doolittle.

☆

CHAPTER 30

SHAKE-UP

O n July 19, 1943, the same man who had led the first American air raid on Tokyo led the first large-scale USAAF attack against Rome. Jimmy Doolittle, who humiliated one Axis capital in April 1942, brought the war home to a second Axis capital 15 months later.

Only five months had passed since Doolittle assumed command of NASAF, the strategic component of Tooey Spaatz's Northwest African Air Forces, but both organizations had grown and matured into effective fighting units. With the invasion of Sicily having taken place on July 10, and the mainland Italy landings in the cards for September, Doolittle was focusing the attention of his bombers on the transportation network, both rail and sea, by which the German and Italian armies could move troops and materiel within the country.

All eyes now turned to Rome as the crossroads of the Italian rail network. In his memoirs, Doolittle notes that "the most important and potentially vulnerable" rail yards in Italy were near the central part of Rome, but hastens to add that so too was neutral Vatican City, the heart of global Catholicism and vast collections of art treasures that were a vital component of Western civilization.

"If they were destroyed, the Allies would probably go down in history as ruthless, barbaric hordes worse than those of Genghis Khan," Doolittle lamented. "While we agonized, the Germans were using the marshaling yards to distribute hundreds of troops into Italy to fight our forces in the coming Allied invasion. . . . If we went after these targets, it would be a challenge for precision bombing. We decided to try."

For the mission, Doolittle put together around 500 aircraft, the largest strike package ever assembled in the Mediterranean. Always one to fly critical missions personally, he was in the right seat of the Flying Fortress piloted by Colonel Leroy Rainey, commander of the 97th Bomb Group. As Doolittle recalled, "We flew in the last plane—'Tail End Charlie.' It was the most vulnerable position in any formation, but I wanted to see the results."

The intended results at the rail yards and airfields met expectations, though unintended damage done to Basilica Papale di San Lorenzo Fuori le Mura led to a round of criticism in the Allied media. Six days after Doolittle's armada came over the centerpiece of his "new Roman Empire," however, Italy's onetime expansionist dictator, Benito Mussolini, was removed from office by Italy's King Victor Emmanuel and replaced by Marshal Pietro Badoglio.

The Battle of Sicily finally ended on August 17, the same day that the Eighth Air Force was flying the dual missions against Regensburg and Schweinfurt, and Roosevelt and Churchill were at the Quadrant Conference summit in Quebec.

For Tooey Spaatz, the six months between the Casablanca Conference and the one in Quebec were consumed with the big picture of supporting the progress of the Allied armies from North Africa to Sicily to Italy, and with building up his NAAF to meet these and future operations.

He was also looking ahead toward the creation of the Fifteenth Air Force, but the invasion of Italy was a prerequisite for this. The success of the Fifteenth hinged on having bases in Italy that would be several hundred miles closer to the Reich than the NAAF facilities in North Africa. The intended location, around Bari and Foggia in the heel of the Italian boot where Italian bases already existed, were closer to Regensburg than were those of the Eighth Air Force, and were within range of the Messerschmitt factories at Augsburg in Bavaria and at Wiener Neustadt, near Vienna. The new bases also meant that future operations against Ploesti, once at the limit of the range of American bombers, could become routine.

The invasion of Italy began on September 3 with British landings on the heel and toe of Italy, and continued on September 9 with major American landings near Salerno on the west coast south of Naples.

Italy's reaction was swift.

King Victor Emmanuel and Marshal Badoglio surrendered immediately.

Germany's reaction was equally swift.

The German army, already constituting the majority of military power in Italy, quickly declared its former Axis partner to be an occupied country, and continued with the previously planned opposition to the Allied landings.

Neither the next phase of the Allied grand strategy, nor the capture of the planned Fifteenth Air Force bases, was easily achieved. The British landings, mainly against undefended Italian positions, went well, but a German counterattack almost pushed the Americans back into the sea at Salerno. Thanks in no small part to the NAAF, the Allies held on, though it took a month of bitter fighting to secure the beachhead and advance to the initial operational objectives.

Through the coming winter and the one following, the story of the ground war in Italy would be one of the Germans using rugged, easily defensible terrain—and using it well—to mount a tenacious defensive campaign that slowed Allied advances to a barely perceptible crawl.

With Bari and Foggia in Allied hands, the Fifteenth Air Force was activated on November 1, though it took until December for the facilities on the ground to be made fully operational. Nevertheless, Doolittle hit the ground running, sending a mission to attack the port city of La Spezia on November 1 and launching an ambitious, 1,600-mile round-trip heavy bomber mission to Wiener Neustadt the following day. The results were good in that the Messerschmitt plant was subsequently off-line for two months.

By Doolittle's reckoning, the Fifteenth opened for business with 11 combat groups and the goal of increasing its strength to 21 groups within four months, although, in order to do this, groups previously earmarked for Ira Eaker's Eighth Air Force had to be rerouted to Doolittle.

"This diversion made Ira Eaker unhappy, but I had no say in the matter," Doolittle observed. "It made good sense to me because, theoretically, we would have better weather and thus could launch more aircraft than Ira could from England, especially in the winter. It was the second time my air force had taken resources away from him. Ira was very annoyed and I couldn't blame him."

It was during this same period that the top Allied leadership met to plan the strategic direction of their efforts for the coming year. Roosevelt and Churchill, along with their Combined Chiefs of Staff, got together again in Cairo on November 23 for the Sextant Conference, their fourth conclave of 1943. They then adjourned to Tehran on November 28 for their first "Big Three" rendezvous with the Soviet Union's Josef Stalin before returning to Cairo for a final week of Sextant, which continued through December 8.

At Casablanca, the Combined Chiefs and their chiefs had agreed in principle to a Combined Bomber Offensive; at Trident they had made it a top priority through the Pointblank Directive; and at Sextant they complained that not enough had been done.

Under the cloudless skies of Cairo, the Sextant conferees looked not at the overcast lying across Europe but at the numbers. Their review of the situation concluded that from February through October 1943, RAF Bomber Command had flown three times as many night sorties as the

Eighth Air Force had by daylight. On December 3, the RAF's Air Chief Marshal Peter Portal told the Combined Chiefs of Staff that Operation Pointblank—the designated prerequisite to the all-important Operation Overlord—was "a full three months behind schedule." This phrase would haunt the Allied leaders and planners all winter.

Out of Sextant, and the preliminary sessions that led to the summit, there also came a major shake-up of the Allied command structure that would be implemented through December and into January 1944. At the apex of the new structure, Dwight Eisenhower was ordered to depart the Mediterranean to occupy the head chair at the new Supreme Headquarters, Allied Expeditionary Forces (SHAEF) in Europe, and therefore of Operation Overlord. As such, Eisenhower was now the supreme Allied commander in Europe and of the invasion of northern France that was to be the central feature of Allied strategic action in Europe during 1944.

In the Mediterranean, Britain's Commander-in-Chief, Middle East, Field Marshal Henry Maitland Wilson, succeeded Eisenhower with the title of Supreme Allied Commander, Mediterranean. Commanding the Allied ground forces in the Mediterranean under the umbrella of the new 15th Army Group was Field Marshal Harold Alexander. Meanwhile, Lieutenant General Jake Devers, who had succeeded Frank Andrews as commander of the ETOUSA, would be relocated to command the Mediterranean Theater of Operations, US Army (MTOUSA).

For air operations, the organizations with the obsolete "Northwest African" designations were to be superseded by a new hierarchy bearing "Mediterranean" prefixes. At the top of the chain of command, NAAF became the Mediterranean Allied Air Forces (MAAF). Within this structure, NASAF became the Mediterranean Allied Strategic Air Force (MASAF), and NATAF the Mediterranean Allied Tactical Air Force (MATAF). The Twelfth Air Force fell under the jurisdiction of MATAF, and the Fifteenth under MASAF.

With this, there was also a reshuffling of personalities in the command structure. The RAF's top man in the Mediterranean. Air Chief Marshal Sir Arthur Tedder, went back to England as Eisenhower's deputy, while USAAF Major General John Cannon took command of both MATAF and the Twelfth Air Force, and RAF Air Marshal Sir Arthur Coningham returned to England to be part of the planning team for Overlord.

Tooey Spaatz was recalled to England *and* to the strategic mission against the Reich, a change for which he had longed for more than a year. As he had been discussing with Hap Arnold for some time, he was named to command the United States Strategic Air Forces in Europe (USSTAF), a newly created parent organization for both the Eighth Air Force and the Fifteenth Air Force, which would coordinate and direct all American strategic air operations.

Before leaving Cairo, Arnold discussed the Spaatz appointment with Eisenhower and the latter's chief of staff, Walter Bedell Smith. As Arnold noted in his diary for December 8, "Both agreed that Spaatz was the man for the job, wouldn't take anyone else, not even Tedder."

Ever since he had left England to command Operation Torch, Eisenhower had wanted Spaatz nearby, and now that he was returning to England, he wanted Spaatz back there with him. For Spaatz, it was the role of a lifetime.

For two others who resided at the top of the chain of command there came a surprising role reversal: Hap Arnold decided that Ira Eaker and Jimmy Doolittle should *trade places*!

Doolittle would go to England to replace Eaker as commander of the Eighth Air Force, while Eaker would be ordered to relocate to the Mediterranean to assume command of MAAF. Nathan Twining would step in to command the Fifteenth.

Eaker was the last to know about the big switch. He knew about Spaatz's appointment to head the new USSTAF, and had actually suggested such an arrangement to Arnold on at least one occasion, but he was unaware that Arnold was about to ask him and Doolittle to exchange places. The others learned of Arnold's plan more than a week before

Eaker did. On December 9, Arnold stopped off at the Fifteenth Air Force headquarters in Bari on his way home from Sextant, where he met with Spaatz, Doolittle, and Cannon. In his diary, Spaatz wrote that they "discussed personnel to be utilized in new set-up. Presented to [Arnold] my ideas of moving present staff to UK with me when assume overall command of Fifteenth and Eighth." He also added that he agreed with the Eaker-Doolittle swap.

For Doolittle, as for Spaatz, the redeployment was a golden opportunity.

For Eaker, who had crafted the Eighth with his bare hands, and who had become synonymous with the Eighth and American airpower in Britain, the change would be devastating—when he finally learned about it, ten days after the Bari meeting.

Arnold communicated with Eaker several times without mentioning the situation. Indeed, he had looked in on Ruth Eaker upon his return to Washington on December 16, had discovered that she was under the weather, and had promptly informed her husband.

"Ruth ill with pneumonia," Arnold wired his old friend. "Will keep you informed. Condition not critical."

"Ruth very much improved," Arnold wrote the following day. "Temperature gone."

On December 14, Eaker met with Portal, who was also apparently in the dark about the Eaker-Doolittle swap. Portal had just returned from Sextant to discuss the return of Spaatz to England. Though Portal had referenced Eaker when he used the phrase "three months behind schedule" at Sextant, Portal now told Eaker only of *Arnold's* expressed displeasure with Eaker's progress.

The following day, Portal wrote to Arnold: "I found Eaker thoroughly alive to the need for earliest possible attack on Pointblank targets and to importance of using maximum force available. I am confident you will see great achievements as soon as weather gives him a chance."

Finally, on the morning of December 19, ten days after Arnold met with Spaatz and Doolittle, Eaker learned of Arnold's decision in an eyes-only cable. James Parton, who was with Eaker at the time, writes that when Eaker received the news, "it was an absolute bolt from the blue."

"It has been decided that an American will take over Command of the Allied Air Force in the Mediterranean position now held by Tedder," Arnold wrote in his memo. "As a result of your long period of successful operations and the exceptional results of your endeavors as Commander of the Air Force in England you have been recommended for this position."

Doolittle noted later that "Ira was very upset when he found out about the decisions and felt that he had been fired."

"Believe war interest best served by my retention command Eighth Air Force," Eaker wired back late on December 19. "Otherwise experience this theater for nearly two years wasted. If I am to be allowed my personal preference having started with the Eighth and seen it organized for major task in this theater, it would be heart-breaking to leave just before climax. If my services satisfactory to seniors, request I be allowed to retain command Eighth Air Force."

Spaatz, who cleared his own memo on the subject with Arnold before sending it two days later, told Eaker: "In view of command assignments, importance of having an American in command of Mediterranean Allied Air Forces, and establishing US Strategic Command in UK, believe best interests in overall conduct of war effort makes necessary your assignment as Air Commander in this theater. Because of close relationship with other services and other nationalities in both theaters and for most effective integration of effort I consider it essential that American air rank and experience be distributed between two theaters."

Doolittle recalled that Eisenhower agreed with Spaatz on the latter point, that "to have Spaatz and Eaker both in England did not spread out the talent sufficiently."

Though Doolittle added that George Marshall "did not overrule him," the chief of staff remained unconvinced of the wisdom of removing Eaker. Apparently, he was alone among those whose opinions mattered.

On December 21, Arnold gave Eaker his final answer. "This move is necessary from the viewpoint of worldwide air operations," he wrote. "No one knows better than I do the difficulties encountered leaving an organization that has been [built] up and most successfully operated under one's personal direction. This is particularly true when the loyalty from top to bottom is unquestioned and the commander has complete cooperation from all of his personnel. Such is your position at this time. The dictates of worldwide air operations necessitate major changes being made. This affects you personally and while from your point of view it is unfortunate that you cannot stay and retain command of the organization that you have so carefully and successfully built up, the broader view of the worldwide war effort indicates the necessity for a change. I extend to you my heartfelt thanks for the splendid cooperation and loyalty that you have given me thus far and for the wonderful success of your organization, but I cannot see my way clear to make any change in decisions already reached."

Arnold's formal orders regarding changes of post reached Eaker, Spaatz, and Doolittle on December 23.

Early on Christmas Eve, as a swan song, Eaker dispatched 670 Eighth Air Force heavy bombers, the largest number to date, against fortifications that the Germans were constructing in northern France. At the time, few people on the Allied side realized that these were being constructed as launch sites for V-1 cruise missiles, and nobody realized how much of a problem V-1s would become after they were first thrown into action in June 1944.

No bombers were lost to the enemy on Eaker's last major act as chief of the Eighth.

That afternoon, taking satisfaction from the mission results, Eaker sat down and penned his terse reply to Arnold: "Orders received will be executed promptly Jan. one. Am in communication [with] Spaatz discussing staffs and matters of mutual necessity."

On January 7, it was the RAF that hosted a farewell dinner for Eaker. Peter Portal was there, as were Arthur Harris, many other RAF officers, and the senior staff of the Eighth Air Force. Parton, who was also present, reports that no notes were taken of the speeches made and toasts offered.

Toward the end of the evening, Portal took Eaker aside to mention that "Colonel Holt" wanted to see him as he passed through Marrakech on his way to his new headquarters in the Mediterranean. Eaker did not know at the time that this was the alias used by Winston Churchill—then in Morocco recovering from pneumonia—when he was traveling incognito. In speeches given in the years to come, Eaker recalled the prime minister's words frequently.

"I can understand your disappointment, young man, at having to leave the Eighth Air Force just when it's achieving its maximum effect on the war effort," Churchill told him. "All in all, [your new post] will be a much larger command, with more responsibilities, than you had in the United Kingdom. . . . The prediction you made to me at Casablanca last February about our combined bomber missions, including 'round the clock bombing, are now being verified. I no longer have any doubt that they will prove completely valid."

CHAPTER 31

HOME FOR CHRISTMAS

B ack in October 1943, Ira Eaker had been planning to dispatch a high-level delegation from the Eighth Air Force to Washington to brief the Joint Chiefs of Staff, but the results of Black Thursday made this imperative.

Wanting to send representative *combat* commanders from both the VIII Bomber Command and the VIII Fighter Command, Eaker consulted with both Fred Anderson and William Kepner. The men whom they recommended were Curtis LeMay of the 3rd Bombardment Division and Hub Zemke of the 56th Fighter Group. One might say that they were two of the rising stars within the operational ranks of the Eighth, but one also might say that their stars had already risen.

Just as LeMay had influenced bomber formation organization throughout the Eighth Air Force a year earlier with his dictum against evasive action, Zemke was implementing his ideas about how fighter formations should be organized to best protect the bombers.

"With the three squadrons positioned around the bomber formations as the mission dictated, we sought optimum flexibility," Zemke wrote in his memoirs. "The flanking squadrons were separated into two sections, often at different levels, while the third squadron, or one of its sections, frequently became a freelance unit. If escorting the leading combat wing, this squadron or one of its sections ranged out some miles ahead. It could also act as a support squadron to the other two, answering calls for assistance."

It did not hurt Zemke's credibility that he was now an ace, having scored his fifth aerial victory on October 4 during a ten-day stretch when his 56th downed 34 Luftwaffe aircraft.

Having both been assured that their absence from England was temporary duty and that they would be returned to their respective commands, LeMay and Zemke flew up to Prestwick on what was to have been the first leg of their flight to Washington. This being November, it should have come as no wonder that weather conditions over Iceland and Greenland were terrible and promised to delay flights on this route for days. Nobody wanted a repeat of the loss of Frank Andrews in Iceland the previous May, so the two air commanders raced to Liverpool, scrambling aboard the liner *Queen Mary* on November 15 just as her gangplank was about to be raised.

LeMay and Zemke, who had known each other before the war at Langley Field, fell into a routine of shop talk and penny-ante gin rummy.

"As we played we talked and I was able to appreciate something of why this man was such a determined and successful commander," Zemke wrote. "Most people judged him by his curt, gruff manner; but he had a sense of humor and a deep interest in a wide range of subjects."

The two men, who had been at odds for shotgun ammunition at Langley Field before the war, apparently formed a cordial relationship. The following spring, LeMay would come to Zemke for an unusual favor. One of LeMay's bomber pilots, Lieutenant Colonel Preston Piper, who had been shot down and rescued, was suffering from a bout of traumatic stress and fixated on a fear of losing his crew again. LeMay asked Zemke to take him in as a fighter pilot—where he would have no crew—and he proved himself in this new role.

LeMay and Zemke met first with Hap Arnold and the top brass of the USAAF at the Pentagon, and then were dispatched on a tour of major commands throughout the United States, to bring them up to speed on what was happening in the European Theater, and to advise men headed overseas on what to expect. The two officers were also called upon to make public appearances to promote the USAAF.

"As for the public attitude about the Air Force, it apparently wasn't very positive or LeMay wouldn't have been sent home to try to improve it," Tom Coffey editorialized in his biography of LeMay. "But at least the Air Force was striking some blows against the German homeland. Where was the Army? Bogged down in Italy. What good were they doing there? . . . On the home front, prices were going up rapidly but wages weren't keeping pace."

LeMay was a powerful leader who commanded the respect, if not the universal fondness, of his men. He was the type of man whose presence at the front of a briefing room would render it so hushed that a pin dropping would have been audible—but, ironically, he was a man who was very much ill at ease as a public speaker in other contexts. Fortunately, he was aided in his grueling public speaking tour by a script that had been crafted for him by Captain Sy Bartlett, the Hollywood screenwriter who had been part of the Eighth Air Force staff and who would become the coauthor of *Twelve O'Clock High*.

At least their being stateside for more than a month meant that LeMay and Zemke had the opportunity to go home for Christmas and to see their families for the first time in more than a year.

Helen LeMay met her husband in Washington and they both flew to suburban Cleveland, where her family lived, and where she and Janie were spending their time while Curt was overseas. As Helen later told

Tom Coffey, Janie insisted that her father sit on the porch with her in the blustery cold for nearly an hour so that the neighborhood kids could see that she really *did* have a father.

Hub Zemke made it to Missoula, where his wife was spending the long months of their separation with his parents. When he was asked to address the Rotary club, he was joined at the head table by his father. As Hub recalled, Benno Zemke "didn't let his guard drop but I knew he was secretly proud that his son had finally had some success [a Distinguished Flying Cross]. Neither my mother nor my wife hid their concern for my safety."

Bob Morgan had come home many months before Christmas and had taken to a public speaking tour like the proverbial duck takes to water. Morgan and his crew arrived in June 1943, carried westward by the *Memphis Belle* nine months after she had taken them to England. Though William Wyler's film about the *Belle* would not be released until early 1944, there was already a great deal of media attention surrounding the bomber and her crew, who had been explicitly ordered to make a publicity and war-bond-selling tour that Ira Eaker called their "twenty-sixth mission."

It began before they landed at Washington National Airport, when Morgan impulsively made a low-level, high-speed pass over the field, scattering a sizable crowd. Once the *Belle* had come to a stop and the men tumbled out, newsreel cameras rolled and flashbulbs popped as the crowd first converged, then parted when Hap Arnold strode through to personally greet them. Morgan at first feared a chewing-out from the chief of the USAAF, but Arnold returned his salute, welcomed him home, and whispered, "That was one hell of a buzz job."

For several days, men used to lunching in mess halls or in bombers bound for Germany attended fancy luncheons with cabinet members and dignitaries of all stripes. At one of these events, Morgan recalled that Arnold took him aside and gave him permission to "buzz any place you want while you're on this tour," adding, "just be careful."

The media had a field day when the *Memphis Belle* buzzed into Memphis and Morgan was reunited with *the* Memphis Belle, Margaret Polk. When pictures were published of the brave pilot kissing his "Belle," there was talk of a wedding, but the USAAF public relations experts decreed that, for the purposes of the tour, the sweethearts should be merely engaged, not already married.

As the *Belle* and her boys crisscrossed the country, they partied at '21' and the Cotton Club in New York, and flew to Hollywood, where they recorded dialogue to be dubbed into Wyler's movie, which had been shot without sound.

Morgan later described their whirlwind tour of cities and war factories across the United States, writing about "parades, speeches to crowds of people, me introducing the crew of the *Belle* again and again from some flag-draped platform with a microphone in the middle. The boys always being charming, humble, brief. The limousines. The hotels. The good dinners and the drinks that never stopped getting poured. And the girls. The girls, girls, girls, girls . . . Who would ever have thought it? We didn't intend it that way. Neither did the girls. Nobody did. It just happened, a spontaneous combustion of all kinds of emotion."

As might have been expected, given Morgan's reputation with regard to relationships, the "girls, girls, girls" got in the way of the longevity of his relationship with Margaret. When she complained, he told her they weren't married yet and she told him they never would be. He later pleaded for her to reconsider, but she never did.

Morgan met Dorothy Johnson, a Biltmore Forest Country Club secretary, during his homecoming visit to Asheville. She reacted admiringly to his low-level passes with the *Memphis Belle*, and to passes made in person. However, when it came to his inevitable marriage proposal, she initially hesitated. He later recalled that he could see her warming up to him on Christmas Day. Two days later, she said yes. Their marriage would last 35 years.

Shortly after the start of 1944, as he was in Washington preparing to return to Halesworth to resume command of his 56th Fighter Group, Hub Zemke heard some very distressing news from a friend at USAAF headquarters. General Monk Hunter—who had been relieved of the command of the VIII Fighter Command in August, and now commanded the First Air Force, with headquarters at Mitchel Field in New York—had pulled some strings in Washington to have Zemke reassigned to *his* command.

"The thought of being confined to a staff desk appalled me," Zemke recalled. "I had no desire to work directly under Monk Hunter. In England it had been my view that he was out of touch with the situation in his command—and General Eaker had apparently come to this conclusion too. . . . Perhaps some officers would have considered this a great posting but I could not have felt more gloomy."

Zemke had not yet received orders transferring him from the Eighth to the First and was still traveling under orders to report back to England. Deciding upon "quick action," he presented his orders to the Air Transport Command and climbed aboard a flight to England. When he reported in to VIII Fighter Command, General Kepner knew about Hunter's pending orders, but Zemke was able to honestly say that he had not yet received them. Kepner, who sympathized with Zemke, told him to make himself scarce for a couple of days while he discussed the situation with the new Eighth Air Force chain of command, meaning Doolittle and Spaatz.

Though he never learned exactly what transpired in the ensuing days, Zemke was ordered back to the 56th Fighter Group a week later.

CHAPTER 32

✪

CALCULATED RISKS

Tooey Spaatz and Jimmy Doolittle reached England from the Mediterranean on the eve of the official activation of their new commands on January 6, 1944.

Spaatz's USSTAF took over the existing headquarters and staff of the Eighth Air Force at Widewing in Bushy Park, which had been Spaatz's earlier home when he had commanded the Eighth in 1942. Meanwhile the title of "Eighth Air Force" was transferred to the existing headquarters and staff of VIII Bomber Command at Pinetree in High Wycombe. As an entity, VIII Bomber Command ceased to exist, and its commanding officer, Fred Anderson, became Spaatz's deputy commander for operations at USSTAF. Having been thoroughly involved in mission planning and operations throughout Eaker's tenure, he would continue to be one of the most vital members of the team, and the principal caretaker of the Eighth Air Force institutional memory that neither Doolittle nor Spaatz possessed.

As 1944 began, the immediate objective to which Spaatz, Doolittle, and Anderson devoted their attention was a secret project called Operation

Argument. Formalized at the Sextant Conference in December 1943, Argument was conceived as the narrowly focused climax of Operation Pointblank. While the latter was openly discussed, Argument was addressed behind closed doors. Its catalyst was the realization that Pointblank was behind schedule and that the days between January and the scheduled May 1 date of Operation Overlord were rapidly slipping away.

Both Spaatz and Doolittle had come to England knowing that Operation Argument was to be their primary focus. The idea was for a weeklong maximum effort against the Luftwaffe, its infrastructure, and the factories that supplied it. For Argument, "maximum effort" meant not a few hundred bombers on a single day as in the Regensburg and Schweinfurt missions but a sustained multiday campaign involving as close to 1,000 bombers as the Eighth could muster—this time escorted all the way to the targets by P-51s.

As the basic mission—breaking the back of the Luftwaffe before Overlord—had not changed, neither had the weather. It had been imagined that Argument might be launched in January, but favorable weather during a northern European January was not something upon which a serious planner of large-scale air operations could depend.

Doolittle, fresh from the sunnier Mediterranean, learned the hard way. An assertive commander not prone to timidity, he was eager to launch the maximum number of bombers as frequently as possible—and was readily encouraged by Spaatz to do so—but he found this more difficult than he had imagined.

The January 24 mission was a case in point, and part of an early turning point in Doolittle's relationship with Spaatz. It was to have been an assault on an unprecedented scale against industrial and transportation targets throughout the Frankfurt metropolitan area. The Eighth launched 857 B-17s and B-24s, roughly triple the number that had been part of the big Regensburg and Schweinfurt missions in August and October. The number illustrated both Doolittle's determination and the increase in the number of men and aircraft. The Eighth began 1944 with 26 heavy bomber groups, compared to 16 in August 1943.

That morning, the skies were mainly clear over the bases in southeast England, but as the armada moved eastward to rendezvous and get into formation, they ran into multiple layers of overcast, which had not been predicted. This made it nearly impossible to form up, and more than 400 bombers had to abort. The remainder were put into a holding pattern over the English Channel, until most of them had to be recalled. Only 56 bombers reached Germany that day, and these were diverted to a secondary target near Aachen.

When Tooey Spaatz learned that 95 percent of the massive strike had been recalled before they had even reached continental airspace, he looked out the window and saw clear weather.

In his diary, Spaatz wrote: "Today is to go on record as completely wasted. Good weather at bases, good weather over target and Doolittle sent no bombers."

He then called Jimmy Doolittle into his office.

"I wonder if you've got the guts to lead a big air force," Spaatz said angrily. "If you haven't, I'll get someone else who has."

Doolittle's response was that he "didn't want to gamble the lives of my men on an uncalculated risk." He went on to point out that if the American airfields had closed down before the bombers came back, the Eighth "could have lost, on one mission, a major part of the force that we had so laboriously built up. It would have been a needless waste of lives and planes."

Making it obvious to Doolittle that he did not agree, Spaatz dismissed the Eighth's commander with a brusque "That'll be all."

Not long after this exchange, a cooled-down Spaatz invited Doolittle to join him aboard his personal B-17 for an inspection tour of Eighth Air Force bases.

On the second morning of the tour, the two generals awakened to "heavy drizzle with minimum visibility."

As Doolittle wrote in his memoirs, "I wanted to head for home before we got weathered in somewhere, but Tooey wanted to visit three more bases first. We did get to two of them, but searching for the third proved impossible because of ever-lowering overcast and decreasing visibility. [The aircraft's pilot, Lieutenant Colonel Bob] Kimmel chose to stay under the clouds and hedgehop over the countryside, hoping to locate himself visually and find someplace to land. Hedgehopping in bad weather has killed hundreds of pilots before and since, and I had lost many friends who had chosen to stay in visual contact with the ground. I was more than somewhat concerned. I'm sure Tooey was, too, but he didn't say anything. Kimmel finally found a pasture that seemed long enough for a B-17 and free of obstructions; he managed to sideslip the four-engine bomber in for a bumpy landing—heading right toward a stone fence. He jammed on the brakes and we stopped only a few feet from it."

"You were right, Jim," Spaatz said, putting his hand on Doolittle's shoulder as they emerged from the plane. "I see what you mean about uncalculated risks."

David Mets, Spaatz's biographer, wrote that the crash landing had proven Doolittle's point that, "were the same thing to happen to the whole force, it would be a disaster. After that, the tension between them lessened." Thereafter, there was also an increased urgency in improved and expanded training for instrument flying.

When Hub Zemke had returned to Halesworth to resume command of the 56th Fighter Group on January 19, 1944, he found that during his two-month absence new 108-gallon drop tanks had arrived to extend the range of the group's P-47s to more than double what it had been when Zemke first arrived a year before. They did not have a range to match the remarkable P-51 Mustangs, but at the time, there were still 1,348 Jugs and just 543 Mustangs in the European Theater, although the number of P-51s had doubled in a month.

Also while Zemke had been away, the 56th Fighter Group became the top-scoring group in the VIII Fighter Command, reaching a total of 200 air-to-air victories over the Luftwaffe—double that of the rival 4th Fighter Group—by the end of January. The 56th, with the cowlings of its

P-47s now painted bright red as though to draw attention to themselves, was evolving into a "home of the aces." Walker "Bud" Mahurin scored his fifteenth in January to maintain his position as the leading ace of the Eighth Air Force. Bob Johnson was only one behind Mahurin, while Francis "Gabby" Gabreski, the commander of the 56th's 61st Fighter Squadron, had scored his eleventh.

The stepped-up tempo of air combat was partially the result of the increasing numbers of Eighth Air Force fighters, their extended range, and a change in battle doctrine. Whereas the more cautious Ira Eaker had mandated that fighters escorting bombers should stay with the bombers, Jimmy Doolittle relaxed the directive to permit American fighters in hot pursuit of Luftwaffe fighters to continue that pursuit. His reasoning was that Operation Pointblank was a war on the Luftwaffe, and any German fighter shot down affected the enemy's balance sheet.

"Fighter pilots are usually pugnacious individuals by nature and are trained to be aggressive in the air," he observed in his memoirs. "Their machines are specifically designed for offensive action. I thought our fighter forces should intercept the enemy fighters before they reached the bombers."

When he visited Bill Kepner at Ajax, the VIII Fighter Command headquarters, he noticed a sign on the wall that read "The First Duty of the Eighth Air Force Fighters Is to Bring the Bombers Back Alive."

"Bill, who dreamed that up?" Doolittle asked.

"The sign was here when we arrived," Kepner replied, blaming Monk Hunter.

"That statement is no longer in effect," Doolittle told him. "Take that sign down. Put up another one that says, 'The First Duty of the Eighth Air Force Fighters Is to Destroy German Fighters.'"

"You mean you're authorizing me to take the offensive?"

"I'm directing you to," Doolittle said.

Kepner then told him that he had been trying in vain for months to sell Eaker on this idea. Indeed, Hub Zemke was among those who had lobbied Kepner for exactly this approach.

Sensing this change, the Luftwaffe interceptors were now increasingly hesitant to engage the American fighters directly, making every effort to slip between the bombers and their Little Friends for fast hit-and-run attacks, or simply waiting until the bombers were beyond the range of the P-47s.

The change of tactics was helping to achieve part of the goal of Operation Argument by compromising the Luftwaffe's effectiveness.

Another factor that made for a qualitative improvement in the fortunes of the VIII Fighter Command was the retention of experienced pilots. It had been Eighth Air Force policy that fighter pilots were allowed to go stateside after 200 flight hours, just as bomber crews went home after 25 missions. With many experienced men reaching this cutoff, Zemke and other group commanders successfully lobbied Kepner to allow pilots to volunteer for a 50-hour extension in exchange for a 30-day home leave.

If Tooey Spaatz can be accused of taking out his frustrations on Jimmy Doolittle after the January 24 mission, those frustrations were inflamed by the pressure that he himself was receiving from above. As they moved to England, Spaatz was now the recipient of the same pressure with which Hap Arnold had relentlessly nagged Ira Eaker. The day before, Spaatz had received a wire from his boss pointedly complaining about the small numbers of bombers being sent out.

"I cannot understand why, with the great number of airplanes available to the Eighth Air Force, we continually have to send a boy to do a man's job," Arnold wrote impatiently. "In my opinion, this is an uneconomical waste of lives and equipment. In the first place, it allowed the Germans to rebuild their only partially demolished facilities, and in the second place, we have to expose our youngsters and our aircraft a second and sometimes a third time to the German fighter and anti-aircraft defenses. These defenses, we all know, are not getting any less effective."

No wonder Spaatz was so frustrated and so harsh with Doolittle the next day.

This memo, though typical of many that Arnold sent and full of facts that the recipient already knew, is important on many levels. It brings into focus the pressure that was felt by Spaatz and Doolittle—and by Eaker before them. None of them wanted to be seen in the position of doing less than was necessary, whatever the reasons why. Also brought into focus by Arnold's January 23 memo was Operation Pointblank's unfinished war against the Luftwaffe. As the numbers of Eighth Air Force bombers increased, so too did the size and effectiveness of the Luftwaffe interceptor force. The best pilots and the highest-scoring aces were being brought home from the Eastern Front and concentrated in large numbers for the Reichsverteidigung (Defense of the Reich) mission.

The battle lines were now drawn for a decisive clash between the Luftwaffe and the USAAF.

With one impatient eye on the weather, Anderson and the Enemy Objectives Unit had drawn up and refined an ambitious target list for Operation Argument that included both Regensburg and Schweinfurt again, as well as factories and Luftwaffe bases across the Reich from Bremen to Augsburg and Wiener Neustadt.

January slipped away entirely, and on February 8, Spaatz told Fred Anderson emphatically that Argument *must* happen by the end of the month. In the official USAAF history, Arthur Ferguson recalled: "Argument had been scheduled repeatedly—every time, in fact, that early weather reports seemed to offer any hope; but each time deteriorating weather had forced cancellation. . . . By February the destruction of the German fighter production had become a matter of such urgency that General Spaatz and General Anderson were willing to take more than ordinary risks in order to complete the task, including the risk of exceptional losses that might result from missions staged under conditions of adverse base weather."

The way that they addressed and dismissed Doolittle's concerns took him back to that day on the deck of the USS *Hornet* when he decided to go for broke—but back then, it had been Doolittle making the final decision. Meanwhile, Doolittle was increasingly concerned that Spaatz and Anderson were depending upon the advice of the maverick meteorologist Irving Krick, who used unconventional "weather typing" based on historical weather pattern mapping. Krick had the confidence of Hap Arnold, but few others—especially not Doolittle, who considered him "full of crap."

Nevertheless, when Krick predicted clear weather over Germany for at least three days beginning on Sunday, February 20, it was good enough for Spaatz. Though Doolittle continued to voice his hesitant distrust for Krick, Spaatz ordered Operation Argument to begin. It was a calculated risk.

On that first day of what soon came to be known as "Big Week," the Eighth Air Force launched 1,003 heavy bombers from all three bombardment divisions, escorted by 835 fighters drawn from the Eighth and Ninth Air Forces. Their targets, mainly aircraft factories—which had been struck the night before by RAF area bombardment—were as far south as Gotha and as far east as Leipzig.

It was late on Sunday afternoon when Spaatz, Anderson, Doolittle, and their respective staffs gathered at Park House in suburban London—where Spaatz and his staff were billeted—to receive the news. It was not expected to be good. Based on the rate of losses suffered over Schweinfurt in October, around 200 bombers were expected to be lost, meaning 2,000 bunks would be empty that night.

However, it did not happen that way. As Colonel Glen Williamson of USSTAF later explained to Charles Murphy of *Life* magazine, "We had been up all night and all day. The reports came in all evening. Group after group reported no losses or only one or two. We couldn't believe it. We were all thinking somebody's going to get wiped out, somebody's going to say he was cut to pieces. When all the reports were in and we added up the totals the figures were unbelievable."

Instead of 200, only 21 bombers were lost. The weather, which everyone had dreaded, had been perfect for precision bombing and target after target had been hit.

What the Eighth accomplished on Sunday was only part—albeit the best part—of the story. Ira Eaker had been brought into the loop, and with him the Fifteenth Air Force. Nominally part of Spaatz's USSTAF command, the Fifteenth was also in the Mediterranean and within the sphere of influence of Ira Eaker's MAAF. Though Nathan Twining commanded the Fifteenth, which was technically under Spaatz's USSTAF, all parties had agreed that operational directives from USSTAF to the Fifteenth would be routed through Eaker so that he would be part of the chain of command, and he agreed to support Argument.

As February approached, the participation of the Fifteenth was complicated by Operation Shingle, the Allied invasion at Anzio, south of Rome, which took place on January 22. Eaker's MAAF was committed to supplying air support, and he had been using the Fifteenth Air Force in these operations. Though he had promised the Fifteenth to Argument, the latter came at a bad time—the Fifteenth was in the midst of helping beat back a German counterattack at Anzio that was on the verge of pushing the Allies into the sea.

Nevertheless, Eaker did muster 126 heavy bombers for a mission to Regensburg. Sadly, while good weather prevailed in northern Europe, the bombers that Eaker borrowed from the Anzio mission ran into heavy weather over the Alps and were forced to turn back.

On Monday, with the weather still clear in the north, the Eighth Air Force launched 861 heavy bombers, supported by 679 fighters. While the targets for Sunday had been mainly related to aircraft manufacturing, the Monday missions went after Luftwaffe fields. However, scattered overcast was encountered over northern Germany, and that meant less-than-ideal results, so the mood in England was not nearly as positive as it had been on Sunday.

Tuesday morning, Doolittle's Eighth launched 799 heavy bombers, with the largest contingent, 333 Flying Fortresses of Curtis LeMay's 3rd Bomb Division, being sent to infamous Schweinfurt. Eaker's Fifteenth, meanwhile, made a second attempt against Regensburg.

As in August, the best-laid plans for a coordinated Regensburg-Schweinfurt strike did not work out. In August, LeMay had pressed on to attack Regensburg, while Bob Williams was delayed by weather. Six months later, it was LeMay who was stymied by weather over England. After several midair collisions as the bombers attempted in vain to get into formation, LeMay was compelled to abort his part of the mission. The Fifteenth *did* manage to get 183 heavy bombers through to Regensburg.

After a gloriously successful Sunday, things had seemed to unravel for the men of the Eighth Air Force—just as they had for Krick's promise of clear skies for three days. Doolittle lobbied for a day of rest for men whom he sarcastically described as "subsisting primarily on an alternate diet of Benzedrine and sleeping pills," and the detested meteorologist gave it to him. The weather for Wednesday, Krick promised, would *not* be good. He was right, and so too was his promise of good weather on Thursday.

For the Eighth Air Force, Thursday was the second biggest day of Big Week, with 809 heavy bombers, supported by 767 fighters, being sent to Germany. Of these, a strike force of 238 reached the terrible skies over Schweinfurt. On Black Thursday in October, a contingent of nearly the same size lost 60 bombers; in February, only 11 were lost.

Friday, February 25, marked the final day of Big Week, with 754 heavy bombers heading out from the bases of the Eighth Air Force. Of these, 267 from LeMay's 3rd Bomb Division reached Regensburg in an assault that was successfully coordinated with 176 heavy bombers of the Fifteenth Air Force.

From Bushy Park, Spaatz singled Eaker out for praise, wiring him that "strike photographs of the Regensburg attack [have been] examined and I consider that superior results were obtained. The Fifteenth Air Force accomplished a superior job of bombing and vital destruction to enemy installations in the face of heavy air attack, without fighter support and with heavy losses. Even without consideration of the 93 enemy fighters shot down by our bombers, the results far outweigh the losses."

Big Week was also big for Hub Zemke and his 56th Fighter Group. Though their P-47s did not have the range to accompany the bombers deep into the Reich, as the P-51s did, their radius of operations was now extended as far as Hanover by new 150-gallon external tanks. On February 24, Zemke was leading the 56th toward the Netherlands, where they expected to rendezvous with the Schweinfurt-bound 3rd Bomb Division, when they received word that the Flying Fortresses were already under attack. Pushing their throttles ahead, the Jugs accelerated to the rendezvous point, where Zemke spotted four Fw 190s headed toward the bombers.

Zemke dove on a Luftwaffe fighter, only to be attacked by the man's wingman. Acting according to protocol, Zemke's own wingman, Archie Robey, engaged and destroyed the German wingman while Zemke continued to dive. Nagged by a gunsight malfunction, Zemke chased the German to treetop level without achieving any hits.

Though Zemke had failed to score, the 56th Fighter Group emerged from Big Week credited with 72 victories against the Luftwaffe while suffering only two losses. By now, the names of 56th's aces, Gabby Gabreski, Bud Mahurin, and Bob Johnson, were starting to become household words back home as the USAAF publicized its heroes. So too was that of the group leader. The 56th was now called "Zemke's Wolf Pack."

During Big Week, the Eighth Air Force flew more than 3,300 sorties, the Fifteenth Air Force flew more than 500, and RAF Bomber Command contributed more than 2,350. The 10,000 tons of bombs dropped by the Americans were roughly the equivalent of what the Eighth Air Force had dropped in its entire first year of operations. Reconnaissance photos showed that those missions had resulted in substantial damage to the German war machine. The Eighth had suffered a bomber loss rate of 3.5 percent, compared with 9.2 percent six months earlier, in October 1943.

Of Big Week, Walt Rostow, the future advisor to presidents Kennedy and Johnson and then on the Enemy Objectives Unit staff, wrote half a century later, "The German single-engined fighter force never recovered from its unlikely defeat by the American long-range bombers. [Big Week] was the week that, in effect, a mature US Air Force emerged."

Reflecting on Big Week in a February 1945 memo to Secretary of War Henry Stimson, Hap Arnold wrote that "the week of 20-26 February, 1944, may well be classed by future historians as marking a decisive battle of history, one as decisive and of greater importance than Gettysburg."

A great deal of positive spin could be taken from the good news— and it was—but the losses were still real people who were known to those who remained, and who knew that the job was not done.

In his memoirs, Jimmy Doolittle asked rhetorically whether the big calculated risk was worth the effort, and answered, "Initially, I thought it was. We saw immediately that the Luftwaffe did not rise against us in the numbers that it had previously. . . . Historians tell us that we broke the back of the Luftwaffe that 'big week' of February 1944, and it never again equaled its prior performance. Even so, our later experience showed that, although we slowed them down, the Germans never did run out of airplanes and were still able to turn them out in underground factories until the end of the war. . . . What hurt the Germans the most was the deterioration in the experience level of their pilots. . . . The German high command withdrew the bulk of its fighter defenses to the great industrial centers inside Germany, leaving only a modest number of fighters in the probable [Operation Overlord] invasion areas."

CHAPTER 33

SMALL BATTLES WON AND LOST

E ven as he celebrated the success of Big Week and a corner turned in the evolution of strategic airpower, Tooey Spaatz learned that he had lost a battle that he thought he'd won in 1939. Five years earlier, Katharine Spaatz, as a precocious teenager, had bickered with her dad about studying in Paris during the school year that would have begun the same week as World War II. In 1939 he had managed to thwart her plans, but in 1944, now 22, Tattie had made good on her desire to travel abroad. She came to England not as a student but as a member of the American Red Cross.

Harvey Gibson, an influential New York financier who had become the American Red Cross commissioner in Great Britain, had devised a scheme to boost morale at American bases in England. The idea involved the "Clubmobile," a vehicle roughly analogous to a modern urban "food truck" that would pay visits to the bases, serving refreshments such as coffee and doughnuts, selling candy and cigarettes, and playing popular music. The Clubmobiles were staffed by young American women whom the Red Cross in its recruiting documents described as "healthy, physically hardy, sociable and attractive." Tattie Spaatz was one of those young women.

As David Mets, Spaatz's biographer, points out, the young women were not supposed to serve in theaters where they had family members, but Tooey was still in the Mediterranean when Tattie first arrived in England. When photos of her hugging her father appeared in *Stars and Stripes,* "she kept a low profile for weeks. But the Red Cross either forgot about her or was kind enough to leave her in England."

Spaatz had also served in the same theater as his son-in-law. The previous year, Tattie's sister, the musically gifted Beckie, had dropped out of the Peabody Conservatory to marry a young pilot named Emmet "Red" Gresham, who went overseas to the Mediterranean to fly P-38s with the 71st Fighter Squadron of the 1st Fighter Group within the Fifteenth Air Force.

On February 25, the last day of Big Week, when the Fifteenth sent part of its force across the Alps to Regensburg, another force attacked targets in Yugoslavia. Red Gresham was flying one of the fighters escorting the latter mission when his external fuel tank erupted in flame. His wingman followed Gresham as the plane fell like a stone. He watched as Gresham tried in vain to pull it up, and as it crashed into a hillside on the Croatian island of Krk in the northern Adriatic Sea. He reported seeing no parachute.

As David Mets noted, when the news reached Gresham's base at Salsola, ten miles north of Foggia, there followed a flurry of cables between Spaatz and Eaker and members of their staff. It was a February 26 memo from Brigadier General Patrick Timberlake of the MAAF staff to Eaker that reached Beckie shortly thereafter. She and her month-old daughter, Edith, were with Ruth Spaatz in Washington at the time.

It seemed for a while that Beckie had joined the growing list of young war widows. Then the miraculous happened. A March 6 communication from her father explained that Red Gresham had indeed escaped the P-38, but had been captured and was being held on Krk. In a story of cinematic improbability, Gresham had clobbered a guard with a rock and had managed to escape from the island, cross the Adriatic, and reach

American lines in Italy. He survived the war but died, still a young man, in 1953.

Jimmy Doolittle, meanwhile, had a son overseas in the European Theater. James Junior was an A-26 pilot with the Ninth Air Force.

"It was a happy time for both of us—the first time we had seen each other in two years," Doolittle wrote of their reunion early in 1944. "We saw each other frequently during the rest of our tours. Later, I had the pleasure of pinning the Distinguished Flying Cross on him for missions he had flown in the South Pacific. I was proud. He had left his unit in the Pacific before the medal and citation could be presented to him. I flew over to his field in a P-38. He looked longingly at it, so I let him take it up for a hop."

In March 1944, Jimmy Doolittle was planning to fly the first USAAF mission against Berlin, just as he had commanded the first against the other two Axis capitals, Tokyo and Rome.

The last time Doolittle had visited Berlin had been in 1939, just before the war, when he reconnected with his friend Ernst Udet, by then in Luftwaffe uniform. In 1944, pages had turned, and the old First World War ace was no longer on the roster. He had committed suicide in November 1941, three weeks before the United States entered the war, despondent over girlfriend troubles and Hermann Göring's having ignored his warnings about the resiliency of the Soviet aircraft industry.

Tooey Spaatz, Doolittle's boss, had reluctantly agreed and told him that he *could* go to Berlin—but then he changed his mind. Doolittle had been thoroughly briefed on the details of Operation Overlord, and the USSTAF commander could not risk his being captured. Indeed, having the famous Doolittle in custody would have also been a propaganda coup for Germany.

The RAF had attacked Berlin, an 1,100-mile round trip from England, often, but Spaatz waited until after Big Week to begin running American daylight missions against the most heavily defended target in the Third Reich. His first two attempts at a mission to Berlin did not work out. On March 3, an ambitiously assembled 748-plane strike force was stymied by overcast and wound up attacking targets of opportunity in northwestern Germany. The following day, only 30 Flying Fortresses of a force of 502 managed to reach the German capital because of the weather-related diversions. As frustrating as this was, it also served to alert the Germans that the Americans were coming to the Axis capital.

When 672 heavies finally came over the Berlin metropolitan area on March 6, the Luftwaffe unleashed its concentrated fury upon the Eighth, and 69 bombers were shot down. Hitler and his minions could look up and see the sky darkened by the Eighth, but for Doolittle's raiders, the loss rates were reminiscent of the dark days of 1943.

Hub Zemke led the 56th on the March 6 mission, escorting the bombers as far as northwestern Germany. Strangely, in an environment where the skies were usually dark with Luftwaffe formations, Zemke spotted only a lone Fw 190 closing in to attack the Flying Fortresses on the trailing edge of their formation. Rolling and diving, he tried to reach the German before he could open fire, but did arrive as the enemy made his first, fast firing pass. As he banked left, Zemke got on his tail, fired a quick burst, and watched the Focke-Wulf go down in flames, one of ten claimed by the 56th that day.

The first successful attack on Berlin by the Eighth came two months to the day after Spaatz and Doolittle had taken up their new posts in England. Though Operation Overlord was tentatively scheduled for May 1, it was postponed until June 5, and delayed to June 6, making the Berlin mission also three months to the day before the Allied invasion of northern Europe.

Rosie Rosenthal's own milestone mission to Berlin came on March 8, when the 100th Bomb Group was part of the force that targeted the Vereinigte Kugellagerfabriken ball bearing works at Erkner, about 16 miles east of downtown Berlin. This was his twenty-fifth and *final* mission, and for his crew, their third and last mission in the aircraft they had dubbed

Rosie's Riveters II. The bomber flew on with other crews for another two months before being shot down. The original *Rosie's Riveters*, meanwhile, had been shot down with another crew in February.

With his 25 missions behind him, Rosenthal was eligible to put the war itself behind him and go home as Bob Morgan had done nine months earlier. However, Rosenthal decided that he was in the war to fight the Nazis, and there were *still* Nazis to fight, so he elected to volunteer for another 25.

During his second tour, Rosenthal, now a major, took over as commander of the 350th Bomb Squadron within the 100th Bomb Group, flying as a command pilot. In this role, he led missions from the right seat of whichever Flying Fortress had been picked as the lead ship in the formation. The pilot in the left seat flew the bomber, while the command pilot's job was making sure that all elements of the group assembled and flew in the proper formation.

By the first week of May, Chick Harding, whom Rosenthal liked but found to lack an aptitude for leadership, had been replaced as commander of the Bloody Hundredth. After an interim commander, Harding was succeeded by Colonel Tom Jeffrey, whom Rosenthal regarded as a "brilliant, charismatic commander, who brought the group together." Under Jeffrey's leadership, Rosenthal felt the 100th was transformed into "a superb group, the best in the air force."

Even as the Luftwaffe suffered from losses of experienced pilots during the spring, its concentration of assets over the targets still made it a dangerous and effective force. They began using the idea of the *Sturmgruppe*, a large force of heavily armed and armored Fw 190s that could overwhelm the defensive armament of a bomber force. In turn, these interceptors would be supported by a large force of Bf 109s flying at a higher altitude, which could then dive to attack USAAF escort fighters as they challenged the *Sturmgruppe*.

To meet this challenge, Hub Zemke developed some tactics of his own. "I reasoned that a force of our fighters arriving at [an enemy rendezvous point] could disrupt assembling Luftwaffe formations to such an extent that they would be unable to reform in time to meet the Forts and Libs," Zemke recalled, proposing that the 56th would then "fan out over a 180-degree arc. An extra section would be maintained in the center so that if one flight called in enemy fighters this section could move out to help. If we went out well in advance of the bombers and employed these tactics we stood a good chance of picking up some of the Luftwaffe units assembling for a mass attack and would be able to break them up."

When he presented his idea to Bill Kepner and his staff at VIII Fighter Command, they "were quite receptive and approved what they termed 'the Zemke Fan.'" It was, however, a work in progress.

The next day, May 12, happened to be a maximum effort against petrochemical industry targets, especially around Merseburg, the center of catalytic high-pressure ammonia synthesis. Among the 735 fighters that supported this effort was a contingent from Zemke's Wolf Pack.

Zemke was flying with Willard Johnson and Preston Piper over Koblenz when they became aware of seven Bf 109s with a 5,000-foot altitude advantage. One German fighter slashed through the formation, claiming the Jug flown by Johnson. As Zemke started to react, the German was back, this time picking off Piper. He was the bomber pilot whom Curtis LeMay had wanted to have transformed into a fighter pilot.

The Bf 109 next turned to Zemke.

"Desperation rather than fear gripped me as I looked for an opening to escape," Zemke recalled. "Two down, one to go. Fear took hold, in that racing jumble of thought the prospect of death spun by. . . . Perhaps my dread would have been all the greater had I known that the pilot I had just seen dispatch Johnson and Piper was the third ranking ace of the Luftwaffe, Major Günther Rall."

With more than 250 aerial victories to his credit at the time, Rall was the Gruppenkommandeur of II Gruppe of Jagdgeschwader 11.

"I took the only possible course to escape," Zemke continued. "With violent movement of the controls, I rolled [my P-47] over with a fast aileron flip and headed vertically for the ground, barrel rolling as I went to make a difficult target for my pursuers. Down, full power, into the realms of compressibility. By the time the altimeter had unwound a couple of times and the airspeed indicator had hit the peg, the Thunderbolt was rumbling and vibrating so much I expected it to fly apart."

It did not and Zemke survived, observing that "perhaps they couldn't catch me; perhaps they thought I was out of control."

His headset, filled with the transmissions of the Wolf Pack, was now fully engaged, and Zemke climbed to rejoin the battle. After dodging four Bf 109s over Wiesbaden, he began working his way toward England. Having climbed to 20,000 feet, he spied another four beneath him over Koblenz. As he circled for a quick firing pass, he watched more fighters join the others, and realized that he was over a Luftwaffe assembly point.

He observed that this was "just what we had been seeking to do in developing the Zemke Fan—but instead of a sizable bunch of Wolf Pack eager beavers poised for the kill there was, ironically, only the lone originator of the scheme. My throttle hand depressed the radio microphone switch. . . . I continued to call for help as the force below me grew to an estimated thirty in number, a whole fighter Gruppe. With each orbit they gained altitude and as they went up so did I, to maintain my [altitude] advantage."

At last joined by two others as backup, Zemke executed a wingover and a fairly steep dive, picked a Bf 109 near the edge of the formation, and opened fire.

"From the tracers my aim was seen to be too far ahead of my target so I continued firing, letting the [Bf] 109 fly right through my bullet pattern," Zemke noted. "Strikes were seen along the fuselage before superior speed necessitated an abrupt pull back on the stick to avoid ramming my victim. Zooming up in a climbing turn, a quick peep over the shoulder revealed the [Bf] 109 in flames and the pilot bailing out."

Zemke rolled, dodged four more trying to attack him, and headed for home. In all, Zemke's Wolf Pack claimed 18 from the enemy while suffering three losses. All three pilots survived, albeit in captivity.

"The Zemke Fan had certainly brought the action we sought," he observed with understatement. "The principal error had been in using only flight strength forces at an altitude where they were vulnerable to attack from above."

Zemke and his Wolf Pack were learning from the experience.

CHAPTER 34

OVERLORD

In looking ahead toward Overlord, Spaatz and Doolittle—and Eaker before them—saw it as the ultimate goal of Operation Pointblank. After Big Week, they began looking at the air war *beyond* Overlord, and the beginning of the largest *ground* operation in American military history. The USAAF men had their own ideas, but Dwight Eisenhower, as the theater commander and architect of the big picture, saw things differently.

The direct support of the ground forces would be the job of Allied tactical air forces, the RAF Second Tactical Air Force and the USAAF Ninth Air Force. For the purpose of the invasion, they had been consolidated under an entity known as the Allied Expeditionary Air Force (AEAF) and commanded by Air Marshal Trafford Leigh-Mallory, formerly of RAF Fighter Command. Leigh-Mallory answered directly to Eisenhower and his deputy, Arthur Tedder, at SHAEF. Serving as Leigh-Mallory's deputy at AEAF was Major General Hoyt Vandenberg, Tooey Spaatz's old classmate from the Command and General Staff School, who went on to serve on the AWPD and later as Jimmy Doolittle's chief of staff at NASAF.

Meanwhile, the planners of Overlord at SHAEF and AEAF began

discussing what role the Eighth Air Force might play in the support of Overlord. It was only natural that they would wish to have the mightiest single component of Allied airpower at their disposal. It was not a question of *whether* they should have the Eighth, but of *how* best to use it to support Overlord—as well as the post-Overlord land battle in Europe.

Eisenhower and Tedder saw the Eighth best used in a *tactical* role, favoring a campaign of interdiction against the transportation infrastructure within northern Europe—and the phrase "isolating the battlefield" came into use to describe the cutting of roads, rails, and telecommunication between the German headquarters and their frontline troops.

Spaatz and Doolittle saw it best used in a *strategic* role, favoring a campaign against the German petrochemical industry, including a growing synthetic petroleum component. They saw fuel as the ultimate bottleneck in the interconnected web of the German war machine. Indeed, petroleum had been high on every USAAF strategic target list going back to AWPD-1.

Those favoring petroleum industry targets, who came to be known to their detractors as "the oily boys," were destined to be overruled by Eisenhower. As Walt Rostow of the Enemy Objectives Unit points out, it was in "an historic meeting" on March 25, Eisenhower "decided in favor of Tedder and marshalling yards on the grounds that the latter would provide some immediate help in the landings and their aftermath, whereas the military effects of the oil attacks might be delayed." Nevertheless, Spaatz was given an allowance to plan the occasional mission against petroleum objectives and he would exercise this option.

However, as the weeks counted down toward Overlord, now scheduled for June 5, Eisenhower decided that instead of merely cooperating with Leigh-Mallory's AEAF, Tooey Spaatz's Eighth Air Force and Arthur Harris's RAF Bomber Command should be placed under the *direct command and control* of SHAEF. Although both men relinquished their strategic mission and their autonomy reluctantly, neither wanted to be seen as having stood in the way of the success of Operation Overlord.

And so it was that the Eighth Air Force reached its now formidable talons into northern France. Less than two years earlier, the Eighth had gone into these skies with trepidation, and against a formidable foe. By the eve of Overlord, the Allies had achieved control of French skies, and would be using their airpower to control events on the ground.

As the end of May approached and Overlord was in the wind, nearly every person in uniform knew that it was coming soon, but of course only a handful knew that the actual day was intended to be June 5. However, the vexing weather, which so bedeviled the airmen, would force Eisenhower to delay the great amphibious undertaking 24 hours to June 6.

One day toward the end of May, Hub Zemke was summoned to Ajax, the VIII Fighter Command headquarters, for a normal group commanders' briefing. There was nothing unusual in that. What was unusual was that this time the commanders were specifically ordered to come by road and told not to fly. After a regular meeting and a dinner, Zemke was driven back to the 56th Fighter Group, which had moved to Boxted in April.

On June 5, Zemke had just landed after a routine fighter sweep over northern France, when he was called to Ajax for another group commanders' meeting. As on the previous occasion, he was told to come by car.

"Immediately on entering Bushey Hall I sensed something was up," he recalled in his memoirs. "Security was tight with guards posted. This was it, tomorrow was D-Day, the long-talked-of cross-Channel invasion. Excitement was high; our briefing thorough. The 56th was assigned to patrol an area from Boulogne to the north of the Seine. . . . The reason for the insistence on road transportation was now plain: each group commander was provided with a large quantity of plans. No risk could be taken with these in the air lest someone got lost in bad weather and end up across the other side. The previous trip to Ajax had obviously been a trial run."

Back in Boxted, as at every Eighth Air Force base in England, intelligence officers were called into the briefing room and the doors were locked. Bases became "as tight as a prison, with guards posted and no one allowed out" as maintenance crews began painting black and white "invasion stripes" on the tactical aircraft.

At 3:30 a.m. on June 6, Gabby Gabreski led the first 56th Fighter Group mission. Zemke, being a man who knew too much about Overlord, like all the group commanders, was forbidden from flying missions early in the day. "I had to sit around and watch our squadrons come and go," he recalled. "It was evening before I was off the hook and could fly on operations."

At dawn, as 156,000 Allied troops crossed the beaches of Normandy against heavy German ground fire, there were more than 12,000 warplanes in the skies above them. Of these, according to General Werner Junck, the Luftwaffe's fighter commander in Normandy, only 160 were German. A year earlier, when Operation Pointblank was in its infancy— or even half a year earlier, when Big Week had not yet transpired—it would have been a very different story. Of those sorties that day, 1,728 were by Eighth Air Force bombers against coastal targets between Le Havre and Cherbourg, and 1,880 were by VIII Fighter Command fighters.

"We expected the whole of the Luftwaffe in the west to be thrown into the battle but as the day wore on it was clear that was not to be," Hub Zemke recalled. "As Eisenhower had prophesied, the planes over the invasion beaches were ours."

"I was up before dawn that momentous day and decided to fly a P-38 over the beaches," Jimmy Doolittle recalled. "Just as we hoped, enemy interception was almost nil, and I saw none. What few enemy aircraft did appear were promptly engaged and the skies were swept clear. . . . I came in under the clouds over the English Channel and turned toward the invasion beaches. The scene below was the most impressive and unforgettable I could have possibly imagined."

Hub Zemke took off at 4:45 p.m. that afternoon for the 56th Fighter Group's seventh and last mission of D-Day. After attacking the Luftwaffe airstrip at Fanville, the P-47s "swept east" toward Dreux and joined P-51s of the 352nd Fighter Group strafing a parked ammunition convoy, but were "interrupted by some Fw 190s."

"I saw a single Fw 190 trying to sneak up on one of our lower elements," Zemke later wrote. "He saw me coming, changed his mind and fled to the west. Because of my superior altitude I rapidly overtook him in the dive. The Focke-Wulf pilot then broke right to engage me and as I came in behind him he tightened his turn, suddenly losing control and spinning down straight into the ground. I never fired a shot."

Just as the land battle of Normandy had barely begun when the sun set on June 6, so had the work of the airmen who flew the 12,000 sorties that day—this maximum effort was only the beginning.

On June 7, one of the more remarkable fighter sorties of the day was flown by Hub Zemke himself. After a dive-bombing attack over Normandy, he had flown south, tangled with some German fighters, and gotten separated from his flight. At that time, he spotted six aircraft and he began to shadow them. Gradually four of the six pulled far ahead of the other two, and Zemke was about to break off his pursuit when the two turned sharply to the southeast. By cutting a corner, he could now pull closer, and when he did, he saw that the two were members of his own group who were shadowing four Fw 190s.

He ordered the two to join him in intercepting the Germans, but the message was garbled and misunderstood, and the Americans broke off the pursuit and vanished into the clouds. Zemke continued to follow the four Germans, who made a turn that allowed Zemke to close in. With a 7,000-foot altitude advantage, he decided to make a quick pass to take out one of the Germans, then dash for home.

He opened fire on the last plane in the flight and watched it burst into flames and go down. Amazingly, none of the remaining three seemed to notice. As he closed on the aircraft whose wingman he had just downed, the pilot rocked his wings. Apparently the flight was maintaining radio silence, and this pilot thought Zemke's P-47 was his wingman! Zemke just rocked his wings back, then opened fire. As this Focke-Wulf went down, Zemke could see that he was running out of ammunition, so he dove on the last two to gain speed before breaking away. They broke first and ran as fast as they could.

Rosie Rosenthal, like Zemke, also flew at the end of the day on June 6, as the command pilot leading the last of three missions flown by the 100th Bomb Group. "As we flew over the channel, we saw thousands of ships in an armada down there; it was so thrilling," he recalled. "You weren't supposed to talk on the intercom unless it was very important, but one of the crew started to pray and we all joined in."

Overlord was a success, a bloody success but a success nonetheless. The role of airpower in general, and of the Eighth Air Force specifically, cannot be overstated. Jimmy Doolittle spoke for all Allied airman when he reflected upon his own firsthand observation of the beachhead and wrote that "what was most personally satisfying was that the hundreds of ships and barges could unload thousands of troops without worrying about enemy aircraft. We had achieved what we had planned and hoped for: complete air supremacy over the beaches."

CHAPTER 35

SUPERFORTRESS

On March 3, 1944, less than two weeks after the conclusion of Big Week, 37-year-old Curtis LeMay became the youngest major general in the USAAF. There was a rumor of an impending transfer back to the States, and a rumor that this was associated with a supersecret airplane.

The Boeing B-29 Superfortress, unproven and not yet flown in combat, would later fulfill its promise as the ultimate strategic bomber of World War II, but in early 1944 it was a trouble-plagued program and an almost unfathomably complex airplane that Hap Arnold and Boeing's Phil Johnson had rammed through its development process almost by force of will. The stress of the program resulted in one of Arnold's four wartime heart attacks, while Johnson later dropped dead of a stroke on the Superfortress factory floor.

As the name suggests, the Superfortress was conceived by Boeing and Arnold as a "supersized" Flying Fortress, half again as large, with twice the gross weight and bomb capacity. It had an operational range in excess of 3,000 miles and was pressurized for routine operations in the stratosphere. While the USAAF called its B-17s and B-24s "heavy" bombers, the B-29 was officially designated as a *"very* heavy" bomber. It first flew in September 1942, but went through a long and troublesome teething period, related especially to the new Wright R-3350, a powerful but temperamental engine that would be the Achilles' heel of the Superfortress program.

The Superfortress would certainly have been effective in the hands of the Eighth Air Force, but it arrived on the scene after the flow of heavy bombers to the Eighth had become a torrent. Arnold intended to save his very heavy bomber for Operation Matterhorn, the strategic air campaign against Japan. This had been heretofore impossible because the USAAF had no bases close enough to Japan for the heavy bombers. The B-29 had the range to reach Japan from bases in China. The question of *when* Matterhorn could begin was one of Arnold's most nagging vexations. At the Sextant Conference, he had promised Roosevelt that Matterhorn would begin in June 1944, though the Superfortress was still far from ready.

Two months earlier, to manage his new weapon, Arnold created a new air force, the Twentieth. To it were assigned the XX and XXI Bomber Commands. Noting the problems that Tooey Spaatz had experienced with Eisenhower's exercising operational control over the Eighth Air Force in Europe, Arnold took the unprecedented step of personally assuming command of the Twentieth Air Force. By placing it directly under himself at the Joint Chiefs of Staff, he would keep it *and* its strategic mission outside of any competing theater chains of command.

In a later conversation with Tooey Spaatz and Ira Eaker that Arnold cites in his memoirs, he explained: "Both General MacArthur and Admiral Nimitz wanted the Twentieth Air Force, but it could not be under either one because we were operating beyond the battle area controlled by either of them—far beyond."

As operational commander for the XX Bomber Command, Arnold picked Major General Kenneth B. "K.B." Wolfe, his Materiel Command troubleshooter who had babysat the Superfortress through its difficult technical development. To lead the XXI Bomber Command, Arnold chose Haywood Hansell, the longtime veteran of the Air Staff and AWPD, who had served briefly as commander of the Eighth Air Force's 1st Bomb Wing and who had been a key preliminary planner of Superfortress operations. The idea was that Wolfe would operate from China, and Hansell's command would be based on Guam and the Mariana islands of Saipan and Tinian—when they were eventually taken from the Japanese. These would provide far better basing for the Superfortresses than China, being about 1,500 miles from Tokyo and easily supplied by large cargo ships.

Wolfe's bombers began reaching India en route to the intended bases near Chengdu, China, in early April, but engine problems threatened to ground most of them and the bases in China weren't ready. Finally, on June 5, the XX Bomber Command flew its first mission, though not against Japan. Flying from India, Wolfe's bombers hit Bangkok. During World War II, Thailand allied itself with Japan, and it was an important link in the Japanese supply line into Burma. Ten days later, Superfortresses flying from China bombed Yawata. It was the first American air attack on the Japanese home islands since Doolittle's more than two years before.

Though Wolfe had been a logical choice for the XX Bomber Command because he knew the airplane, Arnold quickly grew impatient for faster results. As he had nagged and finally replaced Eaker, he nagged Wolfe and eventually sent for Curtis LeMay, who had the tough, no-nonsense reputation that Superfortress operations demanded.

As LeMay said in 1986, "I sure got the message about what [Arnold] expected to do with the B-29s in the Far East. For all the developmental effort that had already gone into the B-29 program, the aircraft had only been in combat for a month and the USAAF was still getting only minimal results. That wasn't enough for Arnold. He made it clear that we finally had a chance to prove something with strategic airpower, but in order to do this, I would have to go to India and see to it that the B-29 lived up to its potential."

Arriving home in July, LeMay was reunited with his wife and daughter for the first time since Christmas, then bundled them off to Nebraska, where he entered into a crash course to learn how to fly a B-29 and how it should be maintained. A month later, he said good-bye to Helen and Janie for the last time until after the war, and headed for India.

Training his crews on tactics that had worked for the Eighth Air Force in England, LeMay gradually began getting the XX Bomber Command into shape and started running missions against Japan. He found, however, that the logistical challenges dwarfed those faced by the Eighth. In England, there was a ready source of fuel and other supplies and a modern infrastructure to deliver them. In China, LeMay found himself more than 1,200 miles from his sources of supply, with no means by land or water to bring in what was needed. The only way that any bases in China could be supplied was by aircraft flying across the notorious "Hump," the Himalayas.

"We were flying seven trips over the Himalayas with every B-29, off-loading as much gas as we could to still get back to India," he explained. "On the eighth trip across the Hump to Chengdu, we would finally take a load of bombs and fly a bombing mission against the Japanese. Because it took so many flights to get our fuel and bombs to China, we could fly only one mission a week against the Japanese."

Meanwhile, during August 1944, as LeMay was beginning his XX Bomber Command campaign, the US Marine Corps was wrapping up the bloody battles that captured Guam and the Marianas from the Japanese. At last having the basing sites for which he had been waiting, Arnold sent Hansell, who arrived on October 12. Robert Morgan, formerly of the great *Memphis Belle*, was piloting the second Superfortress to land on Saipan, coming in that afternoon, hot on the heels of Possum Hansell.

Morgan had seen his first B-29 in March 1943 courtesy of K. B. Wolfe. The *Memphis Belle* had made one of its publicity tour stops at Wichita, where Boeing was still building Flying Fortresses along with the still-secret Superfortress. After the speeches, Wolfe pulled Morgan aside and took him into the hangar, where Morgan first beheld the airplane, at which he "couldn't stop gaping."

After a cockpit tour, he told Wolfe, "I'd like to get into this program."

Wolfe promised to "put him in touch with the right people" after the *Memphis Belle* tour wrapped up. He did, and in October 1943, Morgan took the controls of a Superfortress for the first time. By January 1944, Bob Morgan was newly married to Dotty Johnson and living in Pratt, Kansas, undergoing intensive flight training in B-29s. As he recalled in his memoirs, "The Superfortress may have been a gorgeous specimen of airplane to admire from the outside, and her updated gadgetry could dazzle the mind, but she was not much fun to fly. I guess no combat plane ever built could quite match the B-17 in that department. . . . Flying the Superfort was work, pure and simple."

Given his past combat experience, Morgan was named commander of the 869th Bomb Squadron of the 497th Bomb Group within the 73rd Bomb Wing. The size of the numerals relative to those of Eighth Air Force units indicated how large the USAAF was becoming. Originally earmarked for the XX Bomber Command, the 73rd, commanded by Brigadier General Emmett "Rosie" O'Donnell, was reassigned to spearhead the XXI Bomber Command.

As his overseas deployment approached, Morgan was assigned the Wichita-built B-29 with tail number 42-24592. Had circumstances been different, she might have been given the name *Memphis Belle II*, but Margaret Polk of Memphis was no longer part of Morgan's orbit and 42-24592 became *Dauntless Dotty*. He had hoped to reassemble most of the *Memphis Belle* crew to fly with him aboard *Dotty*, but ultimately had to settle for only bombardier Vince Evans. Johnny Quinlan volunteered to fly as Morgan's tail gunner again, but wound up in a different Superfortress in a different unit.

Saying good-bye to his pregnant wife, Morgan headed west as part of the first wave of Superfortresses, arriving in the Pacific before the Quonset huts had been built to house the crews.

Over the course of the first month, more and more bombers arrived, but no missions were flown against Japan, a fact that was not lost on Hap Arnold, who now badgered Hansell as he had Eaker, Spaatz, Wolfe, and any of his commanders who was not taking the war to the enemy.

"We simply were not ready," Morgan wrote. "Our pilots were still struggling to master the demands of controlling a B-29 in the best of circumstances, and to avert the many mechanical glitches that could, and did, bring those great, fragile birds spiraling into the ocean. On top of that, our fliers had run into an added headache—the swirling demon-winds that seemed to guard the home islands like a mythic beast. It was these winds, in fact, that introduced Allied pilots and thus the rest of the world to the concept of the jet stream."

Morgan added that "the unhappy carrier of this bad news was the newly arrived General Possum Hansell. Possum was a good young professional officer who lacked a certain edge of fire-breathing aggression, which would soon cost him dearly."

The first half dozen XXI Bomber Command missions, flown between October 28 and December 11, were not against Japan but against the then-obscure islands of Natsushima (aka Dublon) and Iwo Jima that lay between the Marianas and Japan. Iwo Jima, whose name was not yet etched in the historical memory, served as a base for Japanese aircraft attacking B-29s at their own bases and en route to Japan.

On the eve of their first mission to Japan, Rosie O'Donnell told Bob Morgan that he would lead the strike and that O'Donnell would fly the mission—in *Dauntless Dotty*'s right seat. He told Morgan that, since he had been through 25 missions over Europe, he would probably get through one more.

At dawn on November 24, the Superfortresses lined up and took off from Saipan's Isely Field, then climbed to 32,000 feet with Morgan leading the first USAAF mission against Tokyo since Jimmy Doolittle's mission 31 months earlier. The targets were industrial enclaves across the city. Of 111 bombers that were launched, only 88 reached Japan without mechanical problems, illustrating the temperamental nature of the Superfortress. Two were lost over Tokyo, but only one of them was lost to enemy action.

The Eighth Air Force was then pounding Germany's industrial plant into desolation, but the job had only just begun in Japan.

Over the next several days, Morgan returned to Tokyo twice, learned that he had become the father of a daughter, and was promoted. In a scene worthy of Hollywood, he received his promotion to lieutenant colonel on the flight line as he climbed aboard *Dauntless Dotty* for the December 6 mission.

For Hansell, it was not a happy time. He found himself having to grapple with mechanical problems, largely inexperienced crews, poor weather, and a boss who seemed not to understand him. By the end of the year, Arnold had made up his mind to replace Hansell with LeMay.

"When I had gone into China, it was with the basic understanding that the XX Bomber Command would get out of there as soon as the better bases in the Marianas became operable and capable of supporting large numbers of B-29s," LeMay told this author. "China had proved to be a horrible, almost impossible, logistical situation."

In fact, Arnold moved LeMay but *not* the XX Bomber Command. After abandoning Chengdu, the command would continue flying missions against Southeast Asia from India for several months while the bulk of the new Superfortresses flowed into the Marianas.

The news of Hansell's dismissal reached the field commanders on January 7, 1945. LeMay flew to Guam for a meeting with Hansell and General Lauris Norstad, Arnold's chief of staff, who arrived from Washington bearing their boss's plans for a change of command.

As Hansell observed in *The Strategic Air War Against Japan*, and as he told this author in conversations many years later, "I think the major factor in the decision to move General LeMay to the Marianas had to do with General Arnold's dissatisfaction with my rate of operations. I wasn't satisfied with it either. I knew it would improve over time, but he was very impatient. He was also aware that if the XX Bomber Command were moved to Saipan, there would then be two commanders—General LeMay and myself—when we only needed one. General Arnold had asked me to stay on as vice-commander to General LeMay, but I didn't think that was a good idea. It wasn't that I didn't have confidence in General LeMay—in fact, I had every confidence in him. I simply felt that he didn't need a second in command, especially one who was in effect being re-lieved from first in command. It is a difficult thing and probably a bad idea to take the commander of an outfit and keep him on in a subordinate position, so I asked Arnold that I be relieved, and I was."

As Bob Morgan observed, Hansell's lack of "fire-breathing aggres-sion" had cost him dearly.

Of LeMay, who had been a larger-than-life figure when Morgan was in England with the Eighth, Morgan noted that "he was just what we needed—a scholar-warrior, a thinker as well as a man of action, a canny and aggressive commander who would beat the Japanese by the force of his will, if nothing else. Suddenly the blood was back in my veins."

CHAPTER 36

LIFE AFTER THE EIGHTH

n the minds of Allied leaders, in the eyes of the contemporary media, and in the hindsight of historical memory, Operation Overlord was the central focus, and the biggest single event, of World War II in Europe during 1944.

The Mediterranean Theater, and the bloody battles taking place there were greatly overshadowed by the events surrounding Overlord. A case in point was the liberation of Rome, the first Axis capital occupied by the Allies, which came just 24 hours before Overlord. The event was eclipsed both in the headlines on the home front and within the Allied strategic perspective on the war.

Since he had arrived in the Mediterranean Theater in January, Ira Eaker's new life found his own strategic perspective intertwined with ground actions. There was the invasion of Anzio, which was intended to outflank the German lines. This operation had gone poorly for the Allies, who came close to losing their beachhead to counterattacks. It took them more than four months to push 40 miles from Anzio to the gates of Rome. MAAF had played a vital—indeed, pivotal—role in these actions, while the heavy-bomber bomb capacity of the Fifteenth proved crucial in saving the Anzio beachhead.

Less dramatic, but no less bloody, was the painfully slow northward slog through the Italian boot against the German Gustav Line defenses, with the Americans west of the Apennine Mountains and the British to the east, which had begun in September 1943. A major roadblock to the Allied advance up the narrow transportation routes through the Italian boot had turned out to be the crossing of the Rapido River. It lay 1,300 feet beneath a mountainous ridge called Monte Cassino, which was capped by a sixth-century Benedictine abbey of the same name—founded by Saint Benedict himself—that the Germans were thought to be using to house artillery spotters. After suffering grievous losses to German guns—including a horrible mauling of the 36th Infantry Division in January—in failed attempts to cross the river and break through the Gustav Line, the Allies were faced with a difficult decision.

In February, as the Allies were stalled and threatened at Anzio and on the Rapido, Field Marshal Harold Alexander gave the order to destroy the abbey under the widely shared assumption that it was a German stronghold. On February 14, Ira Eaker said to Jake Devers, head of the US Army's Mediterranean Theater command, "Let's go have a look."

Flying in an L-5 light aircraft, they passed within a few hundred feet of the ancient mountaintop monastery.

As reported by David Hapgood and David Richardson in *Monte Cassino*, Eaker recalled: "We clearly identified German soldiers and their radio masts. . . . I could have dropped my binoculars into machine-gun nests less than 50 feet from the walls."

James Parton, who was with Eaker at the time, wrote in his biography of his boss, "Flying over the battlefield was just the sort of action Eaker loved. But he had no enthusiasm for bombing the abbey, sharing the views of Clark and Alexander that the ruins would make an even stronger obstacle and that any observation could be done equally well from nearby. But he recognized that this was another occasion when air support of ground action took priority over strategic objectives. He decided to do the job thoroughly."

On the following day, on Alexander's orders, waves of USAAF aircraft dropped 576 tons of bombs, nearly obliterating the building and killing roughly 250 civilian refugees. The monks survived in their cellars far below the main building, and the abbey's great trove of precious artwork had been evacuated to Rome several weeks earlier.

In later years, it was determined that—contrary to what Eaker and Devers *thought* they had seen—few if any German troops had occupied the abbey before the bombing. However, as predicted, they did occupy the ruins afterward. So well entrenched were the defenders that it took another three months for Allied ground forces to finally capture the mountain.

Since the war, this event has been controversial because of the destruction of the abbey, though at the time, Eaker focused on the failure of ground forces to exploit what the use of airpower had given them. In an April 4 memo to Hap Arnold, he wrote: "I feel the Air Forces opened the door to Cassino, but the Ground Forces did not enter. . . . [A] Ground Commander who gets the same percentage of casualties that we in the Air Forces take as a matter of course might be called a butcher."

While the principal mission of MAAF throughout 1944 was the interdiction of German supply lines in Italy, Eaker also used his control over the Fifteenth Air Force to mount a strategic campaign penetrating deeper into southern Europe, including missions to Austria, Czechoslovakia, and Silesia—as well as reaching into distant eastern Europe.

By June, as all eyes were about to turn to Overlord, and with Cassino and Anzio behind him, Ira Eaker turned to one of the more unusual projects of his wartime career. It was this endeavor that found him, on Overlord's D-Day, in neither England nor Italy. He was in the Soviet Union.

Spaatz had picked him to serve as the point man for a strategic initiative called Operation Frantic. It was only a footnote to the history of USSTAF operations, but an illustrative moment in Soviet-American relations as they would evolve in the last year of the war and in the postwar world.

Frantic developed from one of those strategic ideas that look good on paper—in this case, a map of the European Theater. Having a strategic bombing mission land at a base other than its starting point was not new. For Doolittle's Tokyo mission ended in China, just as LeMay's Regensburg mission ended in North Africa. Under Frantic it was imagined that USSTAF bombers flying from either England or Italy could hit targets deeper inside the Reich if they continued on to the Soviet Union at the end of the mission to refuel and rearm.

The idea of a "shuttle-bombing" program was raised by American diplomats in 1943, and in November of that year, Franklin Roosevelt raised the issue personally with Josef Stalin. The Soviets, driven by a distrust of having American combat forces within their territory, agreed in principle, but dragged their feet before finally making bases near Poltava in eastern Ukraine available to the USAAF.

Working with Averell Harriman, the American ambassador to Moscow, Spaatz and Eaker arranged for the initial deployment of B-17s from the 5th Bomb Wing of the Fifteenth Air Force. The long-term plan—or at least the hope—was for full-scale USSTAF air bases to be constructed in the Soviet Union and for operations from these to become routine. The first mission was scheduled for June 2, four days before Overlord. Originally, a June 12 date had been considered, but SHAEF planners thought that news of the mission might distract the Germans from the impending cross-Channel invasion.

As on the first B-17 mission over Europe nearly two years earlier, Ira Eaker considered this mission so important that he decided to accompany it. Parton, who was at Eaker's side during the project, wrote: "It was an assignment he relished immensely, recalling his happy days as a group commander and giving him the chance again to take direct charge of an air operation and lead it into action."

The targets for 130 Flying Fortresses, escorted by 70 Mustangs, included the rail yard at Debrecen, Hungary, and adjacent sites. Spaatz would have preferred targets deeper inside German-occupied eastern Europe, but the suspicious Soviets did not want to have the bombers interfering with their planned ground offensives. No Luftwaffe fighters were encountered, and there was only light, sporadic flak. Only one aircraft was lost, and that was apparently because of mechanical failure.

The first USAAF strike force to reach Soviet soil crossed the Dnieper River in light drizzle and touched down in the early afternoon. Eaker was greeted by Harriman and a man whom James Parton later identified as Colonel General Dimitri Davidovich Grendal of the intelligence directorate of the Soviet air force. Parton observed that Grendal had been sent because of his senior rank to receive Eaker, whose three stars made him the highest-ranking American officer in the Soviet Union—*and* there was also an obvious intelligence component to his having a close look at the American aircraft.

After barely an hour on the ground, Eaker and Parton, along with Grendal, Harriman, and their entourages, climbed aboard a Soviet aircraft for a two-hour flight to Moscow. Having grabbed a quick nap, Eaker and Parton were hustled off to the Kremlin for a midnight-to-dawn meeting with foreign minister Vyacheslav Molotov and other Soviet officials.

After catching another nap, Eaker dashed back to Poltava to preside over the launch of a 5th Bomb Wing mission to Mielec in Poland, but it was scrubbed because of overcast. Plans were made to strike the air base at the Danube River port of Galați, though this mission was postponed until June 6. As he was waiting for the mission's return to Poltava, Eaker received news of the success of Operation Overlord.

Spending the next several days among his airmen at Poltava, Eaker had the opportunity to join them in a volleyball game proposed by Soviet ground crews working at the base. Parton reports that "no one could imagine a Russian general doing something like that."

Despite the primitive conditions at Poltava—typical of Soviet bases, but below American standards—Eaker was initially optimistic that Operation Frantic could be an important part of future USSTAF operations. However, German awareness of Frantic quickly became problematic.

On the night of June 21, after the arrival in Poltava of the first Eighth Air Force contingent from England, the Luftwaffe did what it had not previously been able to do—assault a large contingent of the Eighth's bombers on the ground. In the strike, 47 out of the 73 Flying Fortresses at Poltava were put out of commission, and a substantial quantity of stored fuel was destroyed. Ineffective Soviet antiaircraft fire claimed none of the nocturnal attackers.

The surviving bombers flew on to Italy on June 26, striking the oil refinery and rail yard at Drohobycz, Poland, en route. Eaker wrote to Arnold the same day, telling him, "We must prepare to defend our Russian bases or abandon the project. . . . We all want to destroy the German Air Force—where better then than in Russia where the German has indicated his willingness to fight?"

By now, though, a cloud of pessimism had quickly descended over the project at USSTAF, where doubts were being expressed as to whether Frantic was worth the trouble after all. David Mets, Spaatz's biographer, wrote that by August, Spaatz "had become somewhat disillusioned while still entertaining hopes that he could use the bases there for reconnaissance missions and ground electronic bombing aids, if not as staging sites for bombers and fighters."

Only five additional complete round-trip shuttle missions were completed, with the last one taking place in September. The turning point came when the United States wanted to use the bases to support efforts to deliver supplies to the Polish freedom fighters during the Warsaw Uprising. The Soviet Union opposed this because the uprising was supported by the Polish government in exile, then residing in London, and the Soviets did not wish that government to return to power after the war.

From August forward, the Soviets did everything possible to discourage Operation Frantic. Indeed, Molotov even informed Harriman that the bases had been merely "on loan for the summer."

Even before Frantic afforded him the brief window of opportunity for strikes into eastern Europe, Eaker resumed attacks on Ploesti, beginning with a 230-plane raid on April 5. Using the bases in Italy, which were much closer to Romania than those in Africa used in 1943, the Fifteenth was able to more thoroughly and decisively damage and destroy the refineries.

Within a few months, though, the situation within Romania changed considerably. In August, with the Soviet armies hurtling toward Romania's borders, pro-Nazi strongman Ion Antonescu, who had ruled since 1940, was ousted, and King Michael I ordered Romanian troops to stop firing at Soviet troops.

Ira Eaker, meanwhile, was ahead of the curve. On August 19, he and Nate Twining flew to Bucharest with an armada of Flying Fortresses—not to bomb the Romanian capital but to *land* there. After contacts with officers of the Forţele Aeriene Române, the Romanian air force, who had traveled to visit him in Italy, Eaker flew into the former hostile power to evacuate American airmen who were being released from POW camps. While there, four days ahead of Antonescu's ouster, the Americans took possession of extensive Romanian files documenting the actual results of the missions against Ploesti. Had the Soviets reached Bucharest ahead of Eaker, the Americans might never have gotten their hands on this information.

Eaker, now less optimistic than in Frantic's early days, had developed a new, cautious approach to America's Soviet allies. In this approach, he was right. When they took over a few weeks later, the Soviets showed a complete lack of willingness to share with their American allies any intelligence they gathered in Romania.

CHAPTER 37

★

RIDING THE MOMENTUM

I n the summer of 1944, after early June's dual successes at opposite sides of Europe, Overlord and the liberation of Rome, it was a natural assumption that USSTAF's two strategic air forces should be allowed to return to the strategic mission. Though the direct control over the Eighth by SHAEF, which Eisenhower had insisted upon in April, would continue until September, Tooey Spaatz issued an order on June 8, only two days after the invasion, for Jimmy Doolittle at the Eighth Air Force and Nate Twining at the Fifteenth to prepare for the campaign against the German petroleum industry.

Though he gave Spaatz a great deal of leeway in mission planning, Eisenhower showed less willingness to release his "temporary" hold on the Eighth than Spaatz had anticipated. Eisenhower was worried. The Germans had successfully contained the Allies within the Normandy beachhead for six weeks. This was deeply concerning to SHAEF, leading Eisenhower to integrate Eighth Air Force airpower into Operation Cobra, the breakout plan.

On July 25, to support the Allied ground offensive, Spaatz dispatched 1,581 heavy bombers, supported by 483 fighters and Ninth Air Force medium bombers, to attack German positions in the vicinity of Saint-Lô. Within this massive maximum effort, there was a dreadful error that tarnished the reputation of precision bombing and cost 102 American lives: 35 bombers mistakenly dropped their ordnance behind friendly lines. Among those killed was Lieutenant General Lesley McNair, commander of the US Army Ground Forces, the land equivalent of the USAAF.

Despite the Saint-Lô disaster, Eisenhower was unwilling to back away from using heavy bombers as artillery, nor to relinquish SHAEF control over the Eighth—at least not yet. Lewis Brereton, the commander of the Ninth Air Force, wrote in his diary for June 27: "In a talk with General Spaatz and myself, General Eisenhower stated that he was pleased with the air attack at Saint-Lô and that he considered heavy bombers an indispensable weapon to keep our army moving when they bogged down. General Eisenhower's idea is sound, but the use of heavies in close support is in direct contradiction to what General Spaatz, Doolittle, Eaker [on a visit to France from Italy] and I feel is the proper employment of heavy bombardment. General Spaatz expressed this by pointing out that if the heavies were diverted too long from their strategic program, it would allow targets inside Germany to be rehabilitated."

Another issue that diverted the Eighth Air Force during and after the six-week post-Overlord stalemate was the surprising deployment by the Germans of their V-1 cruise missiles. First launched on June 13, these fast-moving and hard-to-stop weapons created a climate of fear in England by bringing London under continuous air attack for the first time since the Blitz had waned several years earlier. On June 16, Hap Arnold, who was on an inspection tour to England, awoke to one of the "buzz bombs" striking a village five miles from where he was staying. Under Operation Crossbow, the Eighth Air Force devoted a sizable number of sorties to attacking the launch sites in northern France, continuing the strategy until October, when the sites were finally captured by advancing ground forces.

By August, the Allies had achieved unchallenged air superiority over France. Allied armies on the ground were on the offensive and appeared unstoppable. In northern France they were moving faster and liberating more territory more quickly than expected. Operation Dragoon (originally Anvil), the invasion of southern France on August 15, commanded by Jake Devers and staging out of Italy, went far more smoothly than Overlord, and Allied armies streamed north against minimal German opposition.

As had been the case with Doolittle on the morning of Overlord, Ira Eaker could not resist the temptation to have a firsthand look at the Dragoon beachhead east of Marseilles.

"On the day of the invasion I flew a Mustang P-51 single-seater fighter for an hour over the invasion coast," he wrote to his father on August 27. "It was a great sight to see hundreds of ships, nearly a thousand of them, lined up off shore and many hundreds of small boats loaded with troops plowing relentlessly toward the shore. It was also a good sight to see the broadsides fired from the battleships and to see the bombs raining down from our heavy bombers."

He proudly reported that he had dined with Winston Churchill on the eve of Dragoon, and that once again the prime minister had recalled their conversation at Casablanca a year and a half before.

"Mr. Churchill was in rare form and obviously pleased with the way the invasions were going," Eaker wrote. "He referred to our meeting at Casablanca and said that the daylight bombing, about which there was considerable doubt in his mind at that time, had more than matched his fondest expectations."

Though such missions had been interrupted by Eisenhower's having sidetracked USSTAF, the Supreme Commander was finally about to relinquish SHAEF direct control so that Spaatz and USSTAF could move back to the strategic mission. This action was certainly hastened by the quick maturing of the tactical air forces. Indeed, the ground force commanders and the tactical air commanders—including Hoyt Vandenberg, previously the deputy AEAF commander who took command of the Ninth Air Force in August—were developing a closer, more seamless operational relationship, which would prevail through the end of the war.

Meanwhile, both Eisenhower and Spaatz formally moved their respective headquarters from metropolitan London to metropolitan Paris. After briefly relocating to Normandy on September 1, SHEAF formally set up shop in the Trianon Palace Hotel in Versailles on September 20. Six days later, a month after the liberation of the City of Light, Spaatz moved his USSTAF headquarters from Bushy Park to the prosperous suburb of Saint-Germain-en-Laye, about eight miles from Eisenhower and a dozen miles west of the center of Paris. However, Spaatz spent much of his time at Eisenhower's headquarters, both at Versailles and at Reims, after Eisenhower moved SHAEF to that city in February 1945.

Despite their posh addresses, the new quarters occupied by Eisenhower and Spaatz were more modest than the 1,200-room Reggia di Caserta near Naples, which Eaker shared with Harold Alexander and the rest of the Mediterranean Theater staff.

Another aspect of Eighth Air Force operations over France during the summer of 1944 involved dropping supplies to the French Resistance. On July 14, coincidentally Bastille Day, France's national day, Rosie Rosenthal was flying such a mission over the southern part of the country. It was routine for bombers that became separated from their own groups to join other groups for protection, but on this particular day Rosenthal's contingent was joined by a bomber from another group that was outbound on a strike mission. Because the 100th was on a different radio frequency, they could not alert their new companion of their mission, so the specter arose of this aircraft accompanying them to the drop zone and raining bombs onto the Resistance fighters.

Tom Jeffrey, commander of the 100th Bomb Group and the mission leader that day, then sent one of his bombers to circle the formation, come ahead of the bomber with the bombs, and release his parachutes. As Rosenthal recalls, everyone aboard his plane breathed a sigh of relief when the other plane's bomb bay doors slammed shut.

A month later, Rosenthal found himself *in* France.

On the morning of September 10, he was on the flight line, preparing to lead a mission to Nuremberg as command pilot with the 350th Bomb Squadron, when Colonel Jeffrey passed by. He noticed that Rosenthal was not wearing his uniform cap, and called him on this deviation from the dress code.

"Where's your hat?" Jeffrey asked.

"Somebody took it at the officers club last night," Rosenthal explained. "I don't have a hat."

"Here, Rosie, take *my* hat," his boss said. "It's a lucky hat."

The luck of the hat served Rosenthal on the flight to the target and through the bomb run, but the bomber was badly mauled by the Luftwaffe over Frankfurt on the way home, and two engines were knocked out. Another engine failed as they crossed into northern France, making it impossible to return to England, so Rosenthal decided to try for a crash landing. Fortunately, they were now over Allied territory. The bomber came down in a field near Reims, struck a tree, plowed into a canal embankment, and toppled over. Being up front, all four officers were seriously injured and knocked unconscious.

"The next thing I knew, I was in a hospital in Oxford, England," Rosenthal recalled. He had suffered a broken arm and multiple head-to-toe contusions, and was evacuated to the 91st General Hospital.

A few days later, he received a visit from his boss.

"Down the hallway came Jeffrey with three other people from the 100th Bomb Group, and I thought he was going to say 'Rosie, where's my hat?' Instead, he came over, greeted me, and handed me a gallon of ice cream. Our PX guy, Al Paul, was notorious for doing things. I think he swapped a jeep to the Navy for an ice cream machine. I became the hero of the hospital because I dispensed ice cream. Jeffrey never asked me about the hat."

By October, the Eighth Air Force was routinely launching strategic missions involving hundreds of bombers. Doolittle now had 2,100 heavy bombers at his disposal, while Arthur Harris's RAF Bomber Command had around 1,100. As the numbers of bombers steadily increased, bombing accuracy was also improving.

Thanks to the work of these bombers, many German industries, especially the one supplying synthetic petrochemicals, were on the verge of collapse. Attacks on transportation, which had isolated the Normandy battlefields, now moved into Germany itself. German industry, especially the aircraft industry, had survived and flourished after Big Week by its having been dispersed. However, it would not survive without the ability to move components and subassemblies by rail between dispersed factory locations.

In the Mediterranean, it was beginning to be the same story. The Fifteenth Air Force wielded around 1,200 heavy bombers and reported that the percentage of bombs falling within 1,000 feet of the target grew from 18 in April to 32 in June and 50 in August, compared to a progression of 29 to 40 to 45 percent for the Eighth.

There were few strategic targets left in Italy, and many of the targets in the east that had been considered under Operation Frantic half a year earlier were now in the hands of Soviet ground forces. Tactical units within Eaker's MAAF were still attacking German supply lines, but were spending more and more of their time running missions into Yugoslavia to drop supplies to the various partisan bands that were actively waging a guerrilla war against the German occupation.

Eaker established good relations with the partisans. He even received two cordial visits at Caserta, the first unannounced, from the infamous partisan leader Josip Broz Tito, the future strongman of Yugoslavia. On the second visit, Tito and his young mistress were treated to a production of the play *Our Town*. The playwright, Thornton Wilder, was a lieutenant colonel on the Mediterranean Theater planning staff.

CHAPTER 38

★

OUT OF THE FRYING PAN, INTO THE UNKNOWN

After Overlord, as the Allied air forces achieved air superiority over France and gradually chipped away at the Luftwaffe's air superiority over Germany itself, the 56th Fighter Group, Zemke's Wolf Pack, was undergoing big changes. Because most of the air combat was taking place beyond the range of its P-47s, the Wolf Pack had been eclipsed by the Mustang-equipped 4th Fighter Group as the highest-scoring group in the European Theater.

While Hub Zemke himself was ultimately credited with shooting down 15.25 Luftwaffe aircraft (including shared victories), the 56th was gradually losing its top-scoring aces. Bob Johnson, who became the first USAAF ace in the theater to match Eddie Rickenbacker's World War I score of 26, had been sent home to the States in June with 27. Bud Mahurin had been shot down over France after 19.75 kills, but had been rescued by the French Resistance and smuggled back to England. Because of his knowledge of the Resistance, he was forbidden to fly in combat over Europe, and went home in May.

Gabby Gabreski reached 28 to become the top-scoring USAAF ace in the theater, and also reached 300 hours of flight time, the mandatory end of his extended combat career. He wired his fiancée in Pennsylvania to go ahead with wedding plans, and on July 20 he was standing by for a transport to fly him home while P-47s were warming up for a bomber escort mission. He impulsively dropped his bag on the tarmac and decided to "fly just one more." During a strafing run over the Luftwaffe field at Bassenheim, his propeller clipped the runway and he was forced to crash-land. He survived, but was captured and spent the remainder of the war as a POW. The wedding finally took place on June 11, 1945.

Hub Zemke would also later have an impulsive moment that changed his life.

In August, Zemke's longtime executive officer, Dave Schilling, was offered command of the 479th Fighter Group at Wattisham, replacing Colonel Kyle Riddle, who had been shot down over France. Though the 479th was then only a month away from converting from P-38s to P-51s, the most prized fighter type in the USAAF, Schilling reacted angrily. He did not want to abandon his comrades in the 56th.

"Okay, Dave," Zemke said. "You take the 56th and I'll go to the 479th."

In his memoirs, Zemke used the word "incredulous" to describe Schilling's response, and so it was with the rest of the men in the group. Hub Zemke was volunteering to transfer *out* of Zemke's Wolf Pack!

On August 18, he led the mainly inexperienced 479th into combat over France on a bomber escort mission that concluded with a low-altitude strafing attack on a Luftwaffe base east of Nancy. For 25 minutes, the P-38s raked the field, meeting no resistance except small-arms fire. When Zemke finally took them home, the green pilots could claim 43 German planes destroyed and 28 damaged on the ground, most of them He 111 bombers, a score that buoyed the new group's spirits greatly.

In September, after two months of remarkable successes in the ground war in France, SHAEF optimistically launched Operation Market-Garden, an ambitious plan to use airborne troops to capture bridges across the Rhine River in the Netherlands. On September 17, the First Allied Airborne Army began landing a force of more than 34,000 glider and parachute troops in the largest airborne operation in history. However, initial successes turned sour, and within a week the operation was in trouble and the paratroopers were being pushed back.

On September 26, as the ground forces were pulling back, Zemke's 479th Fighter Group, now equipped with P-51s, was part of a force of 320 USAAF fighters providing air support. From 13,000 feet, Zemke spotted a flight of fighters far below, and led a dozen Mustangs in a 10,000-foot descent. Having identified the fighters as Luftwaffe Bf 109s, the Americans engaged, and soon the sky was a swirling mass of airplanes and tracers.

Zemke picked a Bf 109 from the middle of the pack, delivered a series of short machine-gun bursts—and watched the Messerschmitt roll over and the pilot bail out.

After hitting a second German fighter that escaped into a cloud, Zemke found a third flying into his sights. This pilot maneuvered to escape, was hit by a long stream of lead from American guns, and bailed out just before his Bf 109 hit the ground. It was one of 29 German fighters claimed by the 479th that day, a bit of consolation compared to the Allied disaster on the ground.

Zemke's last victory came on October 7, during a maximum effort against the German synthetic petroleum industry involving 1,422 Eighth Air Force bombers and 900 fighters. He chased a Bf 109 that was trying to escape, pushing the throttle to more than 500 miles per hour to overtake the German before he reached the clouds. He saw the Messerschmitt literally disintegrate, perhaps as much from aerodynamic stress as from American bullets.

By this time, Zemke's combat time had been pushed and extended to 300 hours, and he was ordered to stand down as a fighter pilot. He was kicked upstairs to "fly a desk" as the commander of the 65th Fighter Wing at Saffron Walden, an organization that would eventually contain ten fighter groups.

On the morning of October 30, Zemke was on the ramp at Wattisham, his bags packed for his relocation to Saffron Walden, watching the fighters revving for another maximum effort. As spontaneously as Gabreski had done three months earlier, Zemke grabbed his flight gear for "one last show" leading Group A with the 434th Fighter Squadron.

"The day didn't look too bad as we took off, only once we were heading out over the sea, clouds started to build up ahead," Zemke wrote in his memoirs. "By the time we had identified the wing of B-24s we were to escort, great stacks of cumulus rose three to four miles high from the ground. . . . I didn't like the look of those white billows but it was so high we had little choice other than to plunge through if we were not to lose the bombers. . . . As soon as my Mustang entered the mists it began to bounce like a cork."

The violent turbulence threw the Mustang into a spin, from which Zemke recovered, only to find himself plummeting straight down at an accelerating rate of speed. Suddenly the aircraft disintegrated around him and he was "suspended in a misty void," still strapped into his cockpit seat. He kicked free and yanked the D-ring to open his parachute.

As he recalled, "a feeling of blessed relief flooded through me; I didn't consciously think I had just cheated death. Floating down through the cloud came a fleeting thought of those bags packed and waiting at Wattisham and the desk job at [the 66th] Wing. I didn't intend it this way, but I'd fooled 'em!"

The last laugh was on Zemke, though. Flying a desk would have been preferable to what was to come.

He crashed into a swamp at the edge of some woods, smarting from injuries to his knee and arm. As sleet began to fall, he struggled to his feet and staggered into the tree line, where he built a fire to try to dry himself out and stay warm. The following day, limping down a country lane, he was spotted by some civilians, who called the authorities.

Zemke was taken to Auswertestelle West, the Luftwaffe facility at Oberursel, near Frankfurt, where captured Allied flyers were processed. There he was introduced to Hanns-Joachim Scharff, the Luftwaffe's infamous "master interrogator," to whom higher-ranking flyers and well-established aces were typically delivered.

Definitely of the "good cop" school of interrogation, Scharff was a successful prewar automobile salesman who was highly skilled at getting people to do as he wished without them knowing it. Fluent in English, he gained the confidence of his subjects through kindness and courtesy and managed to obtain critical intelligence in casual conversation.

In Zemke's case, Scharff had an extensive dossier on the 56th Fighter Group, complete with casual photos, and knew the details of Zemke's early life in Montana. He also mentioned that he was well aware that Zemke was conversant in German, which was something he had hoped to conceal from his captors.

"There was the satisfaction that the interrogation had been light; as an experienced group commander I had expected the third degree," Zemke recalled. "What really baffled me was just what, if anything, had Hanns Scharff and his cooler crew extracted from me of military value? He never did attempt to enquire about the tactics of the fighter groups or other combat techniques. Air strategy and the future plans of aerial engagement had been raised but soon dropped. . . . Even so, there was a nagging worry in my mind that something had been extracted; Scharff was too wily to permit me to slip through his fingers if he thought I could supply the answers he required."

After his wounds had received attention, Zemke was soon transferred to the Dulag Luft (Durchgangslager der Luftwaffe), the transit camp at Wetzlar for Allied airmen bound for stalags, or prison camps. As the weeks dragged by, Zemke remained at the Dulag, watching hundreds of men arrive and depart. Life at Wetzlar was dull and tedious for a *Kreisgefangener* (POW), the days punctuated only by brown-bread meals and speculation about what was going on in the outside world. The only excitement came in late November, when a few bombs dropped by the Eighth Air Force in a raid on the nearby Leica optical works landed near the camp.

On December 11, Zemke awoke to news that he was being transferred not to a stalag but back to Auswertestelle West. Accompanied by two guards, he was taken north in a third-class car of a regular Reichsbahn passenger train. It was standing room only aboard the train, but the guards pushed in and requisitioned seats for them all. Zemke found himself seated next to a ten-year-old girl who was traveling with her mother and younger sister.

"A certain amount of apprehension appeared on the face of my young companion when she saw *'Kreisgefangener'* stenciled on my clothes," he recalled. "In an effort to ease her discomfort I smiled and struck up a conversation. She was obviously astounded that I could speak German and wasn't a demon who would eat her. We talked about her school, that I had a little son back in America, and other such matters relative to a child's world. At first shy, she quickly gained confidence and proved highly entertaining. My guards observed this exchange with some amusement."

As the train chugged northward, the two chatted and the sun came out. No one was expecting what was about to happen: suddenly "the blissfulness of the moment erupted into carnage."

As Zemke wrote, "Splintered holes appeared in the wood panel opposite with a deafening whip-like crack. The little girl who had been beside me fell across my extended legs, the top of her head a bloody pulp. One of the soldiers opposite pitched forward, a bullet through his middle. People screamed and struggled to escape as, with a violent jolt, the train came to a halt."

It was with immense irony that Hub Zemke found himself on the receiving end of a strafing attack by USAAF P-47s who were out wreaking havoc as part of the war on German transportation dictated by SHAEF. The P-47s had red cowlings like those of his old 56th Fighter Group, but he insisted to himself that it was a coincidence—they *had to* be from another unit.

Zemke joined the tide of humanity that exploded from the car, running helter-skelter, and witnessed much of the attack from outside. His guards were nowhere to be seen, and he thought of escape, but the train was stopped in a narrow canyon surrounded by steep, rocky cliffs.

His eyes fell on the mother of the two girls, who was crouched beside the train screaming for someone to save her children. Zemke rushed up the embankment, dragged the mother to safety behind some rocks, then ran back into the train, where he grabbed the younger sister a few seconds before one of the fighters made another firing pass. When he handed the younger girl to the mother, she screamed for the other child, and Zemke had to tell her that the older sister had died in his lap.

Assisted by a lone German soldier, Zemke dashed back into the train several times to drag people to safety, but when it was over and the fighters had left, the civilians noticed that Zemke was a *Kreisgefangener* and were preparing to stone him to death when a Wehrmacht lieutenant intervened and took him away to a nearby house to wait for a Luftwaffe staff car.

As Zemke later reflected, "No sane pilot would choose to strafe civilians, but the facts were that in this conflict involving a nation's whole economy, the military and civil populations and installations were inseparably entwined. In this total war the women and children of Germany were as much in the front line as those of Britain, Russia and the many occupied countries."

Zemke and his captors reached Auswertestelle West by nightfall, having survived a car wreck—the spooked driver drove off the road when some P-38s passed overhead.

"You certainly had some unusual experiences yesterday," Hanns Scharff said when they met the following day. "You are extremely fortunate to be here."

"Why was I brought back here?" Zemke demanded.

"Your people in America wrote a nice article about you going down in *Time* magazine the other day. This has been picked up by the [senior officers] in Berlin and now they want to see you. They are the officers from the Oberkommando Wehrmacht [OKW, or German general staff]. You are to be taken to the Opel hunting lodge in the Taunus mountains to await their arrival."

Indeed, the December 4 issue had called him the "'fightingest' US pilot commander in Europe . . . the leading US ace operating in Europe." He was credited with an exaggerated 19.5 victories in the magazine, and reported to have been captured.

"Was this some joke or interrogation ploy?" Zemke thought. "What on earth would the OKW want from a mere combat colonel."

As for the latter, Scharff didn't say. As for the Opel hunting lodge, it was the genuine article, owned by the family of the founder of the carmaker, and used by the OKW. Zemke later remarked that the night before, he went to bed dirty and hungry on a straw mattress. That night he took a bath, had his clothes cleaned, dined on fine china, and slept on clean sheets in a real bed.

When the OKW men arrived the following day, Zemke found Scharff a "wily master of dialogue, even among his own countrymen."

They sat down to a wonderful dinner, accompanied by ample supplies of wine and seasoned with small talk. Only after dinner was Zemke asked his opinion of the progress of the war. He pointed out that the German armies were withdrawing on all fronts and that the strategic air offensive was only intensifying. The Germans countered with the talking point of the times, this being that secret wonder weapons would soon win the war for Germany. The Messerschmitt Me 262 jet fighter, which Zemke had encountered just one time, was only the tip of the iceberg.

When talk turned to the Soviets and the Eastern Front, they finally got around to their reason for so cordially entertaining the man whom they saw as America's greatest ace. They had a proposal. They wanted Zemke to *lead* a volunteer combat air force against the Soviets! They promised him that the job would not involve fighting the Anglo-American Allies, and that payment would be generous, and in *gold*.

His answer was simple. "Hell no!"

The OKW men appeared to take no offense, nor did they take no for an answer, continuing to negotiate with Zemke.

The following afternoon, after the last good meal that he would have for many months, Zemke was collected by a Luftwaffe lieutenant for transfer to a permanent prison camp. Traveling through the night, the two were waiting for a train in Hanover when sirens sent them into a *Luftschutzkeller* (air raid shelter) as more than 300 Eighth Air Force B-17s came overhead. By the sound and feel of the continuous thunder of concussions, Zemke quickly ascertained that the rail yard was the target. Once more, he was on the receiving end of the Eighth Air Force bombing campaign.

After the raid, they emerged from the shelter and walked for many miles through a light dusting of snow until they reached undamaged track and boarded a train. The next day, Hub Zemke walked into Stalag Luft I in Barth, near the Baltic Sea, 150 miles north of Berlin, which would be his home for the remainder of World War II.

CHAPTER 39

THE END SEEMED NEAR

G iven the speed of the Allied armies and the crumbling nature of German defenses within France, there was a pervasive optimism that the war would soon be over.

By the middle of December 1944, the 21st Army Group, commanded by Montgomery and comprising the British Second Army and the First Canadian Army, had pushed its way to Germany's border with the Netherlands. The 12th Army Group, commanded by General Omar Bradley and incorporating the US First, Third, and Ninth Armies, was lined up against the German border in Belgium, Luxembourg, and eastern France. Farther south, the 6th Army Group, commanded by General Jake Devers and comprising the US Seventh Army and the French First Army, was pushing toward the Franco-German border in Alsace and Lorraine.

The wishful thinking that the war might be over by Christmas faded with the onset of the heavier than normal winter snows, and was erased completely by a sudden and unexpected German offensive. On December 16, four German armies, composed of more than a dozen divisions and around 200,000 troops, sliced through American lines in the Ardennes highlands of southern Belgium. The Germans took advantage of this moment, knowing that Allied tactical airpower would be grounded by the weather. The offensive overran a huge part of the Allied rear, rendering an image on Allied maps that led to the ensuing struggle being called the "Battle of the Bulge."

"We got our big break on December 24," Jimmy Doolittle recalled. "There was poor visibility over England, but the forecast called for excellent weather over Germany. We dispatched more than 2,000 B-17s and B-24s with an escort of almost 1,000 fighters. Eleven airfields and 14 communications centers were hit with 5,000 tons of bombs. Most of those 3,000 planes returned, one way or another. For those who got back it was a curious Christmas Eve. While they were airborne, the weather over England had grown worse. At some of our bases the weather had grown so thick that they could not land at their home bases. They came down on any airfield they could find open, and wherever they landed the officers and men who belonged to those fields took the visiting crews in and shared their Christmas with them—cigarettes or chocolate or talk of home or whatever else they had."

Though the battle upset the Allied momentum, the German offensive was defeated, the "bulge" eliminated from the map, and the German armed forces on the Western Front, both air and ground, were fatally broken. Overhead, the Eighth Air Force resumed strategic operations. During the week that included New Year's Eve, Doolittle launched an average of more than 1,000 bombers every day.

"By the end of 1944 we had refined our Eighth Air Force operations, which represented more than two years of hard-won experience by Tooey, Ira, and me trying to knock out the German war industries and the Luftwaffe," Doolittle observed in his memoirs. "As we encountered less and less enemy opposition and launched missions with ever-greater intensity, the Eighth became a smooth team that worked together like the movement in a Swiss watch."

The positive spin placed on Eighth Air Force operations in early 1945 would be qualified by discussions of the mysterious German super-weapons to which Hub Zemke's hosts at the Opel lodge had alluded. Most of these never materialized, although the presence of the V-1 cruise missiles and the supersonic V-2 ballistic missiles during 1944 led to the belief that anything was *possible*. One wonder weapon that did present problems for the Eighth was the Messerschmitt Me 262. First encountered in the summer of 1944, it was finally deployed in substantial numbers in March 1945. Jagdgeschwader 7, the world's first all-jet fighter wing, shot down eight of Doolittle's bombers on March 3 and a dozen from a strike force on March 18. Jagdgeschwader 7 launched nearly 60 Me 262s on April 10, and claimed 19 bombers and eight fighters, but lost none of its own. The Messerschmitt jet was a remarkable weapon, but nearly every account of its service career contains phrasing analogous to "too few, too late."

"The speed differential between our fighters and bombers and these aircraft was striking," Doolittle recalled. "If they were produced in great numbers, there was no doubt in my mind that they would become a serious threat. . . . I told Hap [Arnold] that we were not awed by these new aircraft and would continue to try to decimate the German force, reduce production, delay the development of new equipment, and devise plans to successfully combat the new threat if and when it eventuated."

During March 1945, there were 17 days when Doolittle sent out a force of more than 1,200 heavy bombers, including twice when there were more than 1,400. The losses were negligible.

"By the beginning of April 1945, we were running out of targets," Doolittle wrote in his memoirs. "Victory was in the air as the armies of the Allies moved rapidly and pushed back the German defenders. As the official Air Force history notes: 'Most of Germany was not enemy territory any longer.' We still sent out bomber armadas with heavy escorts against old targets that seemed to be able to respond as part of the Nazis' last-ditch defenses, [but by] mid-April the German factories were not turning out war materiel; there were no more oil refineries; the submarine pens were no longer a menace to the Allied navies. Only tactical bombing remained. We were now ready to call a halt to the strategic air war."

The RAF was first to call the halt. Air Chief Marshal Peter Portal observed on April 7—seven weeks too late to save Dresden from the RAF—that "further destruction of German cities would magnify the problems of the occupying forces."

On April 16, Spaatz made it official. The USSTAF commander sent word to both Doolittle at the Eighth and Twining at the Fifteenth, noting that "the advances of our ground forces have brought to a close the strategic air war waged by the United States Strategic Air Forces and the Royal Air Force Bomber Command. . . . From now onward our Strategic Air Forces must operate with our Tactical Air Forces in close cooperation with our armies."

Having told them that the USSTAF mission was now over, he added a pat on the back and a firm directive, stating that "all units of the US Strategic Air Forces are commended for their part in winning the Strategic Air War and are enjoined to continue with undiminished effort and precision the final tactical phase of air action to secure the ultimate objective—complete defeat of Germany."

Hap Arnold's fourth wartime heart attack, which occurred on January 17, 1945—not long after he fired Hansell and sent in LeMay—was his worst. Reacting with denial, as he had on the occasions of the previous ones, he simply crawled into bed and hoped that he would, as he had on the occasions of the previous ones, eventually recover. Chief of Staff General George Marshall, Arnold's old friend and confidant, might have relieved the chief of the USAAF of duty after any of those three, but he had not and would not. On the occasion of the fourth, though, he finally did take action.

On March 19, Marshall specifically suggested that Arnold bring Ira Eaker back from overseas to serve as his chief of staff, replacing Lieutenant General Barney Giles, whom Arnold was planning to send to the Pacific. It was a credit to his reputation that Eaker was the man Marshall had in mind, but the idea would not sit well with Eaker.

Meanwhile, Arnold had already thought about naming an heir apparent, but he had *not* considered Eaker. On February 19, Arnold wrote to Marshall, telling him, "I think that the fellow who goes in and takes Giles' place should be the fellow who will take my place as Commanding General, Army Air Forces. It is a job that cannot be learned over night because of the thousand and one ramifications. However, if you ask who the fellow is who will take my place, I cannot answer at once. Offhand, it looks to me like one of two, both of whom are absolutely essential in the Air Forces in the jobs they are now doing overseas, so I suppose they are both out."

Those two were Spaatz and Vandenberg. James Parton, Spaatz's biographer, recalls that "there seems to be no clear evidence why Eaker was not considered. Perhaps [Arnold] still thought of his protégé as too junior or 'not tough enough.'"

At the time, Eaker still wore the three stars of a lieutenant general, while Spaatz had just received his fourth on March 11. (Three months earlier, Arnold had been one of seven officers—including Eisenhower and Marshall—advanced to five-star rank.)

In March, Marshall ordered Arnold to pick either Spaatz or Eaker and bring him back to Washington. It was not long before the rumor mill spun the word to the command posts of Europe. Eaker recalled in a postwar oral history interview that "being the junior and knowing that General Eisenhower would not want General Spaatz to leave, I could have guessed who was coming home."

The official orders reached Eaker on March 22.

Having been directed to relinquish the Eighth Air Force command that he had built from scratch on the eve of Big Week, Eaker was now being ordered to relinquish *another* combat command on the eve of the victory that he had worked for three years to achieve.

Deliberately insisting that there be no farewell ceremony, Eaker turned MAAF over to John Cannon of the Twelfth Air Force, and left for Washington by way of his old haunts in London. He dined with friends, lunched with Arthur Harris and his wife, and made a last official visit to Portal at RAF headquarters. Eaker reached Washington on March 29, meeting only in passing with Arnold, who was literally on his way out the door for a monthlong inspection tour of Europe.

The next morning, Eaker went to the Pentagon for a two-hour meeting with Marshall, who ordered him to make a round-the-world inspection tour. This would seem counterintuitive, given that the purpose of bringing Eaker to Washington was for him to *be* in Washington when Arnold was not, but Marshall said he wanted him to ascertain "how much of the European air forces we need to transfer to the Pacific to knock off the Japanese, and more particularly, how much can they support logistically."

The chief of staff also wanted Arnold's new understudy to experience the global scope of the war and the role of the USAAF within it.

James Parton wrote: "In sending Eaker on his 'mission,' Marshall was very deft. Several top staff officers, Giles or Kuter for example, could have made the same junket, but they lacked Eaker's immense experience both at building huge air forces, strategic and tactical, and then operating them against air opposition far stiffer than anything the Allies faced in the Pacific. Eaker was listened to with admiration verging on awe and provided respectfully with everything he sought by everyone to whom he spoke in the Pacific, Chinese and Indian theaters. Only Spaatz could have gotten to the heart of the strategic problem as surely. Marshall knew this."

On April 4, after spending Easter with his wife, Eaker headed for Hawaii and the endless Pacific beyond.

CHAPTER 40

$\bigstar$

ROSIE'S LAST MISSION

Rosie Rosenthal had been nearly through with his second tour when he was forced to crash-land in France on his forty-seventh mission, in September 1944. Because of his injured arm, he was taken off flight duty and transferred to the headquarters of the 13th Bomb Wing as the operations officer for Brigadier General Harold Huglin.

"I didn't like it," Rosenthal recalled. "I didn't feel I was contributing."

By the end of the year, he was healed and anxious to get onto a flight deck again, so he asked Huglin to transfer him back to the 100th Bomb Group. The general agreed, and Rosenthal returned to his old outfit as the commander of the 418th Bomb Squadron, the same squadron to which he had been assigned when he'd first gone overseas more than a year earlier. He flew two missions over Germany in late December, and wound up his second tour of duty with his fiftieth mission on January 7, 1945.

As he had reasoned ten months earlier when he had finished his *first* 25, he had come to fight the Nazis, and he wanted to remain until Germany was defeated. Ten days after his second tour was completed, he led the 418th as part of a 700-bomber strike force that set out for Hamburg.

On February 3, he took the right seat of a relatively new B-17G, tail number 44-8379, next to the pilot, Captain John Ernst. They would be the lead aircraft for the entire 3rd Bomb Division in a 1,437-plane assault on Berlin. The massive force took off, circled, and joined the formation in their designated places. The 418th formed with the other squadrons of the 100th Bomb Group, then picked up the other groups within the wing, then other wings within the division, and finally the 948-plane fighter escort.

"Everything went smoothly," Rosenthal recalled. "It was a beautiful day and the sun was shining. It was a thrilling sight to see the streams of contrails as we approached Berlin."

As so often happens when things seem to be going smoothly, the picture abruptly changed for the worse. And so it was for Rosie on that beautiful day. As the bomber stream neared the target, the flak began. A few seconds before "bombs away," Rosenthal's aircraft took a hit, interpreted in eyewitness accounts as having been a ground-launched rocket.

When the bombs were gone, and the bomb bay doors closed, Rosenthal and Ernst sized up the situation. There were fires aboard, and at least one man was dead. Knowing that the aircraft was doomed, Rosenthal radioed his deputy leader, ordering him to take command of the formation. Rather than trying to turn back to England, Rosenthal decided to head east toward the territory that had been captured by advancing Soviet armies. The crew would have to abandon the bomber, and it was preferable to do that over Allied lines—*if* they could make it that far.

Rosenthal ordered everyone to bail out while he maintained 44-8379 in level flight as long as possible. After-action reports from other aircraft described seeing six parachutes soon after the bomb run. A short time later, there was an explosion in the number three engine and the B-17 went down in flames, spinning into the cloud cover at 15,000 feet.

"I had to get out, but I was pinned down by the centrifugal force of the spin. I had to move toward the hatch in the front and force my way out," Rosenthal recalled. "When I got out, I thought I was in heaven. I was away from the plane, the smoke, and the noise. It was quiet and peaceful in the air, and suddenly I hit the ground."

According to USAAF Missing Air Crew Report 12046, Rosenthal went down 15 miles northwest of the town of Neudamm (now Debno, Poland), which is about 50 miles from Berlin. At the time, it was directly astride the fluid front lines of the Eastern Front, and four of the crew were captured by the Germans. Four others, including Rosenthal, landed on the Soviet side.

As he got up, Rosenthal was approached by three soldiers wearing the red stars of the Soviet Army. As one of them moved to hit Rosenthal with the butt of his gun, the American shouted, "Roosevelt, Churchill, Stalin, Lucky Strike, Coca-Cola, *bombing Berlin*." They got the idea that he was an American.

John Ernst had escaped through the bomb bay, but severely gashed his leg as he jumped, and that night his leg was amputated in a German hospital. When he and Rosenthal reconnected at a reunion four decades later, he told of going through this experience without anesthesia. He also recalled watching one of their fellow crew members being lynched by German civilians.

Beginning a quarter century later, the Bloody Hundredth reunions would be an important part of Rosenthal's life. Indeed, as Richard Le Strange noted in his book *Century Bombers*, the first reunion took place in 1968 in Rosenthal's backyard in Harrison, New York, and from this, the 100th Bomb Group Association—still alive and well—was born.

Rosenthal was taken to a Soviet field hospital where his arm, which had been broken a second time in five months, was set in a cast. He then joined other wounded men who were convalescing in a farmhouse, cared for by a woman who fed them hamburgers morning, noon, and night. He assumed that it was horse meat, but didn't care. After another week spent in the hospital suffering from a reaction to Soviet antibiotics, Rosenthal began his journey back to England.

There was nothing simple about Rosenthal's travels. Because there was no direct contact between the Allies on the Western and Eastern Fronts—now just a few hundred miles apart—his repatriation would take him eastward on a circuitous route across thousands of miles.

In Poland, he visited a Soviet air base, where he partied with Red Air Force pilots who compelled him to drink with them, imbibing vodka that he thought tasted more like gasoline. For a time, he lodged with the mayor of a city, who after a few days asked Rosenthal to help him get more food for his family from the local Russian general who controlled everything in the town. It turned out that the general was more inclined to do a favor for an American than for a Pole.

Rosenthal eventually reached Moscow, where he was taken to the American embassy. He lunched with Averell Harriman, the ambassador, and had the opportunity to send a telegram to his family to tell them that he was well. He later learned that a War Department telegram had been sent to his mother informing her that he was missing in action. It had been intercepted by his sister, and his mother never knew that he was missing until he was not.

After months of traveling by surface transportation, Rosenthal was flown to Tehran, where he picked up a series of flights that took him to England via Cairo and Naples in a few days. When he finally reached Thorpe Abbotts, Rosenthal was greeted by Major Marvin "Red" Bowman, the intelligence officer for the 100th Bomb Group.

"Rosie, you're not very smart," Bowman chided him. "We put you in for a Medal of Honor, which you would have had posthumously. You came back and you spoiled it all. All you'll get is a Distinguished Service Cross." Rosenthal replied that he would rather have the DSC than *anything* posthumous.

Time passed, the strategic air campaign wound down, and Rosie Rosenthal never flew a fifty-third combat mission. As the war came to an end, the Eighth Air Force continued to fly additional missions into Europe, dropping supplies and evacuating prisoners, and he flew several of these.

On one such flight, Rosenthal was repatriating a group of French prisoners from Poland to an airfield near Paris. As he neared Paris, he decided that he would "give them a treat" and went off course to make a low-level pass over the city. As he banked to fly around the Eiffel Tower, the prisoners, unused to either flying or having substantial meals, all lost their lunches onto the floor and bulkheads of the bomber.

CHAPTER 41

LeMAY IN THE PACIFIC

After the Battle of the Bulge, the defeat of Germany once again seemed tantalizingly close, despite the difficult winter battles and the fact that the Allies did not secure their bridgehead across the Rhine until the first week of March.

In the Pacific, it was a different story. As 1945 began, the end was *nowhere* in sight. Allied forces were thousands of miles from Japan, and the Japanese controlled nearly as much of the land area of Asia as they had when Jimmy Doolittle first visited Tokyo.

Overhead, the mission to achieve air superiority over Japan ahead of the Allied invasion of the home islands had yet to begin. The Superfortresses of the Twentieth Air Force had barely scratched the surface of the strategic air campaign. When Curtis LeMay formally assumed command of the XXI Bomber Command on January 20, it was with a sense of déjà vu, as if he were seeing the campaign at the same place where the Eighth Air Force's campaign had been more than two years before.

As had been the case for the Eighth in 1943, the Twentieth *was* receiving new aircraft at an increasing pace, but the Superfortress was a temperamental Thoroughbred. By the end of February, the 73rd Bomb Wing had been joined by the 313th and 314th. Then came the 315th, commanded by Brigadier General Frank Armstrong, Ira Eaker's former Eighth Air Force right-hand man.

After a month of running the show, LeMay made substantial improvements, especially in maintenance training, and he was sending missions to Japan several times a week—but he was not satisfied.

"Most of the original design flaws of the B-29 were being addressed at the factory, and the changes I'd made in maintenance procedures in January were starting to be felt," he explained to this author in 1986. "Still, the trouble remained that we had untrained crews and, over Japan, the worst weather I had encountered to date. This was adding up to poor results. In spite of the fact that the force had increased due to the new airplanes that were coming in, it had now become apparent that as long as the weather situation kept up, we weren't going to be able to defeat Japan using high-altitude precision bombing before the scheduled invasion was to begin. We had to do something really different. In other words, we had to use the tools we had in another way. . . . [I]t was now clear that we couldn't possibly succeed by basing our strategy on our experience from Europe. That system wasn't working. It was a different war with different weather and a different airplane. It called for a different solution."

The use of incendiaries to attack Japanese urban areas had been previously considered by the USAAF to the extent that a minutely detailed Japanese city had been meticulously constructed, then destroyed, at the Dugway Proving Ground in Utah. A fact not widely known is that this city was the creation of the Czech-born American architect Antonin Raymond of the New York firm Tuttle, Seelye and Place, a onetime chief assistant to Frank Lloyd Wright who had lived and worked in Japan for almost two decades.

"If there had been any serious planning before the war for the use of incendiaries, I hadn't heard anything about it, and I don't remember any mission that our group flew over Germany where we used them," LeMay recalled. "After sizing up the situation and knowing that I had to do something radical, I finally arrived at the decision to use low-level attacks against Japanese urban industrial areas using incendiaries. Even poorly trained radar operators could find cities that were on or near the coast, and going in at between 5,000 and 8,000 feet instead of 25,000 feet would ensure that all the bombs would fall in the target area. This method solved the weather problem, because instead of getting the force ready and then waiting for the right weather, we would go in under the weather."

By March, LeMay had the resources to launch a maximum effort of more than 300 bombers, and advances in radar technology made a night mission a feasible option—but the crews did not share LeMay's confidence in a low-level nighttime operation.

"We'd be taking off in the dark and bombing in the dark," recalled Bob Morgan, late of the *Memphis Belle* and now flying the Superfortress *Dauntless Dotty*, who was tasked with leading the 869th Bomb Squadron, the tail end of the strike force. "The prospect gave me a feeling of dread. I remembered the low-level missions that had been tried in Europe, and the results—whole squadrons of B-17s blown out of the sky. I kept reminding myself that this wasn't Europe and that our enemies here weren't the Germans. The Japanese had not achieved great accuracy with their antiaircraft guns. They would be expecting us at high altitudes."

At nearly dusk on March 9, 325 Superfortresses from three wings, each carrying eight tons of M69 incendiaries, were launched against Tokyo. On their way north, the crew of *Dauntless Dotty* dialed through the Japanese commercial radio station signals, looking for something to listen to. "We found a station playing American music," Morgan recalled. "That wasn't unusual—the Japanese fascination for Western culture was already legendary, even in wartime. It was the selection of songs that transfixed us. Some Tokyo disc jockey, as unaware of what was coming as our sailors had been that Sunday morning at Pearl Harbor, was innocently playing a string of tunes that predicted what we were about to deliver. 'Smoke Gets in Your Eyes' was playing when we dialed in. We exchanged grim smiles, and somebody muttered a little tensely that smoke would be in a lot of people's eyes in an hour or two. We couldn't believe it when the disc jockey followed that one up with 'My Old Flame.' When he spun out 'I Don't Want to Set the World on Fire,' a few of us started to giggle nervously. We finally switched that radio off."

The waves of bombers swept in at an unexpected altitude and an unexpected hour, starting thousands of fires, which merged into one, consuming around 16 square miles of the Axis capital in flames so bright that for the crews it was like flying a daylight mission.

"Tokyo was already an inferno when the *Dotty* arrived," Morgan remembered. "Great plumes of billowing smoke had climbed for miles into the night sky, but down at ground level the raging fires illuminated things, some of which you would rather not see. Curtis LeMay had been right. The Japanese had not expected us at night, this low. Most of the Japanese Zeros and Ginga fighters still sat, some of them melted, on their airstrips. Of those that had managed to get into the air, the thermal windstorms whipped up by the fires tossed them about the skies like helpless kites. As for the ground artillery fire, it was mostly inconsequential, as LeMay had predicted. The guns were calibrated for the wrong altitudes. We were bombing with damn near impunity."

LeMay had stockpiled sufficient incendiaries to follow up with four additional maximum efforts. Nagoya was attacked on March 11–12, followed by Osaka on March 13–14, Kobe on March 16–17, and Nagoya again on March 18–19. In ten days, the XXI Bomber Command flew more than 1,500 sorties, exceeding the cumulative number of missions in its first five months of combat. Loss rates on similar maximum efforts in the early stages of Eighth Air Force operations were in the double digits. For this week, the Twentieth Air Force loss rate was around one percent, and when it ended, around 25 percent of Japan's industrial infrastructure was shut down.

As Morgan put it, "Finally Curtis LeMay had hit upon a strategy that worked, and gladiator that he was, he bore in now for the kill. Rest and airplane endurance be damned—he'd found a way into the enemy's center, and now he was going to pour fire through it."

"I was not happy, but neither was I particularly concerned, about civilian casualties on incendiary raids," LeMay recalled. "I didn't let it influence any of my decisions because we knew how the Japanese had treated the Americans—both civilian and military—that they'd captured in places like the Philippines. We had dropped some warning leaflets over Japan, which essentially told the civilian population that we weren't trying to kill them, but rather that we were trying to destroy their capability to make war. We were going to bomb their cities and burn them down. We suggested they leave for their own safety."

CHAPTER 42

FROM CANNES TO BERLIN

On April 2, as Ira Eaker was preparing to head west across the Pacific and as Curtis LeMay was tightening the noose on Japan, Hap Arnold and Tooey Spaatz were on the opposite side of the globe dining with George Patton at the Hotel Ritz in Paris. The following day, they flew out to visit Eisenhower at Reims.

After making a tour of Germany and Luxembourg, often accompanied by Hoyt Vandenberg, Arnold flew to Cannes in southern France for a round of meetings with his other senior commanders. The venue was a villa overlooking the Riviera that had been commandeered by the USAAF as a rest-and-recuperation center. For Arnold, his dozen days at Cannes were *supposed* to be just that. He was under doctor's orders to rest up following his January heart attack.

Coincidentally, Tattie Spaatz and her young Red Cross colleagues were based nearby. It was one of the perks of having a father who was the highest-ranking USAAF man based in Europe. In his diary, Arnold wrote of having an alfresco breakfast under clear blue skies, and of Tattie coming to the villa "with two other Red Cross girls and three aviators to swim and enjoy the sunshine."

Spaatz and Doolittle flew in to see the chief on April 12, turning their attention to what the USAAF could do in Europe to hasten the collapse of Germany and, beyond that, what the USAAF should do to bring about the defeat of Japan, and who should lead this effort. Spaatz had suggested, and Arnold had agreed, that when his job with USSTAF was done, Spaatz would go to the Pacific to assemble an analogous organization. Spaatz would command the US Army Strategic Air Forces in the Pacific (USASTAF), which would handle all of the strategic air operations before and during Operation Olympic, the upcoming invasion of southern Japan in November 1945, and Operation Coronet, the invasion of the main Japanese island of Honshu in March 1946.

USASTAF would include the Twentieth Air Force, which was already in the Pacific, as well as the Eighth Air Force, which Doolittle would bring to the Pacific from Europe.

Their meeting in Cannes was reminiscent of the prewar "blank sheet of paper" organizational discussions that had taken place within the Arnold-Spaatz-Eaker triumvirate—except that Eaker was *not there*.

However, he soon would be.

After stops to visit Major General Claire Chennault of the Fourteenth Air Force in China, Eaker had flown to Burma to meet Major General Howard Davidson of the Tenth Air Force, both of them old friends from early Air Corps days. He had then flown westward, via Karachi and Cairo, to Italy, from where he had departed less than a month before.

At three thirty on the afternoon of April 19, Eaker arrived at Arnold's villa in Cannes with Spaatz. It was the first time Eaker had had a chance to sit down face-to-face with Arnold since his boss had relieved him of a command on the eve of its triumph for the *second* time.

Eaker had a lot to get off his chest, and he did so. In his own diary, Arnold used the term "heated" to describe their exchange.

"I didn't ask to go to Washington," Eaker told Arnold.

"Who in the hell ever did ask to go to Washington?" Arnold, by his own admission, "exploded." "Do you think I asked to go there and stay there for 10 years? Someone has to run the AAF. We can't all be in command of [operational air forces] around the world!"

Spaatz, according to Arnold's diary, "stepped in and calmed us down."

They then parted company and returned separately to Washington.

Eaker was back in Washington on April 24, three weeks before Arnold was back in the Pentagon. The chief had taken the long road, stopping in at Fifteenth Air Force headquarters in Italy—where he was told that "they had run out of targets for heavy bombing in southern Germany, Austria, and the Balkans"—spending some time in Brazil, and four days in Florida for a checkup at the USAAF hospital.

During Arnold's hiatus, Eaker had the ironic distinction—upon which he commented at the time—of being the senior USAAF officer in Washington and signing his memos as "Acting Commanding General AAF, in General Arnold's absence."

By April 1945, it was clear to anyone on either side of the vast European battlefield, east or west, that the end of the Third Reich was near. For the men at Stalag Luft I, on the Baltic coast at Barth, there was a sense of Germany's declining fortunes, but in the absence of news, they relied on the currency of rumor. The senior Allied officer at the camp, Colonel Hubert Zemke, late of the Eighth Air Force, was already preparing the men for the end—whenever and however it might come.

Between April and December 1944, when Zemke arrived, the total population of the camp swelled from around 3,500 to about 9,000. To maintain order among themselves, the prisoners organized themselves into a "provisional wing," with an administrative structure headed by Zemke.

These were dire times. Life at the stalag went from bad to worse. After October 1944, the Germans gradually cut the rations to about half as food supplies for all of Germany declined. Red Cross parcels also dwindled, partly because of the damage being done to Germany's transportation network by the Eighth Air Force, but also because the guards were taking the packages for themselves.

By the last week of April, the rumors of the demise of the Reich were substantiated by the thunder of distant artillery fire as the Soviet 2nd Byelorussian Front, commanded by Marshal Konstantin Rokossovsky, moved westward along the Baltic coast. On April 30, the camp commandant, Oberst Warnstadt, informed Zemke that he had been ordered to evacuate the camp within 24 hours and march the prisoners 150 miles to another location near Hamburg. Zemke flatly refused, telling him that the prisoners would fight the Germans before they would endure a forced march.

Both men knew that the scheme was ridiculous, and Zemke convinced Warnstadt that the better idea would be for the Germans to evacuate the camp to save themselves from the Soviets—of whom they were deathly afraid.

That night, the Germans turned off all the searchlights and escaped, leaving the gates unlocked. Zemke, who had planned for this turn of events, now took over, putting men into the guard towers to ensure order among the prisoners and to prevent German troops and civilians from coming into the camp to escape the Red Army. He then sent parties out to make contact with the Soviets, who reached the camp a few hours later. They were in high spirits and celebrating the fact that it was May Day.

The Soviet commander informed Zemke that the prisoners would now be marched 1,500 miles to Odessa to be loaded onto ships for repatriation. If the earlier German proposal had been absurd, this idea was ludicrous, and Zemke told him as much. The British army was only 150 miles to the west.

On May 6, three officers left the camp and made their way to England, where they contacted Doolittle's headquarters and arranged for evacuation by air. A week later, the Eighth Air Force flew 300 sorties to evacuate the prisoners.

Throughout the final two weeks, Zemke maintained his provisional wing organization and orderly control of the camp and its newly liberated inhabitants. According to the US Army Military Intelligence Service, 7,717 American and 1,427 British officers were in the camp, some of whom had been incarcerated for more than three years.

On April 30, as Zemke was bickering with Warnstadt in Barth, Adolf Hitler was in Berlin, murdering his wife of less than two days and committing suicide. When this became known, German commanders in all areas facing west opened surrender negotiations with the British and Americans. Delegations began reaching SHAEF headquarters at Reims on May 4, but Eisenhower told them that *all* German forces on *all* fronts must surrender simultaneously.

Tooey Spaatz was present in the small hours of May 7 when Generaloberst Alfred Jodl, chief of the operations staff of the Oberkommando der Wehrmacht, arrived at SHAEF's headquarters to formally surrender all German forces on behalf of Grand Admiral Karl Dönitz, who had succeeded Hitler as Führer. Walter Bedell Smith signed for SHAEF. Although General Ivan Suslaparov signed for the Soviet Union, the Soviets insisted on a separate signing ceremony in Berlin the following day.

Spaatz and Suslaparov flew to the German capital together in a USAAF C-47. There Field Marshal Wilhelm Keitel, chief of the Oberkommando der Wehrmacht, signed for Germany and Marshal Giorgi Zhukov for the Soviet Union. Initially, it was proposed that Arthur Tedder should sign for the United Kingdom and Spaatz would sign for the United States. However, the Soviets quibbled that Spaatz's rank was not equivalent to Zhukov's. This conundrum was finally resolved by letting Tedder sign on behalf of the United States as Eisenhower's deputy and having Spaatz sign as one of the witnesses.

The celebratory banquet began with Russian caviar, was lubricated by Russian vodka and pilfered German liquor, and lasted until dawn. Spaatz gave the sixth toast: "To the soldiers, sailors and airmen who made this peace possible." A more tipsy Spaatz made the twenty-fifth: "To the women of Russia." In a later toast, after everyone had lost count, he announced, "We stand for honesty, justice, and the rights of the individual."

Shortly after the surrender, Spaatz had an opportunity to debrief Hermann Göring, the chief of the now defeated Luftwaffe. Spaatz sought information about the technical and tactical nuances of the Luftwaffe's successes and failures, asking about topics from the Battle of Britain to the final air battle over the Reich. Göring, however, skewed each query toward blaming Hitler for every disappointment and fiasco throughout the war.

As David Mets, Spaatz's biographer, observed, "Spaatz came away from the meeting with a feeling of skepticism. [His conversation with Göring] was so full of contradictions and mistakes that it appeared as either a deception or a display of remarkable ignorance about the affairs of one's organization. Spaatz, after all, had had a rather good picture of Luftwaffe through Ultra, derived from the words of German air commanders."

While Eaker may have represented Arnold in Washington that week, it was Spaatz who was at the crossroads of history.

CHAPTER 43

SETTING SUN

At the beginning of the second week of May 1945, Americans had two things on their minds, but one vastly overshadowed the other. The former was that Germany had been defeated. The latter was that Japan had *not*.

In his "Victory in Europe" message, broadcast throughout the world, Hap Arnold reminded listeners that "to provide airpower needed for victory over the Axis partners in Europe, the Army Air Forces had to travel a long way over an arduous road," hastening to add that "Japanese industry will have to be battered to the same chaos that engulfed Germany's military machine. That is a campaign barely begun."

For Bob Morgan, who had been in the Pacific since October, the war was already winding down. He flew his last Superfortress bombing mission against Japan on March 30, and his last mission in *Dauntless Dotty*, a weather recon flight, on April 4. He had now flown more missions in the Pacific than with the *Memphis Belle* over Europe.

He had expected to be part of the April 7 mission that mustered 100 bombers against Tokyo, but the new commander of the 497th Bomb Group, Colonel Arnold Johnson, wanted squadron commanders, such as

Morgan, to stop flying combat missions and take up administrative work—flying *desks*. Two days later, Rosie O'Donnell, the 73rd Bomb Wing commander, told Morgan that he might be able to send him stateside—"if you are ready to go."

Suddenly, it occurred to Morgan that he *was* ready. He looked at the color photo of his daughter, Sandra Lea, that he carried. Born at the end of November, she was almost five months old. He had never seen her.

Morgan left Saipan on April 26 with a recommendation from O'Donnell for a promotion to colonel, and two Distinguished Flying Crosses—one for leading the first Tokyo mission and one for flying 26 Superfortress missions. He reached San Francisco on the same day that Hitler committed suicide.

Tooey Spaatz and Jimmy Doolittle were on their way home to the States shortly after VE Day, but it was to be only a stopover on their way to new assignments in the Pacific.

Spaatz almost did not make it. As his biographer, David Mets, points out, he had run out of fuel at the end of the *First* World War, almost ending the life of Lieutenant Spaatz. Then the same almost ended General Spaatz's life at the conclusion of the *Second* World War. The Flying Fortress carrying him, his staff, and his daughter, Tattie, was en route across the Atlantic from the Azores, when they learned that their next stop, Gander, Newfoundland, was fogged in. So was Goose Bay, Labrador. They diverted again, this time to Sydney, Nova Scotia, running out of fuel as they taxied off the field. By evening, Tooey and Tattie had greeted Ruth and Carla at Washington National and everyone was home in Alexandria.

"There is no grander feeling in the world than to return to the comfort of one's hearth and family," Jimmy Doolittle wrote of his own post–VE Day homecoming, and the anticipation of seeing Joe and their younger son, John, who was just finishing his third year at West Point. "For the first time in too many months I was going home."

As Spaatz had flown home with his second daughter, Doolittle came home with his elder son, Captain James Doolittle, Jr. When the two men had reconnected in England a year earlier, Doolittle had observed that his son's presence in the theater "made me think about the future for Joe and me. Both boys wanted to remain in the service after the war, which meant we wouldn't see much of them. John was taking flight training while a cadet at West Point and would also be going to peacetime military assignments on a worldwide basis, just as Jim, Jr., would. I wrote Joe that I thought I might like to stay in uniform until normal retirement if I were offered a commission as a permanent brigadier general. If so, I said, I would like to take an active part in the inevitable reorganization of our defense establishment and the Air Force after the war."

Whatever the postwar world may have held for the Doolittles, Jimmy still had unfinished business in an unfinished war. His first assignment, prior to his long trip to the Pacific, was to make public appearances at rallies—such as one at the Los Angeles Coliseum that he shared with George Patton, which drew a reported million people—in which the job was to convince people that the war really was still *unfinished*.

Doolittle was eager to get on with the finishing. There had been a flurry of headlines and political cartoons suggesting that Japan was really doomed now that Doolittle was coming back to finish that job he started in April 1942. This publicity angered him because he thought it showed only a callous regard for all those who had fought and died in that theater to hasten an American victory.

With the Joint Chiefs of Staff having formally approved the USAS-TAF on July 2, its two senior commanders headed west, Spaatz to Guam, where the headquarters would be located, and Doolittle to Okinawa, where he formally established the new home of the Eighth Air Force on July 16.

It was a coincidence that one day earlier (across the international date line) the Manhattan Project had detonated its first nuclear weapon. As Spaatz and Doolittle both knew, plans were in motion for the 509th Composite Group of LeMay's XXI Bomber Command to stand by to use these weapons to defeat Japan before operations Olympic and Coronet, which were expected to cost the United States a million casualties.

Also ongoing at that moment, in a suburb of a decimated Berlin, was the Potsdam Conference, the last Allied summit of World War II. Out of this came the Potsdam Declaration, which explicitly gave Japan one last opportunity to surrender unconditionally or face "prompt and utter destruction."

On June 13, a month before Spaatz and Doolittle arrived, as part of an extended visit of the Pacific Theater, Hap Arnold had stopped by LeMay's headquarters on Saipan. He saw, as Spaatz and Doolittle would soon see, how much the Twentieth Air Force and the strategic air offensive against Japan had grown since LeMay had taken over at the end of January. New B-29s and crews were flooding into the Marianas like B-17s had into England after Big Week.

During two consecutive nights at the end of May, the XXI Bomber Command had struck Tokyo with maximum efforts involving an average of more than 500 Superfortresses. By June it was possible to undertake a sustained strategic offensive with 400-plane missions flown whenever the B-29s were ready—and after the early maintenance anguish, LeMay kept his force ready *constantly*.

As LeMay explained to this author, "I had a directive which was never changed and was approved by the Joint Chiefs, a list of targets ranked by priority. When we were ready to run a mission, we would get the airplanes loaded with fuel and bombs, and the crews would be briefed and prepared. If the weather was good we'd hit a precision target that had a high priority on the target list. . . . [W]e were hitting the high-priority industrial areas just as fast as we could, bombing both at night [low-flying incendiary missions] and in the daytime [high-altitude precision bombing]."

LeMay told Arnold that he and his staff were convinced there was a chance of defeating Japan with airpower—*without* nuclear weapons, and *without* the invasions. As noted in his diary, Arnold digested what LeMay had accomplished and immediately ordered him to fly back to Washington to personally brief the Joint Chiefs of Staff. Arnold wanted this to be done in advance of a June 18 JCS meeting at which details of the November invasion of southern Japan would be discussed with President Truman.

"I believe that General Arnold always thought airpower could do the job, but he was more convinced than ever after we gave our briefing," LeMay recalled. "The decision to go ahead with the amphibious invasion of Japan had already been made on May 25, and I think Arnold realized, when he visited us, that our strategic air offensive might be the one chance of stopping it. I imagine that he wanted to make one more effort to delay the invasion—or to stop it entirely to prevent the American bloodshed we knew would come with the invasion—so he sent me and two of the staff back to Washington."

Flying a B-29, LeMay touched down at Washington National Airport just before midnight on July 16.

"The next morning we drove over to the Pentagon and presented our plan to the Joint Chiefs of Staff and their staff officers," LeMay explained. "Throughout the briefing, each of them had completely blank expressions on their faces. They paid absolutely no attention to us. Marshall was sleeping or dozing through most of it. Admiral Ernest King, the chief of Naval Operations, reacted with disbelief and a complete lack of interest, just as the Navy brass always had. . . . Nevertheless, we went back to the Marianas and we *did* the job."

By the time that Spaatz and Doolittle reached the Pacific a month later, the decision had been made by Truman and the Joint Chiefs to use the nuclear weapons. Part of Spaatz's immediate mission was to brief General Douglas MacArthur and Admiral Chester Nimitz, the five-star senior officers who commanded the US Army and US Navy in the Pacific, on this decision.

On August 6, the *Enola Gay*, a Superfortress of the 509th, dropped the first nuclear weapon on Hiroshima. When the aircraft returned to Tinian, Spaatz pinned a Distinguished Service Cross on the flight suit of her pilot, Colonel Paul Tibbets.

Having been given an idea of what was meant by "prompt and utter destruction," the Japanese government debated their acceptance of the Potsdam Declaration until August 9, when a second nuclear-armed B-29, *Bock's Car*, flown by Major Chuck Sweeney, departed Tinian for Kokura, diverted to Nagasaki because of the weather, and dropped the second nuclear weapon.

Three days later, Tooey Spaatz contacted Jimmy Doolittle to tell him that if he wanted the Eighth Air Force bombers to be in contact with the Japanese, he had "better get an operation going the next day."

"No, the war's over," Doolittle told Spaatz. "I will not risk one airplane nor a single bomber crew member just to say that the Eighth Air Force operated against the Japanese in the Pacific."

A handful of Superfortresses destined for service with the Eighth had arrived on Okinawa, but they would never fly in combat. Some of the Eighth's P-51 escort fighters did fly a few escort missions for the Twentieth Air Force.

On August 14, with the weather clear over Japan, Spaatz and LeMay returned to conventional weapons with the Twentieth Air Force, striking targets across the country. Doolittle recalled that Arnold had wanted a "1,000-plane raid made against Tokyo" that day, and—counting the escort fighters—there *were* more than 1,100 USAAF combat aircraft in the sky. There were no losses to enemy fire. The following day, the Japanese government accepted the Potsdam Declaration and Emperor Hirohito ordered his armed forces to cease hostilities.

Curtis LeMay told this author many years later that he had "no doubt that the atomic bomb precipitated unconditional surrender and in so doing saved American lives. Even given that strategic bombing could have ended the war without the atomic bomb, I think it was a wise decision to drop the bomb because this action did hasten the surrender process already under way. We were losing people and expending resources every day that the war went on. The Japanese were also losing people. What guided me in all my thinking, and guided all our efforts—the reason the XXI Bomber Command worked like no other command during the war and the thing that kept us going—was the million men we were going to lose if we had to invade Japan. . . . The Twentieth Air Force got the job done before the Allied armies had to do it."

When the Allied armies did land in Japan, it was to accept Japan's formal surrender. On August 29, Spaatz, Doolittle, and LeMay all boarded C-54s in Okinawa for the 1,000-mile flight to Atsugi Airport, near Yokohama. It was an eerie experience to be flying a route similar to that taken for six months by the growing fleet of Superfortresses to land on enemy soil, and be greeted by long lines of Japanese troops standing at attention against the backdrop of urban ruins created by the Superfortresses and the crews who flew the final act in the story of strategic airpower in World War II.

On September 2, these three men, two of whom had served as a commander of the Eighth Air Force, were part of the group who assembled on the deck of the USS *Missouri* in Tokyo Bay for the final surrender. Tooey Spaatz would be remembered as the only officer present at *three* Axis surrenders—Reims, Berlin, and now Tokyo.

"I have no regrets whatsoever that Eighth Air Force bombers did not fly a single mission to bring the war to an end in the Pacific," Jimmy Doolittle reflected in his memoirs. "As far as I was concerned, we had helped to prove the point in Europe. What was important now was to see that the peace could be sustained and that there would be no more Pearl Harbors."

* ✪ *

CHAPTER 44

THE POSTWAR AIR FORCE

All three of the men of the Eighth who were aboard the USS *Missouri* on September 2 were home from the Pacific by the end of the month.

Curtis LeMay came back dramatically, leading three Superfortresses—the others were piloted by Rosie O'Donnell and Barney Giles—flying from Japan via Chicago to a media event at Washington National Airport. Jimmy Doolittle flew in the following day, also in a B-29 and also to a hero's welcome.

In his memoirs, Doolittle wrote that his first postwar priority was to locate the members of his 1942 Tokyo team who had been captured and who were now being released and repatriated. Easier said than done, this was accomplished, and Doolittle threw a party for them—a 1942 promise fulfilled at last—in December 1945. It was the first of what later became an annual tradition that continued through 2008.

Tooey Spaatz arrived in less spectacular fashion, but not unnoticed. In 1982, Ruth Spaatz told David Mets that her husband had come home to Alexandria "bone tired" and ready to retire. But there was no immediate respite.

When the last confetti from the celebrations was swept away, the senior leaders who had forged the victory succumbed to thoughts of giving it all up. George Marshall passed the baton of US Army chief of staff to Dwight Eisenhower, while Arnold wrote to Marshall: "With your concurrence, I should like to request retirement from the Service."

Spaatz, meanwhile, was going nowhere but to sit behind the desk of the commanding general of the USAAF with permanent four-star rank and Ira Eaker at his side. James Parton, Eaker's biographer, observed that "Spaatz was always the designated successor . . . with Eaker loyally continuing as deputy commander and chief of the air staff, though he pined to withdraw."

Once again, on the eve of Arnold's departure, the Arnold-Spaatz-Eaker triumvirate was together within an upper room of the American military establishment. Ironically, their biggest task in the winter of 1945–1946 was disassembling their masterpiece. For decades, they had worked to transform their third-rate stepchild of a land army into a world-class air force, and they had created the largest air force in history—before or since.

Now, with the war completed, they had to take it apart. Between 1939 and 1944, they had increased the personnel count from 23,445 to 2,372,292, and the number of aircraft eightfold, to nearly 80,000. Now this mighty force was to be demobilized. Nine of every ten airmen would become civilians, and aircraft waiting to be cut up for scrap filled vast fields. Of the 30,000 B-17s and B-24s that had only recently rolled off the assembly lines, almost none remained in the inventory by 1947.

Congress was impatient to trim spending on weapons after the war, but at the same time, the triumvirate understood that technological advances would soon render most of their wartime equipment obsolete. The service should be investing in building *future* technology.

Spaatz officially succeeded Arnold as commanding general on February 9, 1946, with one more battle to win.

This was a fight that had started long ago with Billy Mitchell and then was placed on hold through World War II. The idea of a US Air Force fully independent of the US Army, which had once seemed impossible, had been hastened toward realization in June 1941, when Marshall authorized autonomy for the USAAF. Now the ball had to be carried the last few yards and through the goalposts.

The senior leadership of the US Army—Marshall, Eisenhower, and MacArthur—supported what amounted to a divorce of the Army from its Air Forces, but other parts of the overall plan still faced challenges within Congress and within the US Navy.

The process was complicated by the fact that the plan called for a comprehensive reorganization of the defense establishment. Heretofore, the US Army and the US Navy had each been represented by a cabinet-level department, War and Navy. Under the reorganization hammered out over the next two years, the three services would be placed within a single cabinet-level National Military Establishment (Department of Defense after 1949).

Congress finally passed the National Security Act in July 1947, unifying the defense establishment and formally granting the independence of the US Air Force, effective on September 18. With this, Tooey Spaatz became the new service's first chief of staff. His vice chief would be Hoyt Vandenberg, the wartime commander of the Ninth Air Force, who had served after the war on the air staff and as the second director of the Central Intelligence Agency.

Spaatz had already reorganized the service in anticipation of its future independence, creating three combat commands representing the three principal missions of the postwar force. Activated in March 1946, the building blocks of the future US Air Force were the Air Defense Command (ADC), the Tactical Air Command (TAC), and the Strategic Air Command (SAC). Three months later, the Eighth Air Force was brought back from the Pacific and assigned, along with the Fifteenth Air Force, to SAC, where it would remain until SAC itself was dissolved 46 years later.

In 1947, the new US Air Force was a hollow force. So effective had been the two years of demobilization that Spaatz commanded a service that had dwindled from more than 200 groups in 1945 to just *two* that were combat-ready.

It was not just a quantitative decline but a qualitative one as well. According to David Mets, when Spaatz took over, "the funds for research and development were so scarce that the bulk of them had to be diverted to perfecting the current capability of the Air Force, with little left over for work that looked to the future [and] neglect of scientific advance during the late forties was later deemed by some to be the most serious mistake of the Truman years, but the fault cannot be laid at Spaatz's door, for his warnings were clear enough. That same financial stringency was preventing the buildup of conventional forces . . . was driving the US in the direction of adopting a nuclear [only] strategy, which would be the bane of the very groups who had done the most to impose the stringency in the first place."

Soon, however, it would be someone else's problem.

Spaatz had promised Arnold that he would remain in the top job until independence had been achieved, and this had been done. On April 30, 1948, he passed the job to Hoyt Vandenberg and left Washington.

Ira Eaker had joined Hap Arnold on the retired list almost a year earlier. On June 14, 1947, the *New York Times* editorialized that "one of the great commanders of the Second World War . . . will doff his three stars tomorrow. . . . He will be sorely missed in the high councils of security. His retirement at 51, however, is the result of a deep conviction that he can be of more service outside of uniform than in. He intends to devote himself to the cause which he cherishes as earnestly—the cause of making the nation aware of the peril in which it stands if it allows itself to become weak in the air."

In fact, Eaker intended to devote himself to fishing on Oregon's Rogue River. He and Ruth were already on their way west in a new Cadillac to find an appropriate place to build a home for his retirement. It was his idea, not hers. He remembered the area fondly after a prewar summer spent there with the 20th Pursuit Group, while Ruth had grown to greatly enjoy being part of an exciting social life in Washington.

"I didn't really want Ira to retire or to leave," she admitted to James Parton in 1983, "but he was very tired and whatever he wanted suited me."

In the first peacetime months of 1945, Jimmy Doolittle spent a great deal of time on a public-speaking tour in support of the independent US Air Force. Meanwhile, he was encouraged by Hap Arnold to become involved in the formation of a civilian, nonprofit veterans organization for retiring US Air Force personnel that would also serve to promote the role of airpower in national defense. In January 1946, Doolittle became the first president of the new Air Force Association, an entity that still exists, boasting more than 100,000 members.

Meanwhile, Doolittle had run into Alex Fraser of Shell Oil, who invited him to rejoin the company as vice president, board member, and public spokesman—at triple his USAAF salary. He accepted. He left active duty, but remained on reserve status, as he had when he left in 1930. As a lieutenant general, he was the highest-ranking reserve officer in the United States armed forces.

In March 1946, just as he was packing for his first overseas trip on behalf of Shell, Secretary of War Robert Patterson called on him to chair a "Board on Officer-Enlisted Man Relationships."

As Doolittle described it, "The creation of the board was in response to public complaints about the lack of democracy in the Army, instances of incompetent leadership, the abuse of privileges, and the favorable treatment of officers compared with enlisted men during the war. I promptly accepted the invitation."

The press called it the "Doolittle Board," but many people were referring to it as the "GI Gripes Board" because of the nature of complaints that Doolittle and his panel of officers and enlisted men found themselves processing.

Doolittle recalled that his report, handed to Patterson in May, "included a number of items to improve the leadership of the officer corps, including rigorous screening out of incompetents, and an internal policing system to prevent abuse of privileges."

It was a thankless job that had numerous detractors, but as he notes, it "was widely accepted, and in fact, the Army had already been making changes."

Curtis LeMay came home from managing World War II's last major strategic air campaign to a noncombat post as Deputy Chief of Air Staff for Research and Development. As David Mets wrote, Spaatz wanted him in this job in order to "charge him with building relations with the nuclear people, so that the bomber units could get at least enough nuclear information to carry out their mission."

From its inception in 1942 through the end of 1946, the American nuclear weapons program, the Manhattan Project, was controlled by the Manhattan District of the Corps of Engineers, which guarded its secrets even from the USAAF, which was charged with delivering the weapons in wartime.

LeMay was also handpicked by Hap Arnold for another special project *outside* the USAAF. In October 1945, Arnold and Donald Douglas had started Project RAND (Research and Development) to develop leading-edge technology projects that were beyond anything then operational. Their first project was a design study titled *Preliminary Design of an Experimental World-Circling Spaceship*, completed in May 1946, more than a decade before Sputnik. The original RAND staff included LeMay and Lauris Norstad of the USAAF.

"We had a few technical people in the Air Force," LeMay told Tom

Coffey in 1984. "But not near enough of them to do the job. And we couldn't attract people like that into the Air Force. So the organization was a gimmick. The Air Force would give RAND a contract to do certain things, then RAND would hire the talent necessary to do the job at the going rate."

However, it was in a series of operational commands that LeMay would best be known in the postwar years.

In October 1947, now with the third star of a lieutenant general, he returned to Europe to assume command of the US Air Forces in Europe (USAFE). When the war ended, all of the USAAF assets remaining in Europe were consolidated into USSTAF, which became USAFE. It was in Wiesbaden, Germany, near where USAFE was now headquartered, that LeMay, along with Helen and Janie, took up housekeeping in the former home of the father-in-law of Nazi Foreign Minister Joachim von Ribbentrop.

The United States, the United Kingdom, the Soviet Union, and France had divided defeated Germany into occupation zones. Berlin, located within the Soviet zone, was also divided, so the non-Soviet sectors of Berlin were like an island in the Soviet zone. Immediately after the war, the Soviets began physically sealing off from Western Europe the areas of Eastern Europe that they had occupied during the war, creating what Winston Churchill described as an "Iron Curtain."

In June 1948, in an effort to compel its wartime Allies to abandon their Berlin sectors, the Soviets cut off all road and rail access to the city, making it impossible to move food, coal, and other goods into western Berlin. The two million people living in those sectors now faced the prospect of privation and even starvation. Given that the other powers had drastically demobilized while the Soviets had not, it was considered impossible to use military force to escort supplies to the city—although LeMay made preparations to provide air support if this decision was made. This included bringing B-29s to England and secretly stockpiling supplies at bases throughout Europe.

It was at this point that LeMay and USAFE, supported by the RAF, audaciously undertook to fly transport aircraft *over* the Soviet blockade. Lasting for nearly 500 days and continuing after the blockade ended in May 1949, the Berlin Airlift delivered two million tons of supplies and proved itself a triumph for the new US Air Force, becoming an often-overlooked feather in LeMay's cap.

CHAPTER 45

A JOKER AMONG KINGS

Maynard Harrison Smith remained in England after he received his Medal of Honor from Secretary of War Stimson in July 1943. Through October, he flew another four missions, received an Air Medal, and had an oak leaf cluster added to it—for "destruction of enemy aircraft." There were not many men in the Eighth Air Force who received that kind of recognition in five missions. Andy Rooney's article in *Stars and Stripes* called him a hero, and back home, newspapers from the *New York Herald Tribune* to his hometown *Tuscola County Advertiser* applauded his heroism.

He knew that his being discovered on KP on the day of his appearance at the carefully choreographed ceremony had embarrassed the 306th Bomb Group in front of Stimson—and he quickly realized that afterward no one was willing to discipline the great Maynard Harrison Smith. He gradually reverted to lazy insubordination, so they grounded him and gave him a desk job, mainly to keep him out of the way.

Because of him, Thurleigh, home of the 306th, became one of the stops made by journalists doing the rounds of Eighth Air Force bases in England. Smith was an amenable and easy interview, with a colorful tongue and a compulsion for extravagant self-promotion. To poke fun at the public relations fiasco, he often posed for photographs while peeling potatoes, the stereotype of KP duty. He was asked for autographs, to which he added the initials "CMH" (Congressional Medal of Honor) to underscore his importance.

It was his own fellow airmen who tired of him first, and this came rather quickly. In turn, and gradually over time, the man who had been the flavor of the month grew to be less of a tourist attraction, and the journalists moved on to other heroes, who were certainly plentiful within the Eighth in 1944 and 1945.

As Andy Rooney reported, his new audience was off base, where "he posed part time as an intellectual and loved to go to the British pubs in Thurleigh to argue with and lecture to the British civilians." At least one British civilian fell under his spell, despite—or because of—his eccentricities. Smith met and won the heart of Mary Rayner, a young woman from nearby Bedford, whose father was a captain in the Royal Army Service Corps. If there was any doubt that the Medal of Honor was still perceived by Snuffy as the high point in his life, he and Mary were wed on July 15, 1944, the first anniversary of his receiving it.

In March 1945, after being overseas for two years, Snuffy Smith went home to Caro, Michigan. Mary would not join him for more than a month. On March 22, the man who departed for the service in handcuffs was treated to a hero's Main Street parade. The townspeople turned out to see the man about whom they had read, many of them too young to remember his delinquent years.

He met Mary in Albany, New York, where she had relatives, and they never returned to live in Michigan. There was that matter of his still being liable for child support that was *years* in arrears. In his home state, the 35-year-old hero was a wanted man, and he dared not tarry.

Relying on his hero status and his connections from his prewar job with the Treasury Department, Smith got a job with the Internal Revenue Service in Washington, DC, and he and Mary settled down to live the postwar suburban dream in an apartment in Falls Church, Virginia.

But it was not to be the perfect dream. In fact, the postwar life of the prewar playboy was more of an exercise in waking up *from* a dream. The inheritance that had financed his life of leisure had been spent, and the burst of excitement surrounding his Medal of Honor had burned out. He discovered that few people cared for his autograph anymore. As some men turned to the bottle, he returned to pseudoscience. The history of popular culture has been filled with get-rich-quick schemes and with life-enhancing drugs that are too good to be true, and the time line of that history has a small point marked for Maynard Harrison Smith. In the twenty-first century, a certain age-old problem has been addressed by elixirs called Cialis, Levitra, or Viagra and advertised ad nauseam. In 1947, there was Smith and an oily balm that he branded descriptively as "Firmo."

Presumably answering complaints, the Food and Drug Administration raided the Smith apartment, confiscated the Firmo, and arrested the war hero on charges of having "falsely advertised" his product. Inspector Barnard of the FDA told Municipal Court that the preparation "didn't work."

Not long after this incident, Smith left the Internal Revenue Service—his version is that he quit when they tried to make him take a test required for promotion—and went to work for a television shop in Washington.

The strangest of Smith's postwar pranks came in 1952. This one had more to do with lost glory than with his need for money. He and Roland Bennett, a coworker at the television shop, cooked up a strange scheme for the wartime hero to become a hero once again by pretending to "save" a person bent on suicide. All they needed was a suicide victim. Bennett called an ex-girlfriend, and they offered her $500 to be part of the plan. When they convinced Ernestine Lucille Whomble, a 21-year-old mother whose five-month-old had recently died, that she did not have to *actually* kill herself, she decided that she could use the money.

Despite the misgivings of her cabdriver husband, she stepped out onto a sixth-floor ledge at the YMCA Building in downtown Washington.

Smith followed, grabbing her and pinning her to the ledge as onlookers gawked from the street and a news photographer arrived to snap a picture. Finally, they crawled back through a nearby window. Initial news reports were exactly as Smith had hoped. A hero once, he was a hero again.

However, the deception unraveled when Lucille implicated Bennett and Smith during a police psychiatric evaluation. Smith denounced her to reporters, saying that Lucille suffered from "hallucinations of grandeur."

Within a month it was over. Smith and Bennett were arraigned for filing a false police report. They had not actually *filed* a report, but the incident was witnessed by the police. They pled not guilty but were convicted. Snuffy Smith was sentenced to a $50 fine or ten days in jail. He claimed that he could not come up with the cash, and once again the man whose military career had begun in handcuffs and culminated in glory was back in handcuffs.

Smith spent the remainder of his life bouncing from one unsuccessful scheme to another. When his mother passed away in 1956, he inherited that part of his father's considerable estate that his frugal mother had not spent. This restored his finances, while his Medal of Honor kept him on the periphery of the limelight. He was quoted from time to time in newspaper articles waxing nostalgic about the war, and was invited to the occasional reunion of men who had earned the nation's ultimate decoration for heroism.

His wife left him and moved to Hawaii, and he retired to Florida, where the window-ledge fiasco was long forgotten, and where, as he grew old, he could embellish his wartime heroism with impunity.

He died at the Bay Pines Veterans Administration Hospital near St. Petersburg on May 11, 1984, eight days short of turning 73. His obituary in the *Tuscola County Advertiser* was not fact-checked and recalled his Medal of Honor action not as it happened but as he had told it in his later years. The most incredible variation from the truth was that "Smith went up to the cockpit. There he found the pilot and copilot wounded and the aircraft flying out of control. Smith gave first aid to the injured pair and pulled the pilot from his seat. He then piloted the aircraft to England." He had done none of that!

There have been many attempts to fathom this man, to understand what made him tick. In his 1995 wartime memoir, *My War*, Andy Rooney, the man who made Smith famous, summarized his life best when he wrote: "From the time he entered the Air Force he had been in some kind of trouble over one petty matter or another. 'Snuffy' was, in fact, known by the fourteen other inhabitants of his Nissen hut by an Army phrase for which there's no socially acceptable replacement. He was a real fuckup."

Smith seems a strange inclusion to this book, a joker in a hand of kings, but he is here to remind us that sometimes war brings out the best in men. When he is remembered—and he *is* remembered—as part of the legend and lore of the Eighth Air Force in its moment of glory, perhaps we can credit the Eighth itself with the sense of purpose and the sense of identity from which its men drew their strength, with giving Smith the intangible *something* that allowed him to rise above and beyond his own inclinations.

The selflessness of five splendid days in 1943 cannot come close to offsetting his shortcomings, compounded over the decades by sinister selfishness and bizarre foolishness, but the legacy of his service, with an Air Medal with oak leaf cluster and the Medal of Honor for his actions during his five missions, speaks for itself, and his bravery for those brief and shining moments can neither be minimized nor forgotten.

CHAPTER 46

RETIREMENT YEARS

I t is not often remembered in accounts of their lives that Tooey Spaatz and Ira Eaker had each *independently* imagined a future for himself not in Washington but in small-town newspaper journalism.

Spaatz entertained thoughts of returning to Boyertown and buying back his father's newspaper, the *Berks County Democrat*, where he once worked as the youngest Linotype operator in Pennsylvania. Instead, he got a better offer in the same field, being hired by *Newsweek* magazine as its military affairs editor, a platform that allowed him to write on the importance of airpower and reach an audience outside Berks County. With this, Tooey and Ruth bought a home in Georgetown, from which he could mail in his columns.

Meanwhile, Red Gresham, husband to their daughter, Beckie, who had cheated death during the war, died in 1953, leaving her with three small children. She tried to get a job as a music teacher, but because she had dropped out of the Peabody Conservatory a decade earlier to get married, she was without a degree. Tooey and Ruth agreed to take the kids in while Beckie went off to study at the Royal Academy in London.

Eaker had planned to go into business with Glenn Jackson, whom he had met in Medford before the war, and who had served on the Eighth Air Force staff during the war. Jackson's family owned several Oregon newspapers, and he had learned that the Pulitzer Prize–winning *Medford Mail Tribune* was for sale. By the time Eaker and Jackson converged on Medford in 1947, however, the paper's owner was having second thoughts.

Ira and Ruth decided to take a drive down to Los Angeles while waiting for the owner to change his mind. Though Eaker and Spaatz later purchased property for a fishing cabin overlooking the Rogue River, the Eakers remained in California and never looked back to Oregon as a place to settle. The two men acquired the remote plot—31 miles downriver from Grave Creek—from Glen Wooldridge, who had worked as a guide on the river since 1917, and who had bought the property as a goldmining claim. They did build a cabin, at which they entertained many former colleagues, including Curtis LeMay, Fred Anderson, and Nate Twining. The cabin no longer exists, but the site of what was long known as the "Generals' Cabin" still appears on trail maps.

Ruth embraced the bustle of Southern California, and Ira reconnected with numerous friends and acquaintances from his early Air Corps years and from his work with the aircraft industry that sprawled across the region. Then there was Hollywood. Actor Jimmy Stewart had served under Eaker in the Eighth Air Force, as had Sy Bartlett and Beirne Lay, who were putting the finishing touches on *Twelve O'Clock High*, which would guarantee a place for the Eighth in popular culture.

It was Bartlett who connected Eaker with the enigmatic Howard Hughes. The son of a Houston oilman who had become rich by inventing a unique oil drilling bit, Hughes had taken over his father's Hughes Tool Company (Toolco) when still a teenager and had grown it beyond what his father could have imagined. A very wealthy man by his early twenties, Hughes had moved to Hollywood, where he began producing and directing successful Oscar-winning films and bought RKO. He dabbled in aviation, setting an around-the-world record on a 1938 flight, and bought a controlling interest in TWA. Through the aircraft division of Toolco, Hughes designed several aircraft, including a gargantuan wooden flying boat that was nicknamed the "Spruce Goose," and the XF-11 reconnaissance aircraft in which Hughes was almost killed during a spectacular crash in 1946. After this crash, the already eccentric Hughes, now addicted to painkillers, was gradually becoming a recluse.

Nevertheless, he was still something of a legend in Southern California aviation circles when he approached Eaker in 1947 to "join up" with him. In 1935, he had founded the Hughes Aircraft Company (which many sources confuse with the separate aircraft division of Toolco), which became a subsidiary of the Howard Hughes Medical Institute in 1953. Hughes wanted Eaker involved in this entity.

Unlike his other interests, which he micromanaged to their detriment, Hughes kept both the Medical Institute and Hughes Aircraft at arm's length. Thanks in no small part to Eaker's hands-on management, the latter quickly became an extraordinarily successful manufacturer of missiles and electronics, and eventually of communications satellites. In 1954, *Fortune* magazine noted that the company had "a virtual monopoly of the Air Force's advanced electronic requirements."

At Hughes, Eaker also met Tex Thornton, the future founder of Litton Industries, as well as Simon Ramo and Dean Wooldridge, two of the geniuses of early airborne electronic systems. They later joined with Thompson Products to form Thompson-Ramo-Wooldridge Corporation (TRW), which became a Hughes competitor, a world leader in aerospace electronics, and for a time in the early 1960s, the employer of Jimmy Doolittle.

In 1957, after a decade with Hughes Aircraft, Eaker grew exasperated with its founder's increasingly idiosyncratic behavior and resigned. Donald Douglas of Douglas Aircraft, an old acquaintance and a Southern California neighbor, invited Eaker to join the Douglas board and asked him to open an office for Douglas in Washington. Much to Ruth's consternation, he agreed. A decade earlier, he had to drag her out of Washington, but by now she had grown accustomed to Southern California, and he had to drag her back.

As in California, Eaker found himself surrounded by old wartime acquaintances, and highly regarded for his experience and expertise, a role he greatly relished. He and Spaatz, once again neighbors, found themselves to be elder statesmen, invited frequently to consult on projects and give after-dinner talks on airpower matters. For Eaker, more than for Spaatz, this meant frequent lecture tours around the country.

Much more financially comfortable than his old boss, Eaker did Spaatz the favor of getting him on the board of Litton Industries, where he did very well with stock options.

Eaker remained with Douglas until 1961, when he reached the mandatory retirement age of 65. The company closed the Washington office, but Eaker picked up the lease and used that as a base for his consulting activities, walking two miles to work each day. Among his new clients was Hughes Aircraft, in which Howard Hughes no longer had any direct participation, which provided Eaker with an annual paycheck of $50,000. In the meantime, he was also writing a syndicated column for the Copley News Service on defense matters and occasional articles for *Strategic Review*, which kept him in the public eye. During this time, Eaker continued to successfully resist being prodded into writing his memoirs, though history would have benefited from its being on his agenda. He considered it an exercise in vanity. Spaatz also refrained from leaving his insights to posterity in an autobiography.

These two men, Eaker and Spaatz, the officers who had reached the summit of command authority within the Eighth Air Force during the years of its most trying times and its greatest glory, found themselves living near each other in the Washington, DC, area for the better part of two decades, and they remained frequent companions.

Spaatz, like many senior officers then, as now, had missed much from the growing-up years of his children, but he made up for that as a grandfather. Carla, his youngest daughter, settled nearby and her children had plenty of enjoyable hours with "Daddy Tooey" when they were growing up. As with Eaker and his wife, Tooey and Ruth traveled a great deal for speaking engagements and to visit old friends. He slowed down only after a heart attack laid him low in 1972.

Two years later, another, more massive heart attack debilitated the old airman, and he entered Walter Reed Army Medical Center in Bethesda, not far from his home, for his last visit. Eaker visited him every day as he lingered near death. On July 13, 1974, Spaatz snapped out of a semi-comatose state, looked up from his hospital bed, and told Eaker, "I am counting on you to get me out of here." Eaker promised that he would be back the next day with a deck of cards and a bottle of whiskey. Spaatz died shortly after midnight. He was 83.

Eaker was with Spaatz on his last flight as he was taken west to be buried on the grounds of the Air Force Academy, two decades after he had served on the site selection committee that had chosen Colorado Springs.

Though his own health began to decline, Eaker kept up his routine of walking to work until April 1981, a few months before a mild stroke left him unable to walk without a cane. In 1985, he was invited to a ceremony at the Pentagon, where Chief of Staff General Charles Gabriel formally awarded Eaker his fourth star as a full general, a rank that had eluded him during World War II. Gabriel apologized, telling Eaker, "I'm sorry it took so long for a grateful nation to recognize all you've done for us and finally set things right for this great air pioneer, this proven combat leader, educator, strong spokesman for national security. . . . I'm proud to put him back in uniform and make him the Four Star he really deserves."

It was the first time he had ever worn the blue uniform of the US Air

Force. The man who did as much as anyone to achieve its existence had retired before it was born. He passed away two years later, on August 6, 1987, at the Andrews AFB hospital, and went to Arlington National Cemetery in that uniform. A year later, Blytheville AFB in Arkansas, which began as a USAAF field in 1942, was renamed Eaker AFB in his honor. A Strategic Air Command B-52 base at the time, it was closed in 1992 during a round of Pentagon downsizing.

Deluged with demands for his time by both Shell and the government for committees, inspection tours, and public appearances, Jimmy Doolittle remained as active out of the service after the war as he had been during his decadelong hiatus from the uniform before the war. He served with the Joint Congressional Policy Board and the Committee on National Security Organization, and in 1950 he and his wife circled the globe on behalf of Shell, inspecting Shell facilities and showing the red and yellow flag.

Everywhere he turned, Doolittle's opinions and expertise were being called upon, and his congenial nature made it hard for him to refuse. Hoyt Vandenberg used him as a civilian troubleshooter within the US Air Force, and sent him to Korea in 1950 to evaluate the tactical situation during that war's difficult early months. In 1952, President Harry Truman asked Doolittle to chair a study of the placement of civilian airports in urban areas, as their once rural locations were being surrounded in the suburban sprawl that came with 1950s prosperity. Doolittle's insightful recommendations led to the development of the new generation of larger airports farther from city centers that we know today.

When he became president, Dwight Eisenhower, whose wartime skepticism Doolittle had long since overcome, put him on the presidential Scientific Advisory Committee. When rumors surfaced about Communist infiltration of the Central Intelligence Agency, Eisenhower asked him to look into this as well. Doolittle's report, kept classified for years, recommended improvements in professionalism among agents, use of technology, and intelligence sharing between agencies. The last item, foreseen by Doolittle in 1954, remains an issue to this day.

During the postwar years, the personal lives of Doolittle and his wife were indelibly marred by the death of their son, Major James Doolittle, Jr., in 1958. Then the commander of the 524th Fighter-Bomber Squadron, he was found dead of a bullet wound in his office at Bergstrom AFB near Austin, Texas. His death was ruled a suicide. His father wrote in his memoirs of the mental anguish and of asking "why, over and over, knowing that you may never learn the complete truth."

Jimmy and Josephine spent the following years trying to stay busy. For Joe, this meant the introspection of letter writing and remaining connected with fiends. In Jimmy's case, hunting trips took him to South America, Africa—where he was treed by a rhinoceros—and back to Alaska, where he had grown up and where Joe now joined him as a tourist. He had promised her such a trip when they were both in high school.

Their plan had been eventually to retire, far from city lights, to the Monterey Peninsula on California's Central Coast, and they had bought property there in the 1940s. However, when he retired from Shell in 1956 in compliance with the company's mandatory executive retirement age of 60, he joined Simon Ramo and Dean Wooldridge—with whom Ira Eaker had worked at Hughes Aircraft a few years earlier—in Southern California. In 1959, after they formed TRW, they hired Doolittle as chairman of their Space Technology Laboratories division. At that time, and for many years thereafter, TRW was a major supplier to NASA, and to the Los Angeles–based US Air Force Ballistic Missile Division, which was in the midst of developing the Titan and Minuteman ICBMs, and accounting for 40 percent of the total Air Force budget.

In his new position, Doolittle resigned from the various governmental committees of which he had long been a member. He also retired from the Air Force Reserve in 1959. However, he returned to Washington in uniform in 1985 for his formal promotion to full general. The four-star insignia was pinned by President Ronald Reagan and Senator Barry Goldwater, a reserve major general.

Jimmy and Joe lived in Santa Monica until 1978, when they moved to a retirement community in Carmel, a short distance from their property on the Monterey Peninsula, which they had given to their son John and his family. Two years after Joe passed away on Christmas Eve in 1988, Jimmy moved in with John and lived there until his death on September 27, 1993, at the age of 96.

CHAPTER 47

COLD WARRIORS

O f the eight men profiled herein, only three remained in the service long enough to wear US Air Force blue while on active duty,
and after Tooey Spaatz retired in 1948, only two made a career of the new
service.

The Berlin Blockade brought together, albeit briefly, the two men who
had maneuvered against one another over small-arms ammunition at
Langley Field during those innocent prewar days. Lieutenant General
Curtis LeMay commanded the whole show, while Colonel Hub Zemke
arrived at the end of the operation as the commander of the 36th Fighter
Group, the first group equipped with the Lockheed F-80 Shooting Star jet
fighter to be assigned to USAFE.

When he came home from Europe and his months at Stalag Luft I,
Zemke, unlike most Eighth Air Force fighter pilots, elected to remain in
the service. His first assignment took him to the Air Tactical School at
Tyndall Field near Panama City, Florida, as the chief of its Tactics Division. In 1948, the 36th, a wartime Ninth Air Force component, was
equipped with jet fighters and redeployed from Howard AFB in Panama
to the wartime Luftwaffe base at Fürstenfeldbruck. It would remain in

Germany until 1994, but Zemke moved on, first to assume command of the 2nd Air Division—formerly the Eighth Air Force 2nd Bomb Division—at Landsberg, and then back to the States in 1953 to attend the Air War College at Randolph AFB in Texas.

LeMay came back in October 1948 to the command for which he is best known—nine years at the helm of the Strategic Air Command. Created in 1946, SAC had gotten off to a shaky start under the command of General George Kenney, who had to contend with a budget at its nadir and a mass exodus of experienced personnel. Meanwhile, he had been the wartime commander of the Fifth Air Force, which had been engaged in tactical, not strategic, operations. Hoyt Vandenberg, now Air Force chief of staff, felt LeMay was ideally suited for the role, and it turned out that he was right. With the job came a fourth star for LeMay, who became a full general in 1951.

The Berlin Blockade experience, coupled with the reality of the Korean War, which began in 1950, brought about a realization by the American public and Congress of both Soviet intentions and the folly of reducing the numbers and capability of the American armed forces to the point where they were not a serious deterrent to Soviet mischief.

LeMay took command of an organization made up of two heavy bomb groups, only one of which had aircraft—the first of the new B-36 intercontinental bombers—and a dozen medium bomb groups, which were composed of B-29s (once "very heavy" bombers and now redesignated as "medium" in deference to the much larger B-36) and B-50s, variants of the B-29. There were no jet bombers yet, no aerial refueling capability, and no realistic training.

When LeMay left in 1957, SAC had 11 heavy bomb wings, equipped with a rapidly increasing number of B-52s and 28 medium bomb wings, equipped with a force of more than 1,300 B-47 jet bombers. By the mid-1950s, on LeMay's watch, SAC had developed the capability for aerial refueling of its bombers—with KC-135 jets—to fly to targets anywhere in the world. In 1957, to demonstrate SAC's global reach, LeMay sent three B-52s, supported by aerial refueling, on a nonstop flight around the world. Training, once lax, had become rigorous, maintenance was streamlined, merit promotions were introduced, and SAC was maintaining a bomber force on continuous airborne alert.

As LeMay wrote in his memoirs and as he reiterated in conversations with this author, he was certain that if the order had been issued, his command "could have destroyed all of Russia (I mean by that all of Russia's capability to wage war) without losing a man to their defenses. [However,] we in SAC were not saber rattlers. We were not yelling for war and action in order to 'flex the mighty muscles we had built.' No stupidity of that sort. We wanted peace as much as anyone else wanted it. But we knew for a fact that it would be possible to curtail enemy expansion if we challenged them in that way."

Hub Zemke also served with SAC, arriving in 1955 from USAFE to command the 31st Strategic Fighter Wing, flying Republic F-84F Thunderstreaks out of Turner AFB, Georgia. Eleven years after he had been shot down literally on the eve of taking over the 65th, he finally had his wing command. The 31st was well-known for Operation Fox Peter, a series of mass overseas deployments of the entire wing using aerial refueling. Fox Peter One, the first of these, which took the wing overseas to Misawa AB in Japan in July 1952, was led by Colonel Dave Schilling, Zemke's former second in command at the 56th Fighter Group during the war.

In 1957 Zemke took command of the 4080th Strategic Reconnaissance Wing, formed at Turner AFB a year earlier to operate RB-57D Canberra high-altitude electronic intelligence aircraft on clandestine missions over the Soviet Far East and China from bases in Japan and Alaska. At the time that Zemke took over and transferred the wing to Laughlin AFB, it was becoming the first SAC unit to begin operating the Lockheed U-2, heretofore flown mainly by the CIA. He moved on to the North

American Air Defense Command (NORAD) staff in Colorado before the 4080th began its overflights of Cuba during the 1962 Cuban Missile Crisis.

In July 1957, when General Thomas White, the wartime commander of the Seventh Air Force and a longtime fixture on the Air Staff at the Pentagon, took over as Chief of Staff of the Air Force, LeMay left SAC to become White's vice chief. Under Eisenhower administration policy, the role of the service chiefs in the 1950s was administration, while that of the *vice* chiefs was operational. In notes penned in 1964, White later observed that he picked LeMay to run the service because "he was then the commander of the most efficient component of the Air Force . . . he was *the* architect of the Strategic Air Command."

Of White, LeMay told Tom Coffey that "he thought politics was the art of compromise. He would go into battle ready to compromise. I never believed in that. I thought if you believed in something, God damn it, you got in there and fought for it."

In 1961, LeMay's bluntness and disdain for compromise put him at odds with the incoming administration of John F. Kennedy. The new president's handling of the Bay of Pigs invasion of Cuba sapped LeMay's respect for Kennedy. By most accounts, including LeMay's to this author, the two men never got along personally.

Nevertheless, when White retired in July 1961, Kennedy surprised everyone—LeMay included—by naming the vice chief as the new chief of staff. Kennedy biographer Arthur Schlesinger later wrote that "LeMay's popularity in the ranks and on [Capitol] Hill gave him immunity," though Hugh Sidey of *Time* magazine later observed that LeMay "had the toughness Kennedy felt the country needed most," and quoted Kennedy as saying that it was good to have men like LeMay "commanding troops once you decide to go in. . . . I like having LeMay at the head of the Air Force. Everybody knows how he feels."

However strained things might have been between Kennedy and

LeMay, the general's interactions with Kennedy's controversial and opinionated secretary of defense, Robert McNamara, amounted to open animosity. A Harvard-trained accountant and statistical analyst, McNamara was the archetypical "bean counter." He had actually served under LeMay briefly during World War II as a staff officer, and spent most of his postwar career at the Ford Motor Company.

McNamara clashed with Air Force leaders on numerous topics, notably his preference for ICBMs over manned aircraft. He became notorious for canceling the B-70 Mach 3 bomber program, for which LeMay had fought long and hard. He also promoted the Tactical Fighter Experimental (TFX), an aircraft that he felt could serve all the needs of both the US Navy and the Air Force. It eventually became the costly and trouble-plagued F-111, which the Navy never used.

"My quarrel with McNamara was not so much our differences of opinion," LeMay observed in his memoirs. "I've had differences of opinion with a lot of people. My quarrel with him was [that I was] trying to help him and he doesn't want my help. And he does things I've known all my life are wrong."

McNamara became famous—or infamous—for coining the terms "mutually assured destruction" (MAD) to describe nuclear war, and "sublimited war" to describe his concept of strategy for the Vietnam War. It was this latter strategy—which McNamara many years later recognized as a mistake—over which the two antagonists disagreed most sharply.

LeMay favored a decisive use of strategic airpower against North Vietnam, cutting off enemy supply lines at their source, while McNamara favored a limited use of tactical airpower against smaller targets close to the battlefield. By 1965, as the American involvement grew, McNamara acquiesced to attacks on North Vietnam, but deliberately imposed tactical limits on American airmen.

"In Japan we dropped 502,000 tons and we won the war," LeMay told Tom Coffey in 1985. "In Vietnam we dropped 6,162,000 tons of bombs and we lost the war. The difference was that McNamara chose the targets in Vietnam and I chose the targets in Japan."

LeMay has long been controversial for writing in his memoirs that North Vietnamese aggression could be halted by the threat of shoving them "back into the Stone Age with Air power or Naval power—not with ground forces." Frequently misinterpreted, the statement dogged LeMay for years as he was called upon repeatedly for an explanation. In a *Washington Post* interview published on October 4, 1968, he explained, "I never said we should bomb them back to the Stone Age. I said we had the capability to do it. I want to save lives on both sides."

When Curtis LeMay retired from the US Air Force in January 1965, the war had barely begun, but he was adamant about a strategy for ending it. Seven long and bloody years would pass before his ideas were finally implemented. In December 1972, it was Operation Linebacker II, a sustained maximum effort by *Eighth Air Force* B-52s against exactly the same targets LeMay had recommended, that finally brought North Vietnam to the bargaining table.

During the presidential campaign of 1968, two years after he retired, LeMay made his last foray into public life by accepting the spot as the running mate to Alabama governor George Wallace on the American Independent Party ticket. While many of his old colleagues—Tooey Spaatz and Ira Eaker included—counseled him not to do it, he allowed himself to be talked into it because he felt the United States needed a strong alternative to Hubert Humphrey on the Democratic ticket, and he did not feel that the Republican candidate, Richard Nixon, offered this alternative. Humphrey lost, as did the Wallace-LeMay ticket, but they carried five states and won 46 electoral votes, more than any third party in a presidential election since Theodore Roosevelt ran in 1912.

Hub Zemke left the service in 1966, a year after LeMay, retiring as a colonel, while LeMay retired as a four-star general. After three decades, he and Maria divorced in 1973. He bought a ranch near Oroville, in the Sierra Nevada foothills of California, and settled down in the quiet obscurity that LeMay also eventually achieved. Meanwhile, Hanns-Joachim Scharff, the Luftwaffe master interrogator who had interviewed Zemke, also wound up in California in the 1970s, having reinvented himself as a successful mosaic artist. Among his commissions were the floor of the California state capitol and the walls of the Cinderella Castle at Walt Disney World.

Working with Roger Freeman, author of *The Mighty Eighth*, Zemke published two volumes of memoirs in 1988 and 1991. As Freeman wrote in 1988, "In retirement, Hubert Zemke, as befits his outlook, has a habit of dismissing his achievements in life with a joke. Others who have known him accord him substantial honors, in particular recognition as probably the most successful American fighter leader of the Second World War. This, the subject contests, not through modesty but because he does not believe it to be true. He insists that the successes in air fighting were due to the quality of whole organizations and not to one man."

In his final decades, LeMay eschewed the limelight and refused interview requests, but made time for old friends. He and Helen lived for many of those years in Newport Beach, California, then moved into a retirement home for Air Force veterans near March AFB. It was here that he suffered a fatal heart attack on October 1, 1990. Helen passed away 17 months later, and is buried next to him at the Air Force Academy in Colorado Springs.

Zemke died four years after LeMay, on August 30, 1994, at the age of 80. Roger Freeman noted that it had been "Hub's wish that when the time comes his ashes are to be interred beneath a towering sequoia in the Sierra Nevada. . . . While his mortal remains may lie in the forest that he loved so dearly, for those who have known Hubert Zemke, either personally or through the medium of the written word, his presence is elsewhere. Far away, high above the land of his forefathers, where wisps of cirrus form and fade in the frigid blue, the spirit of Hubert Zemke forever soars."

———

The Eighth Air Force continued to soar throughout the Cold War and beyond. The Eighth was within Curtis LeMay's chain of command from 1948, when he took over at SAC, until he retired as chief of staff in 1965, and it remained as Hub Zemke's home for most of those years as well. It was headquartered within the United States until 1970, when it moved to Andersen AFB on Guam. From there, the Eighth managed all of the B-52 missions and SAC refueling operations during the war in Southeast Asia. In 1975, its headquarters moved to Barksdale AFB near Shreveport, Louisiana, where they have remained since.

When SAC was merged into Air Combat Command in 1992, the Eighth went with it. In 2009, when the Air Force Global Strike Command was formed from the nuclear-weapons-capable components of Air Combat Command and Space Command, the entire manned bomber capability of the new organization was placed under the umbrella of the Eighth Air Force.

CHAPTER 48

LAST FOLDED WINGS

Two of the eight, the bomber pilots Morgan and Rosenthal, lived into the twenty-first century, and both saw the sixtieth anniversary of the Pearl Harbor attack that had changed the course of their lives.

Bob Morgan's postwar world began to unravel in 1945 on the same day that he stepped off a C-54 in San Francisco on his way back from the Pacific and phoned his wife.

"Why couldn't it have been you instead of my brother?" were the first words that he had heard her say in six months.

"What?"

Dorothy's brother, Harry, her only sibling, had been killed in the Battle of the Bulge, and this had devastated Dotty. For reasons that could be better analyzed theoretically than truly understood, she blamed her husband for Fate's reaper having taken Harry rather than Bob.

"I hung up the telephone feeling as though a flak burst had engulfed me," he recalled.

A week later, coincidentally the same day that the war ended in Europe, Morgan returned to his wife and young daughter in Asheville.

They chose not to address the issue of Harry, though the incident permanently shadowed their marriage.

At seeing Sandra Lea for the first time, Morgan overflowed with all the joy that he had imagined, and that was good, but he was still in the USAAF, and after 21 days he was reporting for a series of reassignments. The first took him and his family back to MacDill Field near Tampa, where he had lived with his third wife, Martha Stone. This lasted for only a few weeks, and he spent the next several months bouncing around to various locations up and down the East Coast. It seemed to him that the USAAF didn't know what to do with a Superfortress pilot who had completed his overseas tour.

Morgan mustered out of the service in September 1945, about a week after the Japanese surrendered on Tokyo Bay. He then took Dotty and Sandra back to Asheville with every intention of putting down roots for the rest of his life and joining the family business, which his father assumed he would do. He hesitated, however, harboring resentment toward his brother, who managed the company, and who had never been in uniform. As he put it, "Dave had gained control of the company while I was off fighting the war."

Vince Evans, who had flown with Morgan in both Europe and the Pacific, urged him to consider a job flying for TWA, but Morgan imagined a life for himself that did not include being away from home. Finally, at his father's urging, he joined the company and settled down amid the realities of the 1950s, when the United States was prosperous and "the American Dream" was coming true. He and Dotty bought a house and a four-door Pontiac, built a bigger house, watched Sandra grow and be joined by her siblings, Robert and Harry—and ignored the darkness gathering in the room.

Under David's guidance, Morgan Manufacturing and its furniture subsidiary expanded to meet the demands of a boom that seemed endless. Perhaps inevitably, the company became overextended and quality began to ebb.

Bob Morgan, like many veterans, was nagged by bad memories and bad dreams of his wartime experiences—which he repressed as best he could. They had yet to invent the phrase "post-traumatic stress," but he had it. He drank more than he should have. He and Dotty argued about the drinking and about which church to attend, and went through frequent separations. They avoided serious talk of divorce—because of the kids. Then she became pregnant again. Their youngest was born in 1958, a decade after their next oldest. She was named Peggy after Bob's sister, who had died of polio shortly after the war ended.

As the separations grew longer, Morgan began having brief affairs with other women. On a business trip to Memphis, he reconnected with Margaret Polk, the original Memphis Belle. She was coming off a failed marriage of her own, and even Bob Morgan thought she was drinking too much. Nevertheless, they had a fling, stayed in touch, fought, and eventually called it quits a second time.

In the meantime, the *Memphis Belle*, that most famous of the Eighth Air Force warplanes, had survived the wrecker's ball. When the USAAF was through with her, she was sold to the City of Memphis for $350, flown a few times, abandoned at the Memphis airport, and rescued for display by the American Legion, who put her on a pedestal near the National Guard Armory in 1950.

Along about 1964, Bob Morgan became romantically involved with a young woman at Morgan Manufacturing, and his own brother fired him. In his memoirs, he recalls reaching out to the great televangelist Reverend Billy Graham, whom he had first met a number of years before. As he put it, Graham convinced him that "God still loved me even when I was as awash in guilt and remorse as a man could be."

Graham also put Morgan in touch with a man who knew a man who eventually hired him at a Volkswagen dealership in Virginia. During a tour for dealers of the company's headquarters in Germany, he found himself talking with a German dealer who had flown with the Luftwaffe during the war. "We started comparing notes on our war histories," Morgan recalled. "I told him what bombing missions I had flown, and the dates, and he, through an interpreter, told me what his fighter assignments had been. Finally we came across one engagement—it was over the submarine pens at Saint-Nazaire—that he and I had shared, and perhaps tried to kill one another. Had his Focke-Wulf been one of those blurs past my cockpit window?"

Bob's marriage to Dotty finally ended in divorce in May 1979 after 35 years. A month later, he made Realtor Elizabeth Thrash his fifth wife. During the dozen years before she succumbed to lung cancer, Elizabeth was at Bob's side as his career path took him back to the side of the *Memphis Belle*.

Long after the death of William Wyler, the director of the *Memphis Belle* documentary, his daughter Catherine Wyler teamed up with David Puttnam to produce a dramatic film, titled simply *Memphis Belle*, based on the story of the bomber. The Morgans, along with all of the other surviving crew members, were invited to England to watch the filming and to attend the 1990 premiere. Bob Morgan was disappointed that the film's director, Michael Caton-Jones, had ignored their suggestions and he felt the result was a film that was "historically inaccurate."

Morgan also found himself entwined with the fate of the real *Memphis Belle*. Though the aircraft had been donated to the US Air Force Museum in the 1970s, she remained in Memphis, gradually deteriorating and being stripped by vandals. A decade later, Morgan became involved with the local Memphis Belle Memorial Association as they raised money to move her to a pavilion on Mud Island in the Mississippi River in 1987.

After Elizabeth's death from lung cancer in 1992, Morgan married his sixth wife, Linda Dickerson, beneath the nose of his old airplane. They had met during the filming of *Memphis Belle* while she was working as a publicity assistant to aircraft collector Dave Tallichet, who supplied the original Flying Fortress that stood in as the *Memphis Belle*.

During his final years, Bob Morgan finally discovered his niche, that being a reprise of his moment of glory. He traveled the country—and the world—making public appearances, signing prints, and pressing the flesh as the man who had once commanded the legendary *Memphis Belle*.

It was at the airport in Asheville in 2004, as he returned from a round of air show appearances, that he suffered the fall that led to his death on May 15 at the age of 85.

The postscript to the *Memphis Belle*'s story is that she continued to deteriorate at Mud Island until 2005, when the Memorial Association relinquished her to the National Museum of the US Air Force, which brought her to its facility at Wright Patterson AFB in Ohio for restoration.

After the surrender of Germany, Rosie Rosenthal was the last of the eight to muster out of the wartime Eighth Air Force. He went home to a new job as the operations officer for the USAAF Air Transport Command, but just as he had served a second tour of duty on the flight deck of a Flying Fortress and had begun a third, he was not ready to quit. It was the summer of 1945, and the war in the Pacific was still raging, with no end in sight.

"With my background in combat, I could do more good flying combat against the Japanese until the war ended," he reasoned.

He decided to go to the Pentagon and to present himself to General Fred Anderson, the onetime VIII Bomber Command leader who had been Tooey Spaatz's right-hand man during the last phase of the air war. He was now part of the planning staff for the strategic campaign against Japan. Anderson agreed with Rosenthal and cut orders for him to report to MacDill Field to learn to fly a B-29.

However, the war ended before Rosenthal concluded his flight training, so he finally went home to Brooklyn. He was welcomed back to the Madison Avenue law firm where he had been before the war. As the principals made their way back from wartime service, and new faces were added, the firm had become Poletti, Diamond, Rabin, Freidin and Mackay, and had recruited Franklin Delano Roosevelt, Jr., to its team. The son of the late president had recently returned from the US Navy and had been shopping for a firm at which to hang his hat.

On the face of it, Rosenthal had landed on his feet in a big way and could easily have settled down to a distinguished career in a high-profile firm. However, by his own admission, he was "more tired than I thought. . . . I didn't realize how fatigued I was."

A couple of months after he returned to Madison Avenue, Rosenthal learned of opportunities for attorneys with the International Military Tribunal that was about to convene in Nuremberg. The Allied Powers had agreed to take the unprecedented step of putting high-ranking members of Germany's Nazi leadership on trial for violations of international law and for crimes against humanity.

The format of the trial called for two judges each from the Soviet Union, the United States, the United Kingdom, and France. In turn, each of those countries assigned a lead prosecutor, who would employ a team of prosecuting attorneys. As the American lead prosecutor, President Truman picked Supreme Court justice Robert Jackson, who had served as United States Attorney General for a year under Roosevelt, and who had come to Europe in the summer of 1945 as leader of the American delegation that helped form the tribunal. Rosenthal applied for a slot on Jackson's prosecution team and was hired to return to a German city that he seen only from three miles in the sky.

Foremost in his recollections of the formation of the prosecution team and their journey to Nuremberg was not the job at hand, nor the Nazis whose doctrines and practices had so angered him, but a particular very attractive woman.

When he was first introduced to Phillis Heller at an initial orientation meeting before embarking overseas, she gave him a cold shoulder the likes of which he had never experienced. His second memory was of her arriving at the pier in Brooklyn three hours after the ship to Bremerhaven was supposed to have sailed. Fortunately for her, the ship was three hours late in embarking, but she nevertheless cut it so close that her luggage was literally thrown on board the ship.

At a cocktail party held that evening for the prosecutors, she discovered who he was and explained that a Columbia Law School classmate of hers had worked at Rosenthal's firm and had told her all about this man named Bob Rosenthal. Ten days later, when the ship docked, Bob and Phillis were engaged. Their efforts to get married were initially complicated by the fact that the anti-fraternization regulations of the American occupation government in Germany severely restricted civilian as well as military marriages. They finally received permission, and were married in Nuremberg in September 1946. They lived to celebrate their sixtieth wedding anniversary.

The Nuremberg Tribunal, meanwhile, tried the two dozen highest-ranking Nazis between November 1945 and October 1946 and sentenced half of them to death. During the course of those trials, the Jewish kid who had enlisted to fight the Nazis found himself across the table from them as their prosecutor. Hermann Göring, who had long been Adolf Hitler's second in command, and who was the highest-ranking Nazi Party man to survive the war, was among those whom Rosenthal faced down at Nuremberg.

As the *New York Times* recalled in its obituary of him after he died on April 20, 2007—four years ahead of Phillis—Rosenthal had said that "seeing these strutting conquerors after they were sentenced, powerless, pathetic and preparing for the hangman, was the closure I needed. Justice had overtaken evil. My war was over."

★

SELECTED ACRONYMS

AAF: Army Air Forces (short for USAAF)

AEAF: Allied Expeditionary Air Force

AWPD: Air War Plans Division (also the acronym for documents prepared by the division)

ETOUSA: European Theater of Operations, United States Army

MAAF: Mediterranean Allied Air Forces

MASAF: Mediterranean Allied Strategic Air Force

MATAF: Mediterranean Allied Tactical Air Force

MTOUSA: Mediterranean Theater of Operations, United States Army

NAAF: Northwest African Air Forces

NASAF: Northwest African Strategic Air Force

NATAF: Northwest African Tactical Air Force

NATOUSA: North African Theater of Operations, US Army (later MTOUSA)

SELECTED ACRONYMS

RAF: Royal Air Force (United Kingdom)

SHAEF: Supreme Headquarters, Allied Expeditionary Force

USAAF: US Army Air Forces

USASTAF: US Army Strategic Air Forces in the Pacific (aka US Strategic Air Forces in the Pacific)

USSTAF: United States Strategic Air Forces (Europe)

BIBLIOGRAPHY

In addition to the books listed below, sources include official USAAF communications, which are identified by date when referenced, as well as interviews in the collections of the Columbia Oral History Collection at Columbia University and the US Military History Institute at Carlisle Barracks, Pennsylvania. Special thanks are gratefully given to Colonel J. A. "Bill" Saavedra, USAF (Ret.), of the Air Force History Office in Washington, DC, and to Rita Easlick of the Caro, Michigan, Library.

Arnold, Henry Harley. *American Airpower Comes of Age: General Henry H. "Hap" Arnold's World War II Diaries*. Edited by John W. Huston. 2 vols. Collingdale, PA: Diane Publishing, 2002.

———. *Global Mission*. New York: Harper & Brothers, 1949.

Arnold, Henry Harley, and Ira Clarence Eaker. *Army Flyer*. New York: Harper & Brothers, 1942.

———. *This Flying Game*. New York: Funk and Wagnalls, 1936.

———. *Winged Warfare*. New York and London: Harper & Brothers, 1941.

Atkinson, Rick. *An Army at Dawn*. New York: Holt, 2002.

BIBLIOGRAPHY

Caidin, Martin. *Black Thursday*. New York: E. P. Dutton, 1960.

Coffey, Thomas M. *Decision Over Schweinfurt: The US 8th Air Force Battle for Daylight Bombing*. New York: David McKay, 1977.

———. *Hap: The Story of the US Air Force and the Man Who Built It: General Henry H. "Hap" Arnold*. New York: Viking Press, 1982.

———. *Iron Eagle: The Turbulent Life of General Curtis LeMay*. New York: Random House, 1986.

Copp, DeWitt S. *A Few Great Captains: The Men and Events That Shaped the Development of US Airpower*. Garden City, NY: Doubleday, 1980.

———. *Forged in Fire: Strategy and Decisions in the Air War Over Europe, 1940–1945*. Garden City, NY: Doubleday, 1982.

Craven, Wesley Frank, and James Lea Cate, eds. *Army Air Forces in World War II*. 3 vols. Washington, DC: Office of Air Force History, 1947, 1948, 1951.

Doolittle, James H., with Carroll V. Glines. *I Could Never Be So Lucky Again: An Autobiography of General James H. "Jimmy" Doolittle*. New York: Bantam, 1991.

Eisenhower, Dwight D. *Crusade in Europe*. New York: Doubleday, 1948.

Ferguson, Arthur. Chapters regarding the strategic air war in the European and Mediterranean Theaters in *Army Air Forces in World War II: Europe*. Edited by Wesley Frank Craven and James Lea Cate. 3 vols. Washington, DC: Office of Air Force History, 1947, 1948, 1951.

Freeman, Roger. *The Mighty Eighth: A History of the Units, Men, and Machines of the US 8th Air Force*. London: Cassell, 1979, 1986, 2000.

Freeman, Roger, with Alan Crouchman and Vic Maslen. *Mighty Eighth War Diary*. London: Jane's, 1981.

Halberstam, David. *The Best and the Brightest*. New York: Random House, 1972.

Hansell, Haywood S., Jr. *The Air Plan That Defeated Hitler*. Atlanta: Higgins McArthur/Longino and Porter, 1972.

Hapgood, David, and David Richardson. *Monte Cassino*. New York: Congdon and Weed, 1984.

Johnson, Bruce. *The Man with Two Hats*. New York: Carlton Press, 1967.

Julian, Thomas Anthony. *Operation Frantic and the Search for American-Soviet Military Collaboration*. Syracuse, NY: Syracuse University (PhD dissertation), 1968.

Lay, Beirne, Jr., and Sy Bartlett. *12 O'Clock High*. New York: Harper & Brothers, 1948.

LeMay, Curtis. *America Is in Danger*. New York: Funk and Wagnall's, 1968.

LeMay, Curtis E., and Bill Yenne. *Superfortress: The Boeing B-29 and American Airpower in World War II*. Yardley, PA: Westholme, 2006. Originally published by McGraw Hill, 1988.

LeMay, Curtis E., with MacKinlay Kantor. *Mission with LeMay: My Story*. Garden City, New York: Doubleday, 1965.

BIBLIOGRAPHY

Le Strange, Richard, with James Brown. *Century Bombers: The Story of the Bloody Hundredth*. Thorpe Abbotts, England: 100th Bomb Group Memorial Association, 1989.

Matloff, Maurice. *Strategic Planning for Coalition Warfare, 1943–1944*. Washington, DC: Center of Military History, United States Army, 1990.

Maurer, Maurer, ed. *Air Force Combat Units of World War II*. Maxwell AFB: Office of Air Force History, 1983.

Mets, David. *Master of Airpower: General Carl A. Spaatz*. Novato, CA: Presidio Press, 1988.

Mikaelian, Allen. *Medal of Honor*. New York: Hyperion, 2002.

Morgan, Robert, with Ron Powers. *The Man Who Flew the* Memphis Belle. New York: Dutton, 2001.

Parton, James. *Air Force Spoken Here: General Ira Eaker and the Command of the Air*. Bethesda, MD: Adler and Adler, 1986.

———. *History of MAAF (Mediterranean Allied Air Forces)*. Washington, DC: USAAF, 1945.

Pogue, Forrest C. *United States Army in World War II, European Theater of Operations: The Supreme Command*. Washington, DC: Office of the Chief of Military History, 1954.

Rooney, Andy. *My War*. New York: Random House, 1995.

Tate, James P. *The Army and Its Air Corps: Army Policy Toward Aviation, 1919–1941*. Maxwell AFB, Alabama: Air University Press, 1998.

———. "The Army and Its Air Corps: A Study of the Evolution of Army Policy Towards Aviation, 1919–1941." PhD dissertation, Indiana University, 1976.

Tillman, Barrett. *Above and Beyond: The Aviation Medals of Honor.* Washington, DC: Smithsonian Institution Press, 2002.

United States Strategic Bombing Survey. *The Effects of Strategic Bombing on the German War Economy.* Washington, DC: Overall Economic Effects Division, United States Strategic Bombing Survey, 1945.

USAAF. *Army Air Forces Statistical Digest, World War II.* Washington, DC: Director, Statistical Services, USAAF, 1945.

Yenne, Bill. *Big Week: Six Days That Changed the Course of World War II.* New York: Berkley/Caliber, 2013.

———. *Hap Arnold: The General Who Invented the US Air Force.* Washington, DC: Regnery, 2013.

Zemke, Hub, and Roger Freeman. *Zemke's Stalag: The Final Days of World War II.* Washington, DC: Smithsonian Institution Press, 1991.

———. *Zemke's Wolf Pack.* New York: Orion Books/Crown Publishers, 1988.

INDEX

INDEX

INDEX

INDEX

INDEX

INDEX

INDEX

★

ABOUT THE AUTHOR

Bill Yenne is the author of more than three dozen nonfiction books, especially on aviation and military history. For Penguin Random House, these have included *Big Week,* the story of the turning point in the air war against Germany, and *Aces High,* the dual biography of Dick Bong and Tommy McGuire, the top-scoring American aces of World War II, which was described by pilot and bestselling author Dan Roam as "the greatest flying story of all time."

General Wesley Clark called Mr. Yenne's recent biography of Alexander the Great the "best yet." *The New Yorker* wrote of *Sitting Bull,* Mr. Yenne's biography of the great Lakota leader, that it "excels as a study in leadership."

Mr. Yenne has contributed to encyclopedias of both world wars and has appeared in documentaries broadcast on the History Channel, the National Geographic Channel, and ARD German Television. A member of the American Aviation Historical Society, he lives in San Francisco, and on the Web at billyenne.com.